A HISTORY OF INTOXICATION

A History of Intoxication

OPIUM IN ASSAM, 1800-1959

KAWAL DEEP KOUR

MANOHAR
2019

First published 2019

ISBN 978-93-88540-25-4

Published by
Ajay Kumar Jain *for*
Manohar Publishers & Distributors
4753/23 Ansari Road, Daryaganj
New Delhi 110 002

Printed at
Replika Press Pvt. Ltd.

To
My Mother Charanjit Kaur, and
Husband Capt. Surinder Singh,
The Driving Forces of My Life!

Contents

Illustrations

Figure

Maps

Tables

Acknowledgements

THIS BOOK HAS been a journey of sorts. During this scholarly sojourn, I have benefited from a vast range of experiences which have added to my knowledge and at the same time, made me more persevering as a human being. I owe a considerable gratitude to all who made this journey an intellectually stimulating experience.

My deepest gratitude is to my supervisor, Arupjyoti Saikia. His meticulous comments, his enduring belief in my ability and his generous support have enormously contributed to the shaping of the present work. This intellectual debt to him I can never repay.

I am very grateful for the help I received from the various librarians and archivists at Assam State Archives, Department of Historical and Antiquarian Studies, Guwahati; libraries at Cotton College and the K.K. Handique Library at Gauhati University; the National Archives at New Delhi; the Central Secretariat Library, New Delhi; the Nehru Memorial Library at New Delhi; the National Medical Library of All India Institute of Medical Science, New Delhi who guided me through their treasure prove of documents and records on which this work has been based. Jayanta Nath has meticulously drafted the maps that appear in the volume. I am especially grateful to Baishya da and late Hira Sonowal of the Assam State Archives for all their help.

Apurba Jeevan Baruah, DIG, Assam Police ensured I had a safe and enriching field visit and stay at Tinsukia. The enthusiasm and support for my research that I received from my local host Akhil Barua of Makum and his NGO was a great incentive. I was humbled by the hospitality I received from the family of Ghanakanta Gogoi of Mamoroni village.

My colleagues and faculty members at the Department of Humanities and Social Sciences of the Indian Institute of Technology, Guwahati, have helped and motivated me in myriad ways.

My deepest appreciation goes to Sardar Pritpal Singh, ADG, Assam Police, for all his encouragement and support. Discussions with him were always illuminating.

My husband Capt. Surinder Singh, who has been a fierce critic and anchor, is the reason that this volume has been possible. I will remain indebted to my mother, Sardarni Charanjit Kaur. This book would not have materialized without her wishes and prayers and staunch support through all my years of turmoil. To my family, I owe special thanks for their affection and encouragement.

KAWAL DEEP KOUR

Note on Usage

BY ASSAM, I refer to the Brahmaputra valley. More specifically, the *ryotwari* areas of Kamrup, Darrang, Nowgong, Lakhimpur and Sibsagar are the areas covered in the present work. The former names of the places as Nowgong, Gowhatty, Gauhati, Calcutta have been retained in the book.

Terms such as *tribe* have been used to convey historically specific meanings. They have been used within quotation marks.

Glossary

Abkaree	:	Excise revenue collected from drugs and liquor
Afing	:	Opium
Afu-toli	:	Poppy lands
Anna	:	Unit of currency. Equivalent to 1/16th of a rupee.
Aus	:	Early maturing variety of rice
Bari	:	Homestead
Behar opium	:	Opium grown in the Gangetic delta of Bihar and Bengal in the nineteenth century; procured by Government and circulated to different provinces as excise opium
Bepari	:	Term used to refer to Assamese merchants
Bigha	:	Measurement of land. 1/3rd of an acre
Burkandez	:	Mercenary soldiers who fought for the Mughal army
Char/Chapori	:	Sand banks near the river. Fertile and extensively cultivated during winters.
Charas	:	Pure resin which is a preparation from the hemp plant, also called hashish.
Chattak	:	Unit of weight. Equivalent to 58.32 grams
Dhapat	:	Tobacco
Ganja	:	Preparation made from the flowering tops of cultivated female parts of the hemp plant
Gossain	:	Spiritual preceptor
Haat	:	Village market
Hookah	:	Apparatus for smoking, a bamboo pipe
Kamrupa	:	Ancient name for Assam.
Kanee	:	Local name for crude opium
Kani Nibarani Sabha	:	Opium Eradication Assembly
Kania	:	Opium eater
Kanikholas	:	A house where raw opium was processed and consumed by a group of opium eaters.

Keyas	:	Local term applied to Marwari traders
Laopani	:	Rice beer
Mahaldars	:	Owner of the revenue division
Malwa opium	:	Opium grown in the princely states of western and central India which was outside the pale of the monopoly of the British government till the 1820s.
Masha	:	0.9071856 gram
Maund (40 ser)	:	37.324 kgs
Mehal	:	Revenue division
Mod	:	Liquor
Mogah	:	Muga variety of silk
Mouzas	:	Fiscal unit
Paan-tamul	:	Betel-leaf and nut
Phatika	:	Home brewed wine
Poorah	:	Unit of land. 1 *poorah* = 3 acres
Rati	:	1.75 grains (1 grain = 0.064799 gram)
Rupit	:	Fertile land
Ryots	:	Peasant
Ryotwari	:	System of land revenue where the revenue settlement was made directly with the cultivators.
Sadr	:	District Headquarter
Sali	:	Transplanted variety of rice
Sattra	:	A Vaishnavite monastery
Sattradhikar	:	Chief Priest of the Vaishnavite monastery
Ser (80 tolas)	:	933.10 grams
Tola	:	11.664 grams

Abbreviations

ACOECR	*Assam Congress Opium Enquiry Committee Report*
ALA	Assam Legislative Assembly
ALC	Assam Legislative Council
AOECR	*Assam Opium Enquiry Committee Report*
ASA	Assam State Archives
DHAS	Department of Historical and Antiquarian Studies
NAI	National Archives of India
RCO	Royal Commission on Opium
SSOT	Society for the Suppression of Trade

CHAPTER 1

Introduction

THE ASSAMESE CALL it *Kanee/Kappa,* following the mode of its preparation and intake (being reduced to a dry state, the opium paste was spread on narrow slips of cloth and later rolled into small bales). For many years before the British occupation of Assam, the 'hubble-bubble'[1] had served as a favourite pastime after a hard-day's labour at the swampy rice fields. Alongside *paan-tamul* (betel-leaf and nut), *kanee* emerged as a stimulant and social lubricant as well. Small gardens of the white and red flower adorned the *bari* (homstead) of most households. They grew 'luxuriantly' as affirmed by a colonial correspondence in 1793.[2] An interesting conjecture attributes that the habit of opium smoking was introduced to the Chinese by the tribes of Assam who had long been addicted to its use.[3] Whatever may have been the mode and method of its spread, opium eating and smoking found a devoted cult in the Brahmaputra valley. However, it never attained the status of connoisseurship as in China, where the Chinese perfected and refined opium smoking into an art and craft. Contrast it with the penny-wise Assamese peasant – who grew poppies and savoured his daily dose of mild stimulation. To him, it entailed recreational and pharmacological properties; the aesthetics neither interested nor enthused him.

Assam had so much in common with its distant neighbour, China. Most importantly, it was naturally gifted with the climate and soil to grow tea plants. It was with this discovery of tea that the province of Assam in the North-East Frontier of British India aroused interest among the colonial officials. (The Assam Tea Company was set up in 1839 when the first opium war was beginning in China.) By the 1840s Assam's configuration within the realms of the imperialism of Britain was made. Its integration is a part of the story that the 'addiction' to tea in Victorian Britain added to the contours of the

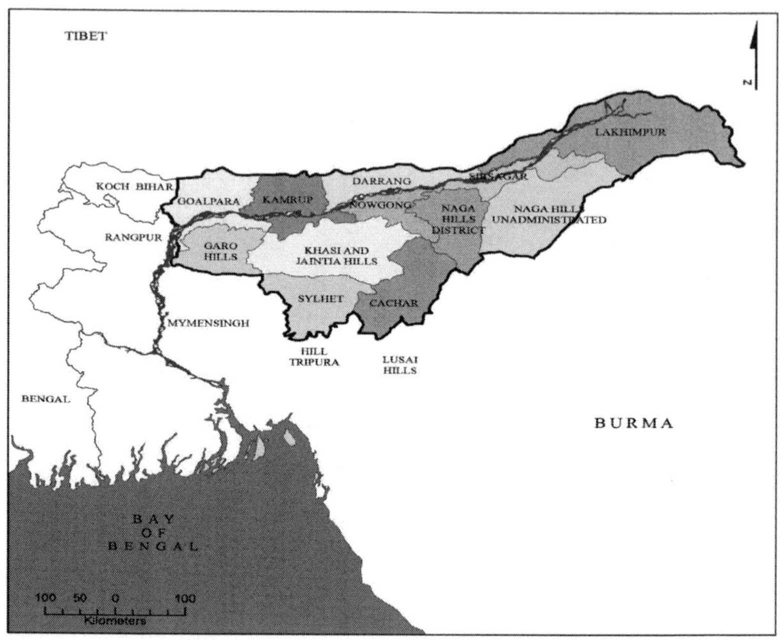

MAP 1.1: DISTRICT MAP OF ASSAM SHOWING THE TERRITORIAL DIVISIONS AS IN THE YEAR 1850. MAP MADE BY AUTHOR.

empire in the Indian subcontinent. Towards the mid-eighteenth century, poppy was the 'golden crop' which spurred Britain's imperial ambition. Acres of land in Bengal and Bihar were teeming with the alluring white and red poppy flowers yielding the juice that would be made into opium *golas* (balls). However, opium was not molasses, it was mind-altering, a psychoactive. Britain had already witnessed the worst phase of opiate use. China was flooded with opium and simmering with discontent over its teeming populace of opium 'addicts'. However, the mercantilist mind was reminded of the immense profits that 'opium for tea' was accruing in China for the empire, which was soon to be disbanded. New routes and markets had to be explored and developed.

Assam's contiguous tracts with Burma and continuing upto Yunnan (famed for its cultivation of best varieties of poppy) was alluring enough. Captain Thomas Welsh's *Report on Assam* hinted at the possibility of the manufacture of 'merchantable opium' in Assam.

This was validated around thirty years later, when David Scott's (the first Agent to the Governor-General, North-East Frontier) remarks on *kanee* – 'in point of purity, probably equal to that of Patna or Benaras',[4] aroused great curiosity at Calcutta. Subsequent surveys and mapping revealed a culture highly accustomed to its use as a medicine and a stimulant. By the turn of the twentieth century, this 'plant of joy' famed as 'Gods own medicine'[5] became a powerful metaphor of dysfunction.

Opium symbolized profits and power. It was capable of inducing physiological and psychological changes in an individual user, effecting changes in the political and social landscape of the region. In turn, they influenced it attributing it with a host of meanings – medicinal, religious and social; economic and political. Each connotation affecting a major change in the way it was perceived. The missionaries preached it was 'evil'. To the medical men, opium was a 'poison' – fatal to the mind and body. Opium eaters of Assam became addicts by the mid-nineteenth century. Opium use was made morally and legally unacceptable. The rhetoric found a suitable comprador in the Assamese intelligentsia who pleaded, argued, protested and finally fought for opium suppression and then eradication. Whether it was in the violent aftermath at Phulaguri (in Nowgong) following the opium anti-cultivation decree of 1860 or the *Nikaniakaran Parva* (Temperance Festival) launched as a part of Non-Cooperation movement in 1920, opium found itself influencing and delineating the course of events – economic or political of the day.

Intoxication and intoxicants remains a neglected study area in India. There is a similar dearth of research on mind-altering substances in Assam, the present north-east province of India. While there have been meticulous research articles, mostly focused on trade and production, they have been by far too little.

This study of the history of intoxication focusing on opium in Assam for the period 1800-1959, narrates the trajectory of opium consumption and its regulation in the Brahmaputra valley of Assam. Moving away from being trade and production centric – the present study attempts to address the centrality of opium in the socio-economic and political life of the people during the period within the scope of the study. The focus of this study is the opium eaters of the Brahmaputra valley of Assam, covering the *ryotwari* areas of Kamrup, Darrang, Nowgong, Sibsagar and Lakhimpur – majority of who were the small peasants. They had, prior to the imposition of monetized economy, led a frugal existence. His indifference to entrepreneurial adventures was interpreted as his 'indolence', and opium consumption was the rationale of such behaviour. Opium use was proclaimed a vice and opium users were labeled as 'social wrecks'. The colonial propaganda of such 'terrible' consequences of 'free cultivation of poppy' led to the anti-cultivation decree in 1860 and the pouring of *abkaree* opium (excise opium) in Assam. The justification was found in the excessive use of opium by the people, which had resulted in lazy and indolent habits of the peasantry in Assam.

To the peasants, it signified blatant disregard of their way of life. Consolidation of British rule resulted in the introduction of monetized economy and forced commercialization of agriculture. To the cash starved peasant, poppy crop ensured that he would be able to render his payments on time. The local Marwari traders were quick to advance credit facilities for the cultivation of poppy. Many of them were earlier chiefly involved in the trade of mustard and some were participants in the opium trade of Bengal, loans were regularly distributed amongst the cultivators for ensuring deliveries. Figures available for the year 1852 (introduction of *abkaree* opium) refer to the apparent importance of poppy as a prime commercial crop. Lakhimpur and Nowgong were the chief exporters of poppy. In 1852, Nowgong had around 3,000 acres of total cultivated acreage under poppy. Not surprising, therefore, that the anti-cultivation decree of 1860 saw violent protest at Phulaguri against the decree. Surprisingly, it failed to evoke any concerted response from the Assamese intelligentsia,[6] who chose to tread a moderate path. Nevertheless, the likes of Hemchandra Barua's mildly satirical composition *Kaniyar Kirtan* and Lakshminath Bezbarua's satire *Arzi* attempted to appeal to the sense and sensibilities of the people accustomed to the use of opium.[7] It is pertinent here to mention that the middle class in its formative years chose to avoid a confrontationist approach, which has led contemporary historical understanding to designate them as collaborators in the colonial enterprise in the twentieth century. With the creation of the Legislative Councils, the Assamese intelligentsia certainly rose up to the occasion and brought forth issues of concern to Assam in the council. Elite activism played an important role in ensuring the success of the anti-opium movement. They were able to take advantage of the political ferment and of the international campaigns against opium. The process of opium suppression became concomitant with the objective of freedom from imperialism and restoring provincial pride.

The Historiography: Opium in Context

As Andrew Sheratt observed, drugs are 'peculiar substances'.[8] The trajectory from approval to denial has been common to all of them. What is also remarkable with them is the fluidity of roles – they can be medicine, stimulants, money, power and social menace. The use/ abuse dichotomy was evident in the anti-opium agitation, which generated tremendous intellectual outpourings in the form of pamphlets and reports arguing for and against prohibition, drawing on the influential pharmaceutical shift, which turned the tide from acceptance to one of opprobrium. An attempt to understand such volatility takes us through vast ranges of scholarship on which rests the understanding of the power and influence of psycho-actives on societies, economies and cultures.

Addictive Consumables, Commerce and Contour of Empire

Imperial expansion was intertwined with the dynamics of trade and networks of production consumption and exchange of psychoactive substances. Exploring this vital dimension in a very succinct manner is Sidney Mintz's *Sweetness and Power* that documents the link between the rise of Britain's colonial empire, industrialization and the increase in the British consumption of tea and sugar.[9] Sugar, to Mintz, was a 'drug food', capable of stimulating and modifying mental activity and which played a very critical role in fostering a culture of conspicuous consumption in England. In another interesting work, Barry Higman[10] focuses on the 'transformative power' of a single commodity, marking a shift from diversified agriculture to sugar monoculture. This provided a fillip to a variety of triangular trades along with altering European tastes and consumption; increased European interest in the tropical colonies, which contributed vitally to the Industrial Revolution.

Woodruff Smith's[11] work on early modern European consumption mannerisms has unfolded the larger historical processes of the conjunction between the use of drug foods and the rise of capitalist world market. To Smith, it reinforced adoption in Europe of tea and sugar as necessities, led to increased demand for both products thus helping to foster British imperialism in Asia, plantation slavery in the West Indies and economic growth in Europe and America. Smith's other work[12] attempts a 'second historiography' of consumption apart from the economic dimension – that of 'politeness and manners', in shaping consumption mannerisms. Analyses of transforming notions of comfort, convenience and gentility in Europe have been the subject of intensive scrutiny. How the fervour for tea in Europe was to lead to a furore in Asia is further elaborated in an essay by Solomon Bard[13] on two imperial commodities, which were the mainstays of commerce of the British East India Company in the nineteenth century. His is an attempt to examine the role of tea in relation to opium and he further explores the conspicuous consumption of tea in Britain. This led to the British Government in India becoming the largest drug trafficking syndicate in the world during the latter part of the century. As he sums it up, 'if there had been no tea, there would be no war'. The social contexts of psychoactive substances – tea, coffee, kola and betel to alcohol, tobacco and cocaine along with their trade, taxation and control have been subjects of intensive analysis by Jordan Goodman, Andrew Sheratt and Paul Lovejoy.[14] Their work asserts the centrality of drugs to the formation of civilizations and the growth of world economies.

David Courtwright's[15] is a comprehensive-geographic and chronological account of the 'psychoactive revolution' that had its roots in the transoceanic commerce and empire building of the early modern period. It also traces the legal, social, political and medical histories of the drugs that he discusses. It focuses on the highly selective nature of the global drug commerce and how psychoactive trade benefited mercantile and imperial elites through fiscal returns and creating dependencies. This engaging account weaves together in a succinct manner the complex portrait of how psychoactive substances are not only part of human experience but in many ways fundamental to our view of civilization. The 'Psychoactive Revolution' which Courtwright articulates involved transoceanic movement. This led to the proliferation of the taste and thereby use across geographic boundaries. This movement of commodities is the foci of Kenneth Pomeranz and Steven Topik's[16] work. They discuss the consumption of chocolate, tea, coffee, cocoa and opium by the Europeans, which subsequently transformed their meanings, and location of production. In consuming countries, they created a culture and in producing countries, they became mere commodities.

Rudi Mathee[17] builds up an impressive account of the encounter of the peoples of Safavid and Qajar Iran with alcohol, opium, tobacco, coffee and tea. Interestingly to him, they are a mark of a 'vibrant rather than an atrophying society'. They open up new avenues of understanding the society. His analysis gives precedence to non-cultural factors, notably economics and geography. The deployment, appropriation and redefinition of mind-altering substances by colonialist forces to aid in domination, exploitation and dispossession of indigenous societies and their traditional forms of drug use is Michael Steinberg, Joseph Hobbs and Kent Matthewson's[18] study. They have elaborated on the impact of the import of drugs into indigenous societies; the introduction of new drugs or new forms of drugs. Further insight into an understanding of the impact of drug food trade on the development of European economies and indigenous societies has been effectively outlined by William Jankowiah and Dan Braindburd.[19] This study has facilitated understanding of how in the early stages of cultural contact, drug foods were important trade items and in many instances only ones acceptable to the natives.

Medical Topographies: Perspectives on Addiction and Drug Diplomacy

Inherent in the concept of addictive consumables are notions of disease and addiction. This has laid the foundation of social and legal restraints and international monitoring and surveillance. Pharmacy and medical journals of the mid-1880s are beset with multifarious opinions, which enabled the globalizing of the circuit of information. It had also helped shape strong temperance sentiments worldwide.

Roger French and Andrew Wear[20] document the mid-nineteenth century epistemological shift, which radically altered notions of the science of medicine. It documents the professionalization of medicine. Medicine became 'scientific' and 'rational' as opposed to that based on natural philosophy since the Middle Ages. The adoption of the 'germ theory of disease' in the later nineteenth century which became attached to the rhetoric of reform was spearheaded by the British Medical Association and it's mouthpiece, *The British Medical Journal* (*BMJ*) and *Lancet*. David Arnold's[21] significant work examines the nature of relationship between the nature of science, technology and medicine in conjunction with the development of British engagement in India. It offers a comprehensive perspective of the role of imperial science in shaping the contours of the empire and the ramifications thereof. Biswamoy Pati and Mark Harrison[22] provide an interesting insight into the 'medicalization' of the colonial power which also reflected utilitarian reformism. Harrison particularly, stresses on how medical topographies identified the vulnerability of newly conquered regions. He asserts, as to how it was all about 'asserting power, marking out cultural differences between the ruler and the ruled'. An essay by Amar Farooqui[23] based on the findings of the report of the Royal Commission on Opium 1893, focuses on the colonial perceptions of the utility of opium as a medicine. He also discusses the 'manipulative element' in the colonial construction of popular 'indigenous' discourse about opium. The Royal Commission's findings have been the foci of introspection on discussions centering science and morality in colonial India. Winther's[24] study is based on the findings mentioned in the Commission's Report. It analyses the contrast between the practices of science in the metropolis and the periphery. It further attempts at integrating science, ethical and economic interests of the colonial Empire. Based on these is an understanding of the political and economic imperatives of the colonial government in the nineteenth century.

For John Logan, the nineteenth century, which witnessed industrialization, colonialism, nationalism, liberalism, was also the 'Age of Intoxication'. In his essay,[25] he investigates the trend of intoxication perceptible amongst different strata, the elites and also those at the lowest rung of the social ladder. This, as his essay contends, led to the emergence of the first organized temperance movements voicing concern over the problem of addiction. Concern over opium use and abuse/addiction in the Victorian society is the focus of Virginia Berridge and Griffith Edwards's[26] monograph. The ubiquity of opium rendered it susceptible to myriad meanings, particularly its rampant use by the working class. She presents examples of middle class denunciations of the use of opium as a stimulant by working class adults. This is characterized as a justification for control, legislative controls and goals.

Geoffrey Harding's[27] innovative 'moral-pathological' model of addiction builds up his argument that the open availability of opium for non-medicinal use was decried by the newly emerging class of medical and pharmaceutical professionals. They ranted at the self-medication practices of the working classes and attempted to establish monopolistic control over the drug's supply for medicinal purposes except until prescribed by a qualified physician. This shifting perception of opiate use from 'intellectually stimulating experience' to 'self destruction tendencies' following the development of the 'disease model of drug addiction'. This is the subject of study in a thoughtful work by Louise Foxcroft.[28] Through an examination of the cultural and medical representations of opiate use, Foxcroft demonstrates that ideas about drug addiction were born out of a combination of both medical and moral concerns.

Medical and ethical concerns were influential in shaping late Victorian attitudes towards race, reform and empire. Jonathan Brown's[29] insight into the evangelical anxiety over the opium trade, which they believed, was detrimental to the progress of Christianity. He remarks that the activities of the Society for the Suppression of Opium Trade (SSOT) might be considered part of the 'consolidationist' schools of empire. For the SSOT, the empire was a laboratory for moral legislation. It desired a more thorough interference in the eastern culture than did the imperial bureaucracy and as Brown asserts, it played a major role in driving the international drug system underground, perhaps this to them 'constituted progress'. William MacAllister[30] situates the historical development of international drug control efforts within political, economic, social, intellectual, cultural and interpersonal contexts. Studying the history of drug regulation in a global arena, it traces the intractability of the 'drug problem'. It provides a frame through which one catches an illuminating glimpse of the modern world.

Opium and the Regional Complexities

China has been a major influence on the world understanding of the 'opium menace'. Much has been written about the Chinese addiction to opium. Standard historical narratives on opium link it to the 'political and social chaos' and the Chinese encounter with 'modernity'. Polemic writings hinge on Britain's moral failure alongside condemnation of opium as evidence of damage done by British imperialists. Written almost twenty years after the Treaty of Tienstin in 1858, Edward Fry's[31] essay captures the intersection of British imperial interests with the controversial trade with opium. Joseph Edkins[32] presents an interesting reading on the dynamics of the opium trade. It encompasses a study of the trade triangle between Britain, China and India. David Owen[33] and John Hill's[34] work holds the Europeans responsible for introduction of a 'vice' on a large scale in China and they portrayed the role of merchants, British, Indians in collaboration with the Chinese for profits rather than looking at it from a mere perspective of 'deliberate policy' of the Empire.

A good work to begin understanding the use of opium in China is a work by Herbert Giles.[35] He presents a wonderful exposition of what opium meant to the Chinese, quoting extensively from

Chinese literature on opium. John Fairbank,[36] an authority on Anglo-Chinese relations, who emphasizes on diplomacy, namely negotiations, through treaties as an alternative form of foreign domination. Commenting on the nature of imperialist aggression in China, he elaborates his argument in 'The Creation of the Treaty System'[37] where his perspective is –'cultural conflict between China and the West' and he expounds the theory of 'synarchy' as an exposition of China's absorption of imperialist aggression.

Highly critical of Fairbank's assertion is Tan Chung.[38] To him, it was neither cultural nor commercial class but the opium traffic that precipitated a major crisis and the treaty system that Fairbank expounds were vehicles of 'Imperialist invasion'. He remarks on the characteristic of the triangle trade which provided 'Indian opium for the Chinese, Chinese tea for the Britons and British raj for the Indians'. In effect, his work is regarded as an 'alternative and contemporary to the Western theoretical framework' and refinement to the earlier works of David Owen, Jonathan Spence and Michael Greenberg, all of whom had noted the existence and significance of a triangular trade, involving opium and British imperialism connecting South and East Asia.

A welcome development has been the engagement of scholars with the opium question on a regional level and this has spawned standard works in English on the issue, although there does exist a vast body of scholarly work on the subject in Chinese literature. Wong[39] has provided a most sophisticated analysis of the significance of opium traffic for British imperialism to date. His findings confirm that the opium sales to China were indispensable for the maintenance of British paramountcy in India and the foundations of British imperialism in general. Carl Trocki[40] re-examines the basic issues concerning the relationship between opium in Britain, India and China. He considers opium as an 'incubator of capitalism' in Asia. The ability of opium to provide consistent, large amounts of revenue for the imperial enterprise, coupled with it's engendering a critical mass of capitalists who profited from the trade. They were the ones who provided a vital support for the imperial lobby throughout the nineteenth century. Barry Miligan[41] offers a potent argument that analyses the ambiguous nature of opium, it was invaluable as an item of commerce, yet it interrupted the free flow of trade between these two great commercial empires. In Britain, it was an accepted analgesic throughout the nineteenth century though the medical profession considered it an addictive and debilitating. This reflects, as Miligan argues, the ambivalent attitude of the English towards the 'Orient – exotic, yet threatening'.

The review of literature available on China has revealed a major spurt of revisionist works in recent years which have followed as the discourse shifts from one of Orient *vs* Occident/West *vs* East and Modernity *vs* Tradition, treating the problem as primarily one of foreign relations between the dynamic nation state of imperial Britain and the stagnant feudal state of imperial China. It is exclusively focused on politics and the diplomacy of opium trade that has been a significant theme of all major standard works. Most of these works have stressed on the foreign relations, elite politics, etc., while also attempting to accommodate the complexity of social relations created by the drug use. Timothy Brook and Bob Wakabayashi's[42] work belongs to the new genre of writings on China. It explores opium in China within political and social contexts rather than moral stances and diplomatic views, drawing on original archival sources. In a non-polemic tone with focus on range of organizations such as the East India Company, the provincial Chinese anti-opium elite groups, League of Nations, the National Anti-opium Association, it highlights the systematic and comprehensive character of drug-control structures and stress their capacity for operating in the political realm and their awareness that it was necessary to do so.

Frank Dikotter, Lars Laamann and Zhou Xun[43] questions the premises of the 'narcophobic discourse'. Their study depicts opium as a 'culturally privileged intoxicant' and argues that smoking of opium was a conscious choice for which the users sought reliable, not infinite, supplies of the drug. They rather assert that 'Chinese were not victims of an international opium plague', but were rather drug users who made disciplined choices based on moderate usage. Treading new ground is Yangwen Zheng's[44] social history of opium use in China. The focus is on the 'social life' of the drug in question, as she attempts to unravel events in the life of, to use her terminology,

'Mr. Opium'. The work is an attempt to carve a biography of opium, within the cultural and social constructs. She has drawn extensively on original Chinese archival sources, which lends novelty to the work, which investigates 'who smoked opium and why?' Alan Baumler[45] explores the changing discourse of opium in China and explores the intimate relationship between opium and China's social and political life. He explores the emergence of drug addiction, following the development and transmission of new theories of addiction to attempts by the Chinese Government to purge the country of the 'opium evil' while examining the international context of China's anti-opium efforts.

The South Asian Connection

Emdad-ul-Haq's[46] work offers an understanding on a range of issues that are pertinent to the understanding of the origins and development of drug abuse and illicit trafficking in Pakistan, India and Bangladesh. He scrutinizes the historical context of the opium menace, colonial policies, internal controls and international regulatory mechanisms and attempts to investigate the proliferation of the drug menace in present times including geostrategy.

Ronald Renard[47] offers a systematic and comprehensive analysis of the socio-economic and political impact of production, trade and use of illicit narcotic drugs in Burma. Burma's history of narcotics has been one of varied policies regarding narcotic use, including colonial networks of production, consumption and distribution, regimes of monitoring and suppression, the Government policy and it's impact on drug control and eradication strategy.

Opium is a rather neglected domain in all-India studies, and even more so, are neglected the analysis of opium consumption in India. Om Prakash,[48] illuminates an otherwise ignored aspect of the opium production and distribution. The focus is the Dutch Cultivation System in Java and their being predecessors of trade of Bengal opium to Indonesia and China. This was before the assumption of monopoly rights by the English East India Company. He explores possibilities of capital accumulation and indigenous entrepreneurship, which the Dutch Cultivation system had generated in Java.

Regarding the production and trade of opium in India, John Richards'[49] work has been highly illuminating. Richards suggests that the report reflects the cultural tensions and conflicts negotiated between British colonizers and the Indian colonized subjects. In another work on the peasant production system of opium,[50] Richards focusses on the opium cultivation, as an export cash crop while throwing interesting insight into the indigenous capitalist enterprise of the Malwa traders which the British could never manage to monopolize. This has been the subject of exposition in Amar Farooqui,[51] – a wide-ranging study on opium production and trade in the Malwa region during the nineteenth century. His work analyses the involvement of Indian merchants and the importance of Malwa opium in fostering new economic and political relations. The British attitudes towards a rival opium monopoly in the West and finally the growth of capital accumulation which favoured the rise of Bombay, has formed the focus of his subsequent work.[52] As Farooqui's emphatic assertion sums up all, 'Without opium, there would be no Bombay'.

Among the works on narcotics which have been highly influential in building up an understanding for the present study is Jim Mill's[53] captivating insight into the conflicting interests of colonial state and its subjects. It looks at ways of how drug production reshaped the ecology of rural Bengal. The resistance to the colonial ambition of regulating the *ganja* trade, which is the subject of another of his study into the economics of cannabis trade and prohibition.[54]

Opium, Empire and Assam

There are yawning gaps in the literature that exists for a comprehensive study of opium in Assam. References to opium though available in both English and Assamese writings, there is certainly dearth on any independent work on the subject. Nevertheless, in one such early work, the issue has been taken up as part of investigations of empire and Assam.

Shrutidev Goswami[55] attempts a chronological exposition of 'opium evil' in Assam. It traces in certain detail the cultivation of opium and the circumstances leading to the prohibition of the private cultivation of opium poppy. This move culminated in resistances of the peasants of Phulaguri against intervention in their mode of sustenance. Alongside are a mention of the evolution and the 'fatality' of British policy with fiscal interests being its cornerstone the main trends of British revenue policies in Assam being expounded in his volume[56] on revenue administration in the early years of the British rule in India. Aspects of revenue accruing from opium and *abkaree* (excise) have been dealt with though a detailed insight is warranted. Yet it fills a crucial gap in understanding the revenue policies and has contributed immensely to shaping up arguments for the present work. It builds on his argument of the 'transitional crisis' which led to alienation of the peasants from their traditional environment[57] and reflects on how the policy of intervention precipitated a crisis in the agrarian landscape and invited resistance. 'Dhewa' or fight for justice as the historians of Assam eulogire it as a counter to the vilification of the Phulaguri uprising by historians of the Raj as 'kania bidroh' (opium-eater's revolt). A monograph on the uprising of Phulaguri by Benudhar Kalita[58] locates peasant's resistance to the sense of deprivation and alienation. Though as he says the Britishers termed it as 'kania bidroh', yet it was the first attempt on the part of the peasants protest against colonial exploitation. He analyses in detail the production of opium in Assam till 1860, the year it was prohibited. Heramba Barpujari offers a chronological evaluation of the British opium policy in Assam.[59] It offers an insight into the official apprehension regarding evolution of an opium policy in Assam following diverse stratum of stakes, which led to the proliferation of the opium problem in Assam.

Amalendu Guha[60] typifies the opium issue as illustrative of an 'Imperialism of Opium', which became the main plank of the nationalist struggle in Assam. He has tried to identify the opportunist shifts in the official policy from prohibition of private cultivation to introduction of *abkaree* further to revenue maximization while progressively reducing the supply of opium. He emphasizes that it was not welfare but a 'monopolist's profit maximizing price policy' that guided the government in this matter. He deplores the apathy of the intelligentsia and their policy of 'prayer and petition' towards the anti-opium agitation which was being initiated in Assam by the resident American Baptist missionary in the nineteenth century. It was not until Assam was drawn into the vortex of nationalist struggle by Gandhi's action-oriented strategy of prohibition of intoxicants that the intelligentsia was infused with a spirit of radicalism. He further elaborates on the influence of contemporary political and economic issues in colonial and post-independence in Assam. [61] For historian Rajen Saikia, opium was a 'sticky' issue where he analyses the opium issue in Assam in context of middle class sensibilities.[62] He reiterates that the opium policy of the Government was influenced by revenue considerations. He discusses in considerable detail the nationalist reactions to the opium question. He maintains that the Assamese elite had been expressing well-informed reactions against opium. Although as he maintains, there was no consensus or unanimity of views among the leaders who represented various interests or their social programme.

Engagement of Assamese literature on opium began in the late nineteenth century. Several works display a strong tradition of an engagement with the issue of social degeneration and reveal a concern for the propagation of socially relevant messages. Facilitating an understanding of the nineteenth century reformist discourse are two Assamese satirical texts by Hemchandra Barua[63] and Dutiram Hazarika.[64] They enable an evaluation of the thought-world of nineteenth century colonial Assam towards issues of social reform. One can safely argue that they belong to an innovative reform agenda and resort to the use of satire, wit and humour. Acknowledgement of the evils of opium eating also echoed in the literary outpourings of the twentieth century, which sought to combine entertainment and reform through satire and wit. Capturing the transition, decay and degeneration in the cultural and political construct of the Assamese society is Indira Goswami's captivating *Datial Hathir Une Khowa Howdah.*[65] The narrative is set in the period around India's independence in Assam and revolves around life in a *Sattra* (Vaishnavite monastery). It captures the many transformations in the society following land reforms and offers an encyclopaedic view of the customs, beliefs, rituals, food habits of the people including the opium-addicted people in the *Sattra*. It also illustrates the favourite and common place habit of the Assamese people, which is the chewing of raw areca nut with betel leaf and lime.

Historiography of opium in Assam has 'demonized' it's use – a striking resemblance with that which occurred to opium in China in the nineteenth and the twentieth centuries. The narrative of opium use as responsible for the moral and physical weakness of the Assamese has been reverberating ever since the colonial times. Historical understanding has thus so far been grappling with lop-sided perspectives which have denied the existence of any moderate or occasional use. They seem to be unanimous in accepting the colonial viewpoint of 'all opium use is harmful'. Such perspectives have been challenged with success elsewhere. This study has also attempted to question this image and revisit the belief that 'Assam was poisoned by opium'.

Survey of Sources

The present study is based on extensive archival research.[66] These archives give access and help imply various conclusions pertaining to ranges of questions that the present study attempts to address. We may begin with a brief survey of scope and nature of the archival records.

Extensive topographical and cartographic surveys rank as the most important sources facilitating forays into building an intellectual framework for an investigation into the geographic and economic significance of Assam. Mapping of natural landscape, geology, vegetation, climate, agriculture, land tenures, river systems reflect the Company's central concerns with trade and commerce and expansionist endeavours in the mid-eighteenth century. In the survey and exploratory records of the eighteenth and nineteenth centuries, one finds mention of long lists of products, prices, information about trade routes, descriptions of coastal and inland marts along with the political information.

There was a careful monitoring of production, circulation and consumption of opium during this period. A range of annual reports, classified either as *Annual Report on the Administration of Assam* or *Annual Excise Administration Reports* contains exhaustive statistical data on excise regulations for opium and other intoxicants. The proceedings from various departments or branches of the colonial state along with the proceedings from the Assam Legislative Assembly and Council debates complement the official statistics. There are other ranges of documents, viz., correspondences of the colonial state relating to resolutions and memorandums on excise administration, proposals towards checking opium smuggling in Assam, measures towards suppressing opium smoking, intelligence notes of the Special Opium Detective Agency or reports on cultivation of *ganja*, which are key indicators of the opium story.

A number of commissioned studies from the colonial period, viz., *Minutes of Evidence of Report of the Royal Commission on Opium, 1895*; *Botham Committee Report 1913*; *The Assam Opium Enquiry Committee Report 1933; The Assam Provincial Banking Enquiry Committee 1929-30* and the *Congress Opium Enquiry Committee, 1925* facilitated engagement with various issues related to opium in Assam. These reports reflect the shifts in the policy of the colonial government towards the issue of intoxication in Assam. The popular perception on opium is also carefully recorded in these works.

The *Assam Pradesh Congress Committee (APCC) Papers* for the period 1921-47 offer insights into the ways the opium issue was handled within the ambit of nationalist struggle. These papers, primarily consisting of important memoranda, telegrams, correspondences between the APCC and the Central Congress Committee, assist in tracing the developments related to the genesis of the anti-eradication movement under the Congress leadership.

Parallel and related to these are some useful collections housed in the National Archives of India. Amongst the most important sources for the study of narcotics are two combined volumes of the opium proceedings available from 1790 to 1856. These proceedings were produced under the administrative supervision of the Indian Home Department till 1863. After that, a separate Revenue Branch (1864-1924) looked into the government revenue. Revenue, which accrued from sources other than Land Revenue, viz., customs, salt, stamps, *abkaree*, etc., was transferred under the administrative control of the Indian Financial Department. Extracts of British parliamentary debates and British diplomatic documents facilitate study of the trajectory of the opium question in colonial Assam within a wider international context.

The Assamese newspaper, viz., *Asamiya*, launched in 1918 by Chandra Kumar Agarwalla, and *Tinidiniya Assamiya*, a tri-weekly edition of *Asamiya*, published for just over a decade from 1930 to

1942, archived at Department of Historical and Antiquarian Studies, Assam, are particularly useful for perspectives on popular perceptions towards the opium problem. It offers useful analysis of the Congress coalition government politics following the launch of the massive Opium Eradication Campaign from 1938. Campaigns of the Opium Eradication Assemblies were widely reported in the press. Focus was given on the treatment of addicts. Another important feature was the advertisement of popular medicines, which claimed to cure opium addiction.

Opinions and programmes of the worldwide evangelical missions and the anti-opium tirade spearheaded by the SSOT were reflected in their mouthpiece *The Friend of India*. They worked in close collaboration with the American Baptist missionaries at Assam. The latter articulated opinions against the vice of intoxication in their publication of *Orunodoi* in the nineteenth century. This literary journal played an important role in initiating social criticism in colonial Assam by embarking on a propaganda against the use of opium. One can briefly mention some key essays like 'Evils of Opium' (January 1846) followed, by 'The Death of an Opium-eater' (May 1846), *Kani Lukor Katha* (June 1860), *Kani Erabor Katha* (June 1861) which found place in this journal.

Medical literature dealing with opium during the period under study is voluminous. These medical journals, viz., the *Lancet*, *British Medical Journal*, and the *Edinburgh Medical and Surgical Journal* mostly belonging to the late nineteenth century Victorian England, are littered with scores of experiments, notes, commentaries, debates and warnings on opium as therapy and tonics. Highly polemic in tone in their reference to the issue of opium in Assam, they contain several elaborate articles offer revealing insights towards understanding of the concept of opium addiction, opium addicts, and the disease model of addiction, viewing opium addiction as a social problem.

Organization of the Volume

The overall goal of the research is to establish a meaning for opium within the imperial-colonial context of the nineteenth and twentieth centuries and the combination of challenges it posed to the government, the polity and also the socio-economic structures that were defined and re-defined by it. While it has also been my attempt to illuminate, as to how opium came to occupy a central place in the 'cultures of consumption' as also in the socio-economic and political life of a people. How it became embedded in societal ethos where it not only served as a social lubricant; soon to metamorphose into a narco-identity for the people of Assam, will also be discussed.

In order to attempt this task, the present volume is based on explaining several queries that revolve around: the complex network of imperial commodities and the emerging economic geography of Empire in colonial Assam; how the opium question was interwoven with imperial ideologies and colonial governance; the emerging pattern of distribution and consumption of opium in colonial Assam and to explore the creation of drug dependency in a social context; the competing forces of Empire, which played a key role in the production and distribution of opium; national politics alongside international drug diplomacy and seek to answer how these together shaped the discourses of opium in Assam; the wider implication of opium production and consumption in the agrarian economy and attempt a review of the narrative of the nationalist critique of intoxication.

In order to address the issues outlined above, I have structured the volume in the following order. It begins with scrutinizing the role of addictive consumables – sugar, tea and opium to the understanding of imperialistic behaviour in Chapter 2. Drug commodities have played a central role in the making of the modern world and the intertwined interests of trade and expansion was woven around imperial tastes – sugar, tea and then opium. Examining the strategies of governance in Chapter 3, is an attempt to highlight the colonial curiosity to investigate the physical landscape including medical topographies which present socio-economic and political perspectives of climate, vegetation, diet, disease and medicine. These were intimately bound up with British attitudes of racial distinctions and hierarchies. In its colonial context, it was all about asserting power, marking out cultural differences between the ruler and the ruled and to establish them as inferior and passive.

Chapter 4 scrutinizes the geopolitical advantages that the colonial government was keen to utilize. With direct routes to China under threat, the search for alternative passages was intensified. The imperial eye struck gold with the discovery of tea in Assam. Exploratory surveys proved that Assam was an invaluable opium – with its poppy fields and direct access to Yunnan in China. Imperial concerns were quick to identify a culture of consumption with commercial significance in a colonial frontier. Undoubtedly the volume argues, the prevalence of a tradition of experimentation with various stimulants – from rice beer to tobacco and betel nut chewing facilitated opium's easy infiltration into the social and cultural life of the Assamese. This was attended with social, economic, and later on political ramifications. The identification of the indigenous Assamese races rendered unproductive as mentioned in colonial accounts and upheld by a section of Assamese intelligentsia was regarded as the consequence of relentless use of opium, which needed immediate remedial intervention. This follows an engagement with the significant facets of British policy in Chapter 5 regarding issues of intoxication – monitor the abuse of stimulants and other intoxicants like liquor and drugs (apart from opium) by introduction of *abkaree* regulations and exploring the ramifications, which is the subject of study of the subsequent chapter. Peasant resistances, Assamese anti-opium propaganda, temperance societies, missionary involvement, official policies of appeasement reveal the multi-stranded dimensions of the issue of intoxication in Assam have been appraised in this chapter. This forms the background for Chapter 6 which examines international context of Assam's anti-opium efforts in the midst of a great prohibition campaign conducted by M.K. Gandhi. It discusses a repertoire of techniques including legislative activism for elimination of 'the great evil called opium' from Assam. In 1939, the Congress Coalition Government launched the Opium Prohibition Campaign, which leads us into Chapter 7 which scrutinizes the various facets of the prohibition within the ambit of the issues of public health with an implicit political agenda of the contemporary government, the Congress Coalition Ministry. Chapter 8 is a re-look into the narrative of the decay and destruction believed to be the consequence of opium use. By examining the data available from various official sources including statistics of rural agrarian economy, it has been attempted to offer an alternative perspective to the narrative of opium intoxication in Assam.

Notes

1. *Hubble-Bubble* refers to smoking of tobacco with a hookah – a long pipe attached to a container filled with water which was used to cool the smoke. Due to the presence of water, on smoking, the pipe let out a gargling sound.
2. 'Report on Assam, 1794, From Captain Welsh to Edward Hay, Esq., Secretary to Government, dated 6 February 1794.' Nagendra N. Acharya, *Historical Documents on Assam and Neighbouring States,* New Delhi: Omsons Publications, 1983, pp. 8-14.
3. Don Sinibaldo De Mas, 'England, China and India', in Hartmann H. Sultzberger (tr.), *All about Opium*, London: BiblioBazaar, LLC, 2009 (rpt.), p. 102.
4. Alexandar Mackenzie, *History of the Relations of the Government with the Hill Tribes of the North East Frontier of Bengal*, New York: Cambridge University Press, 2012, p. 388.
5. William Osler, *The Evolution of Modern Medicine: A Series of Lectures Delivered at Yale University on the Siliman Foundation in April 1913*, New Haven: Yale University Press, 1913.
6. The Assamese middle class was the 'compound product' of a Western system of education, tea plantation society and colonial administrative machinery. Many of them were educated at Calcutta which was the nerve centre of training in English education and culture. The early Assamese intelligentsia included the likes of Haliram Dhekial Phukan (1802-32), Jajnaram Phukan (1805-38), Dinanath Bezbaroa (1813-95), Harakanta Sarma Majindar Barua (1815-1902), Anandaram Dhekial Phukan (1829-59), Gunabhiram Barua (1834-94), Hemchandra Barua (1835-96), Madhab Chandra Bordoloi (1847-1907), etc. The ambivalence in their attitude towards the colonial rule is hence discernable. Rajen Saikia, *Social and Economic History of Assam, 1853-1921*, New Delhi: Manohar, 2001, pp. 159-87.
7. Refer, Hemchandra Barua, *Kaniyar Kirtan: A Play in Assamese on the Evils of Opium-Eating*, Guwahati: Hem Chandra Prakashan, 2003 (rpt.); and *Bezbarua Granthavali*, vol. I, Guwahati: Sahitya Prakash, 1968.
8. Jordan Goodman, Andrew Sheratt and Paul Lovejoy (eds.), *Consuming Habits: Deconstructing Drugs in History and Anthropology*, New York: Routledge, 1995, p. 1.
9. Sidney W. Mintz, *Sweetness and Power: The Place of Sugar in Modern History*, New York: Penguin Books, 1986.
10. Barry Higman, 'The Sugar Revolution', *Economic History Review*, 53(2000): 213-36.
11. Woodruff R. Smith, 'Complications of the Common Place: Tea, Sugar and Imperialism', *Journal of Interdisciplinary History*, 23(1992): 259-78.

12. Woodruff R. Smith, *Consumption and the Making of Respectability 1600-1800*, New York: Routledge, 2002.
13. Solomon Bard, 'On Opium and Tea' (paper presented at the International Conference on Lin Zexu, Opium War and Hong Kong, Hong Kong, December 1998).
14. Goodman, Sheratt and Lovejoy, op. cit.
15. David Courtwright, *Forces of Habit: Drugs and the Making of the Modern World*, Harvard: Harvard University Press, 2010.
16. Kenneth Pomeranz and Steven Topik, 'Economic Culture of Drugs', in Kenneth Pomeranz et al. (eds.), *The World that Trade Created: Society, Culture and the World Economy, 1400 to the Present*, New York: M.E. Sharpe Inc., 2006, pp. 74-97.
17. Rudi Mathee, *The Pursuit of Pleasure: Drugs and Stimulants in Iranian History 1500-1900*, Princeton: Princeton University Press, 2005.
18. Michael K. Steinberg, Joseph J. Hobbs and Kent Mathewson (eds.), *Dangerous Harvest: Drug Plants and the Making of Indigenous Landscapes*, Oxford: Oxford University Press, 2003.
19. William Jankowiah and Dan Braindburd, 'Using Drug Foods to Capture and Enhance Labour Performance: A Cross Cultural Perspective', *Current Anthropology*, 37(1997): 717-20.
20. Roger French and Andrew Wear, *British Medicine in an Age of Reform*, New York: Routledge, 1991.
21. David Arnold, *Science, Technology and Medicine in Colonial India*, vol. III of the *New Cambridge History of India*, Cambridge: Cambridge University Press, 2004.
22. Bisawmoy Pati and Mark Harrison (eds.), *The Social History of Health and Medicine in Colonial India*, New York: Routledge, 2009.
23. Amar Farooqi, 'Opium as a Household Remedy in Nineteenth Century Western India', in Biswamoy Pati and Mark Harrison (eds.), *The Social History of Health and Medicine in Colonial India*, New York: Routledge, 2009, pp. 229-37.
24. Paul Winther, *Anglo-European Science and the Rhetoric of Empire: Malaria, Opium and the British Rule in India, 1756-1895*, Oxford: Lexington Books, 2003.
25. John F. Logan, 'Age of Intoxication', *Yale French Studies*, 50(1974): 81-94.
26. Virginia Berridge and Griffith Edwards, *Opium and the People: Opiate Use in Nineteenth-century England*, New Haven: Yale University Press, 1999 (2nd edn.).
27. Geoffrey Harding, 'Constructing Addiction as Moral Failing', *Sociology of Health and Illness*, 1(1986): 75-85.
28. Louise Foxcroft, *The Making of Addiction: The 'Use' and 'Abuse' of Opium in Nineteenth Century Britain*, Hampshire: Ashgate Publishing, 2007.
29. Jonathan B. Brown, 'Politics of the Poppy: The Society for the Suppression

of the Opium Trade, 1874-1916', *Journal of Contemporary History* 8(1973): 97-111.

30. William MacAllister, *Drug Diplomacy in the Twentieth Century: An International History*, New York: Routledge, 2000.
31. Edward Fry,'China, England and Opium', *Contemporary Review*, 27(1876): 447-59.
32. Joseph Edkins, *Opium: Historical Note*, Shanghai: American Presbyterian Mission Press, 1898.
33. David E. Owen, *The British Opium Policy in China and India*, New Haven: Yale University Press, 1934.
34. J.S. Hills, *The Indo-Chinese Opium Trade*, London: Henry Frowde, 1884.
35. Herbert Giles, *Some Truths About Opium Smoking*, Cambridge: W. Heffer, 1923.
36. John K. Fairbank, *Trade and Diplomacy on the China Coast: The Opening of the Treaty Ports, 1842-54*, Harvard: Harvard University Press, 1953.
37. John K. Fairbank (ed.), *The Cambridge History of China*, vol. X, Cambridge: Cambridge University Press, 1978.
38. Tan Chung, *China and the Brave New World*, Durham, NC: Carolina Academic Press, 1978.
39. J.Y. Wong, *Deadly Dreams: Opium and the Arrow War (1856-1860) in China*, Cambridge: Cambridge University Press, 1998.
40. Carl A. Trocki, *Opium, Empire and the Global Political Economy*, New York: Routledge, 1999.
41. Barry Milligan, *Pleasures and Pains: Opium and Orient in Nineteenth Century British Culture*, Charlottesville: University Press of Virgina, 1995.
42. Timothy Brook and Bob T. Wakabayshi, *Opium Regimes: China, Britain and Japan, 1839-1952*, California: California University Press, 2006.
43. Frank Dikotter, Lars Laamann and Zhou Xun, *Narcotic Culture: A History of Drugs in China*, London: C. Hurst and Co., 2004.
44. Yangwen Zheng, *The Social Life of Opium in China*, Cambridge: Cambridge University Press, 2003.
45. Alan Baumler, *The Chinese and Opium under the Republic: Worse than Floods and Wild Beasts*, Albany: State University of New York Press, 2007.
46. Emdad U. Haq, *Drugs in South Asia: From the Opium Trade to the Present Day*, New York: St. Martin Press, 2000).
47. Ronald D. Renard, *The Burmese Connection: Illegal Drugs and the Making of Golden Triangle: On the Impact of the Illegal Drug Trade*, vol. 6, London: Lynn Rienner Publishers, 1996.
48. Om Prakash,'Opium Monopoly in India and Indonesia in the Eighteenth Century', *Indian Economic Social History Review*, 1(1987): 63-80.
49. John F. Richards, 'Opium and the British Indian Empire: The Royal Commission of 1895', *Modern Asian Studies* 2(2002): 375-420.

50. John F. Richards, 'Indian Empire and the Peasant Production of Opium', *Modern Asian Studies*, 1(1981): 59-82.
51. Amar Farooqi, *Smuggling as Subversion: Colonalism, Indian Merchants and the Politics of Opium*, New Delhi: New Age International, 1998.
52. Amar Farooqui, *The Opium City: The Making of Early Victorian Bombay*, New Delhi: Three Essays Collective, 2006.
53. James H. Mills, 'Cannabis in Colonial India: Production, State Intervention and Resistance in Late Nineteenth-Century Bengali Landscape', in Michael Steinberg, John Hobbs and Kent Mathewson (eds.), *Dangerous Harvest: Drug Plants and the Transformation of Indigenous Landscapes*, New York: Oxford University Press, 2004.
54. James H. Mills, *Cannabis Britannica: Empire, Trade and Prohibition, 1800-1928*, Oxford: Oxford University Press, 2005.
55. Shrutidev Goswami, 'The Opium Evil in Nineteenth Century Assam', *Indian Economic Social History Review*, 3-4(1982): 365-76.
56. Shrutidev Goswami, *Aspects of Revenue Administration in Assam*, Guwahati: Spectrum Publications, 1987.
57. Shrutidev Goswami. 'The Phulaguri Uprising: Some Reflections', in Joyashri Choudhary (ed.), *Souvenir: North East India History Association*, Nagaon: Khagarijan College, 2009, pp. 29-38.
58. Benudhar Kalita, *Phulagurir Dhewa (the Uprising at Phulaguri)*, Deurigaon: Nagaon, 1961.
59. Heramba K. Barpujari, *Assam in the Days of the Company, 1826-1858*, New Delhi: Spectrum Publications, 1980.
60. Amalendu Guha, *Medieval and Early Colonial Assam: Society, Polity, Economy*, Calcutta: K.P. Bagchi, 1991.
61. Amalendu Guha, *Planter-Raj to Swaraj: Freedom Struggle and Electoral Politics in Assam, 1826-1947*, New Delhi: Indian Council of Social Science Research, 1998.
62. Rajen Saikia, *Social and Economic History of Assam, 1853-1921*, New Delhi: Manohar, 2001.
63. Hemchandra Barua, *Kaniyar Kirtan*, Guwahati: Hemchandra Prakashan, 2003 (rpt.).
64. Dutiram Hazarika, 'Rasik Puran' (unpublished manuscript), Guwahati: Department of Historical and Antiquarian Studies, 1877.
65. Indira R. Goswami, *Datial Hathir Une Khowa Howdah (The Moth-Eaten Howdah of the Tusker)*, tr. Indira Goswami, New Delhi: Rupa, 2002.
66. These include the Assam State Archives, West Bengal Archives, The National Archives, New Delhi and the British Library including resources at Department of Historical and Antiquarian Studies (DHAS), Assam, the Central Secretariat Library, New Delhi and the Nehru Memorial Library, New Delhi.

CHAPTER 2

Tastes that Turned History: Tea, Sugar and Opium – Intersecting Stories and Intoxicating Connotations

SCHOLARS INVESTIGATING MANKIND'S long and complex relationship with 'mind altering' substances have agreed that the use of drugs[1] have been ubiquitous and omnipresent in human history. In different regions of the world, psychoactive substances have not only been acceptable but often are also an integral part of religious practices, social and cultural life. Their interaction with different geographical and social settings was facilitated by their inclusion in the global stream of commerce, which set in motion a 'psychoactive revolution'. As two leading American anthropologists, Sidney Mintz and Eric Wolf have showed, that modern commerce in commodities resulted in more than mere economic exchange. Since the rise of the modern world economy, commodities have, in a fundamental sense, shaped the politics, culture and social structure of people around the globe.[2] Concluding his study of sugar's modern history, Mintz comments, 'the first sweetened cup of hot tea to be drunk by an Englishman was a significant historical event, because it pre-figured the transformation of an entire society, a total re-making of it's economic and social basis'.[3] Addition of sugar to tea altered European culinary tastes and in turn fuelled interest and investments in tropical colonies.[4]

From the late eighteenth century onwards, opium became a key commodity in the expanding commerce between Asia and the Atlantic nations, thereby becoming enmeshed in the economies and cultures of the regions. Exchange of psychoactive substances was a lucrative and deliberate indulgence. The medical, hedonic, habituating and in some cases, nutritional properties made them ideal products and reliable sources of profit. The conjunction between the consumption of tea, sugar and opium[5] as commodities with varying but certain 'pharmacologic' properties and the birth of modern colonialism offers insight into the interconnections between the larger trends and movements in history. The commodification of drugs thus became the basis of a promising profiteering trade.

Sugar, Tea and Opium

It was through the networks of distribution that the stories of sugar, tea and opium were set to intersect and inter wine with the British colonial empire in Asia. What linked the commodities were the shifting patterns of dietetics that sugar and tea[6] fostered in England associating it with wide-ranging discourses from culture of health to culture of respectability, to becoming symbols of patriotic zeal.[7] There exists sufficient evidence to document the enormous increase in sugar trade, in consequence of the increased consumption of tea. The 'Psychoactive Revolution', which David Courtwright mentions, is what triggered the mass consumption market, followed first by massive mercantile pursuits and later by an advocacy for imperial dominion in Asia and Africa. Consumption mannerisms have been significant indices of power relations, a view echoed in Sidney Mintz's classic study of sugar where he has explored the impact of commodities in shaping patterns of economic dominance, in challenging and in many instances, reverting the prevailing order. Mintz claimed that sugar in nineteenth century England pioneered the principle of mass consumption. The growth of sugar plantations in the Carribean Islands played a catalyst in propelling the demand for tea.[8] Tea was introduced in the second half of the seventeenth century,[9] and its general employment was not adopted without bitter opposition.[10] Over time, it came to characterize British ideas of gentility and respectability in the eighteenth and the nineteenth centuries; a historical incident attended with wide-ranging ramifications. Tea came to be regarded as a necessity, the enhanced consumption of which was upheld in a great measure by custom and which essentially dependant on the use of sugar for enhancing its taste and flavour. By the early years of the nineteenth century, tea drinking was no longer a luxury, it was hailed as the 'national drink'. Consumption triggered production and trade. Incidental to the increased demand for tea was an upsurge in the demand for exotic Chinese ceramics for the 'tea and sugar' ritual. Its widespread adoption in Britain and Europe[11] greatly led to an upsurge in the demand for both the products – tea and sugar – fuelling the need for economic expansion in Asia and the Indies.

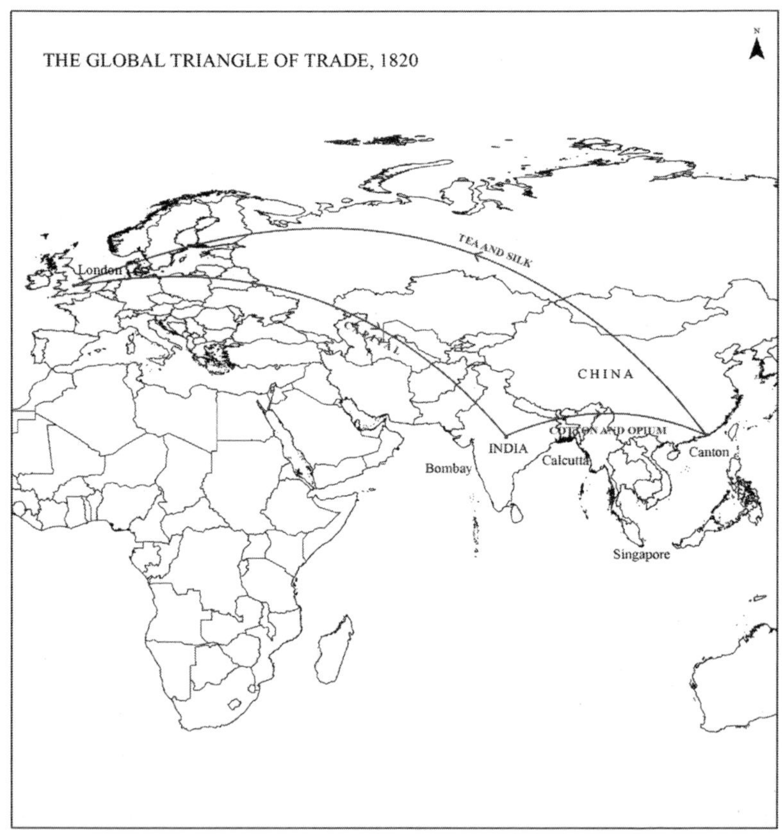

Source: David Meyer, 'The Global Triangle of Trade', in *Hongkong as a Global Metropolis*, Cambridge: Cambridge University Press, 2000, p. 36.

MAP 2.1: MAP SHOWING THE MID-NINETEENTH CENTURY TRIANGULAR TRADE NETWORK BETWEEN ENGLAND, INDIA AND CHINA.

Expenses on tea from China were annually draining England of its precious metals including silver from the Spanish colonies.[12] China accumulated vast amounts of silver, which became the standard global trading currency of the period.[13] An effective solution[14] to the drain of metals from Europe was revealed in the export of two Indian commodities – raw cotton and opium. Opium sales to China rocketed year after year.[15] Opium proved an amazing commodity. The pattern of economic growth and capital accumulation in the East and the West were reversed towards the end of the eighteenth century with opium making a significant contribution towards reshaping of the trade balance. In fact, drugs and the trade in intoxicants like cocoa, tobacco and opium have acted as facilitators in the formation of the British Empire and in the creation of a global capitalistic economy. However, the conjunction of 'relentless commodification' of drugs, their redefinition and appropriation as powerful symbols of exploitation and domination provides an interesting insight into the basis of intentional intoxication, where the 'Addiction' of one leads to 'Corruption' of the other. Herein, lay the crux of the economics of opium, politics of the Empire and its role in effecting a metamorphosis of landscapes and livelihoods.

Interestingly, the three linked commodities – sugar, tea and opium – share a similar trajectory of attraction and repulsion. Beginning their careers as exotic but with significant therapeutic properties,[16] it was their 'downward filtration' as articles of mass consumption,[17] which led to their being denounced as potent agents of physical degeneration, social turmoil and moral failing. The 'use/abuse dichotomy', the demarcation between 'pleasure/aesthetic qualities' and 'medicinal side/euphoric side' were all located within the eighteenth-century European discourse of science and medicine,[18] assigning to the commodities meanings within the prevailing discourse.

The process from elite to mass consumption is suggestive of their geographic and cultural fluidity with symbolic connotation with each mutation. Although trade was a prime catalyst in the 'Europeanization'[19] of commodities, the tentacles of the Enlightenment era prosperity and the notion of progress which it spawned up provided a thrust to the desire for control, not only over distribution but also production of commodities so as to ensure their constant availability. The medical/botanical debate, motivated by necessity of control over production, further spurred the demand for such commodities. Along with the movement of plants, which followed the growth of botanical sciences, it was peasant agriculture and tropical plantations that were patronized to ensure increasing supply of crops for the world market.

Europe was enriched by a range of products – tobacco, maize, potato, cocoa and beans – from the 'New World'. Tea took them towards Asia, where China was the home of the brew whose lure proved more enchanting than either spices or textiles. The English East India Company outmanoeuvred the Dutch to monopolize the entire tea trade with China, which was to inaugurate a long phase of confrontation between the two countries.[20] This was in stark contrast to the spirit of commercial enterprise of the British. Attempts to establish diplomatic relations to ensure free and direct access to the tea trade, was met with stiff resistance by the Chinese, who viewed with suspicion all foreigners and also the expansionist policies of Europe in Tibet, the East Indies, Philippines, Burma and Nepal.[21]

As China became a 'silver lined black hole of European commercial desire', in opium,[22] the British finally found something that the Chinese would buy in large quantities. Opium turned the balance, establishing itself as a powerful commodity financing British economic and political expansion. This was done by structurally linking the economies of China, India and Britain in a trade triangle. By 1773, the establishment of an opium monopoly in India ensured and regulated supply, with profits from opium trade being ploughed to pay for exports of tea from China.

Contours of a Beverage and a Poison: Imperial Eye in the Land of Golden Gardens

The growth of tea plantations in India forms a significant phase of British colonial expansion, where the science and politics of the Empire worked in conjunction to lubricate wheels of colonial expansion, capitalism and the creation of a modern state.[23] Until 1820, all tea came from China, and it was not until 1858, that the

Company began to ship Indian tea to London.[24] The British recourse to opium for tea launched a serious economic concern in China that grappled with adverse balance of payments. The measures taken by the Chinese government began with Emperor Guangzhou's edict of 1729, banning the imports of opium. Chinese campaigns to prohibit opium during the years 1837, 1838 and 1839, culminated in Commissioner Lin's arrival at Canton, and the confiscation and destruction, by his orders of the smuggled opium. This afforded the pretext for the first Anglo-Chinese war. The results of the war developed themselves in the Chinese rebellion, the utter exhaustion of the Imperial exchequer, the gigantic dimensions assumed by the opium trade and ultimately to the growth of tea plantations in its Indian colony.

Growing Chinese belligerency to English mercantile pursuits was viewed as a threat to the 'cultural economies of consumption'. The Charter Act of 1833 made possible for European settlement to allow for direct control over cultivation of such crops as tea, coffee and indigo. This provided an impetus to the British East India Company towards exploring avenues for growth of plantations elsewhere than in China. Official correspondences reflected apprehensions over the increasing tensions at Canton and the Chinese attempts to sabotage the tea trade. This made it imperative for the East India Company to chart 'unknown vast jungles of a strange land', thus, intricately connecting the 'consuming histories of taste to the fruitful disciplines of colonial enterprise'.[25]

> [T]his exceedingly valuable branch of English commerce has been put in jeopardy by ignorance of China, by unnecessarily taking offence and by making retaliation on the part of our residents there. If the trade is lost, either a great boon will be given to the people of this country, who have been so habituated to the use of tea, will be deprived of one of the most necessaries of life – unless we shall find an adequate supply from some territory, over which foreigners have no control, a substitute country which has nearly the same physical circumstances and soil as the district of China – and this idea naturally turns our thoughts to *Assam*.[26]

The Land of Golden Gardens now lay within the domain of the 'New Imperialism' of Britain, as an 'agricultural estate of the tea drinking Britons'.[27] Tea apart, the strategic position of Assam with a common frontier with Tibet, China and Burma was wrought with financial and commercial advantages. Late eighteenth and nineteenth century exploratory accounts of the North-Eastern Frontier reveal the existence of a thriving commercial intercourse between Assam, the neighbouring tribal hill states, China and Tibet.[28]

Large-scale importation of labour into Assam began from 1860 onwards, which was undoubtedly an expensive venture. The failure of the British government to mobilize local labour and the apathy and indolence of the natives, consequent to their 'unlimited use of opium' was a cause of much concern and anxiety. This apprehension of the use of opium and it's assuming 'epidemic' proportions so as to adversely affect the fortunes of the tea plantation industry, echoed in the reports of C.A. Bruce. In 1843, he pleaded to the British government to prohibit the private cultivation of poppy, lest it would 'affect our future prospects in regard to tea.'[29] Col. Vetch's testimony before the Select Committee in 1859, echoes Bruce's apprehension, '[T]here is no sort of cultivation [tea] more congenial to European ideas, habits and constitution. Opium is an obstacle to tea production, which causes debility in the constitution and degeneracy in the race.'[30]

In 1860, private cultivation of poppy was banned in Assam.

A Case for Opium in Assam

No unanimity exits regarding when and how opium was introduced in Assam. The reference to the use of poppy in Assam dates back to the time of the Ahom–Mughal conflict, though it is asserted that it was known even during the days of Sankardeva who is said to have 'removed one of his disciple, Surya Saraswati from the office of the Bhagavat for his addiction to opium'.[31] The *Baharistan-i-Ghaibi*[32] refers to the Mughal general, Raja Ram Singh, who sent a packet of *aphu-guti* (poppy seeds) to the Ahom general Lachit Barphukan, to indicate the innumerable number of Mughal soldiers to which the latter retorted by sending a piece of pestle and mortar with which the seeds could be easily reduced to powder.[33] Credence to the theory that the Mughal incursions in Assam had facilitated the introduction of opium in Assam is contained in the

Buranjis[34] which contain references to presents from the *Paadshah* (meaning the Mughal Emperor of Delhi), which included *afing*[35] (opium) among other articles. According to historian, S.K. Bhuyan, the cultivation of poppy and the habit of its consumption in Assam might have been imported by the bordering tribes from China where the production of this drug was prevalent since ancient times.[36] He further attests to the presence of a thriving commerce between the *mudois* (Assamese merchants) with the neighbouring hill tribes and with China and Tibet. Assamese merchants went to Yunnan in China by the line of trade through Sadiya. In fact, it was the lucrative trade with Tibet and China passing through Assam that was perhaps the reason why the Indian kings (Turko-Afghan) and the Ti-Shans had attempted to capture the Brahmaputra valley. In his account of the *Sattra* institutions of Assam, Satyendranath Sarma tells us that within the precincts of a *Sattra*, addiction to opium eating, smoking and drinking was not tolerated. Though the habit of drinking was nowhere reported, the other two vices were found among the devotees, who were penalized heavily for such indulgence.[37] A chronicle records that sometimes criminals were compelled to swallow opium tablets as a sort of punishment during the rule of the Ahoms.[38] Maniram Dewan records that it was during the reign of the Ahom king, Lakshmi Singha, that the poppy seeds were introduced from Bengal and cultivated at Beltola in Guwahati.[39] It was believed to be consumed only by the royal house and the aristocratic families.

Notwithstanding this disagreement about the origin of opium in Assam, at least, in the last few hundred years, as opium came to be consumed in Assam two forms: eating (*kanikhowa*) and smoking (*kanipankhowa*) were prevalent.[40] When opium is eaten in small pilules, or made into a decoction by mixing it with water, the process is known as *kanikhowa* or *kanimolikhowa*. When it is smoked, after mixing the opium decoction with dried betel-leaves, the process is known as *kanipankhowa*. The process of smoking by a hookah is said to have popularized the habit of smoking, although, opium eating has been the preferred mode of consumption at the later stages of addiction, as the preparation of opium for smoking takes a considerable time.[41]

Initially confined to the upper echelons of the society, opium was a status marker. The participation of the lower classes made opium visible as a socio-economic problem. This was attended by a host of economic, social, administrative and legal ramifications for Assam. As an anti-opium rhetoric gained prominence by the second half of the nineteenth century, which was strengthened by the missionaries zeal and colonial ideology of paternalism in the mid-nineteenth century. This mission in Assam found zealous adherents in English-educated Assamese elites, foremost being the trio of Anandaram Dhekial Phukan, Gunabhiram Barua and Hemchandra Barua. Post 1857 witnesses the development of the colonial policy of non-interference with the native customs and traditions. Colonial appreciation and acknowledgement of the magnitude of the problem was followed by a vigorous native anti-opium propaganda. The colonial administration, however, adopted the declared intention in the Bengal Resolution (1813) that of *maximum revenue from the minimum consumption*. This ambiguity was in fact a characteristic of British colonial policy and was well-reflected in all its proclaimed attempts at *righteousness before revenue* merely served to disguise the commercial intentions of the British East India Company.

In 1860, as mentioned earlier, the private cultivation of poppy was banned. However, it was estimated that in 1864-5, around 143,500 lakh rupees was collected from the sale of opium to the labouring population. Certain tea planters held licenses for the sale of opium to the labour. Opium was used as a tool to induce and enhance labour productivity, apart from pacifying hostile recruits and also for retaining them.[42] Was it a ploy manoeuvred by the British tea planters to induce the labourers to work in the tea plantations, which later boomeranged?[43] Studies conducted on the conjunction of the use of drug foods with the rise of capitalist world market have revealed a vital link between the introduction of drug foods and the rise of capitalist economies. A close relationship has been revealed between the type of subsistence and the stimulants used.[44]

And opium was Britain's panacea with embedded denotations – stimulant, palliative, profit and power – with each changing notion of European ideology affecting a major shift in the meanings of opium. It was this 'polymorphorous nature' that gave opium its distinctive character in the exposition of the interweaved narratives and made it the 'scandal of the empire'.

Notes

1. Commonly understood, a 'drug' is a substance that produces significant physiological and psychological changes. They can be sedatives, analgesic and stimulants, which can be put to both therapeutic and non-therapeutic use, the boundaries are fluid though.
2. Alfred W. Mcoy, 'Historical Review of Opium Production: Opium as Commodity Policy Implications of Historic Pattern', <www.druglibrary.org/schaffer/heroin/historic.htm>(30.12.2008).
3. Probably, the first work in English devoted to a single commodity was R.N. Salaman's, *History and Social Influence of the Potato*, London: Cambridge University Press, 1949. It dealt with its origin, domestication, worldwide diffusion and political fate in European life. Potato was discovered in 1538 by a Spanish soldier, Pedro de Cieza de Leon, in the Cauca valley of Columbia and was introduced in Europe as a curiosity. Along with maize, the potato was instrumental in solving the food problem of the growing population of Europe in the eighteenth century, thus reducing the danger of periodic famines. This was followed by many other such works on sugar, tea, drugs – hard and soft – bananas, tomato, beans, etc. S. Mintz and C. Du Bois, 'The Anthropology of Food and Eating', *Annual Review of Anthropology*, 31(2002): 99-119.
4. The growing demand for sugar towards the end of the fourteenth century was the result of growing European craving for sugar especially after the discovery of its use as a sweetener, which greatly enhanced the taste and flavour of tea and coffee. Sugar plantations came up on the Mediterranean Coast – in the islands of Cyprus and Sicily followed by the Spanish and Portuguese investments in sugar plantations on the Atlantic islands and finally in the Americas. The rise of sugar plantations coincided with the worst forms of exploitation of the indigenous people. Candice Goucher et al., 'Commerce and Change: The Creation of the Global Economy and the Expansion of Europe', in *The Balance: Themes in Global History*, Boston: McGraw Hill, 1998, pp. 491-508.
5. The earliest Western mention of tea is found in a work from 1559 by the Venetian author and administrator Giambatista Ramusio. Seventeenth-century health literature in Europe, established a discourse related to morality and society, where tea and sugar were viewed with disfavour. Mintz calls sugar a 'drug food'. See, Sidney Mintz, *Sweetness and Power*, London: Penguin Books, 1988.

6. The adding of milk to tea was reported in France around 1680 but that practice was not originally connected with adding sugar. See, Ukers H. William, *All About Tea*, London: Martino Publishing, 2007, pp. 35-49. John Coakley Lettsom, in his 'Natural History of the Tea-Tree' (1772), wrote about the various benefits that accrued from drinking tea. He recommended tea as an alternative to 'vegetable infusions' on the grounds of superiority in 'taste and effects'.
7. In 1783, the annual consumption of tea in England about 5,000,000 lbs and the tea duty was 27 per cent. In 1784, Mr Pitt lowered this duty to 12 per cent, thus, extending the use of tea among the poorer classes of society. Tea and sugar consumption were considered to be patriotic as they supported the British Empire. See, Martin R. Montgomery, *On the Comparative Consumption of Tea, Coffee, Sugar, Wine, Tobacco, Brandy and Rum*, London: Parbury, Allen & Co., 1832, p. 52.
8. A Report of the Select Committee of the House of Commons in 1830, mentions that from the years 1710-1810, the East India Company reported sales of tea amounting to 750,219,016 lbs valued at 129,804,595 pound sterling.
9. The Portuguese were the first Europeans to gain the right to trade with China and the first to drink tea. Around 1514, they reached the South China coast and were the first to introduce tea to Europe. K.F. Kiple and K.C. Ornelas (eds.), *The Cambridge World History of Food*, vol. 2, Cambridge: Cambridge University Press, 1999.
10. Tea, coffee, coca were regarded as 'satellites of alcohol', because of caffeine, which as per Charles Fernet's definition of caffeine drinks, causes mental irritability, attacks of dizziness, palpitation and digestive troubles. In 1643, an attempt had been made in the Parliament to forbid its use. See, 'A Clinical Address on Drug Addiction: Given at the Annual Meeting of the British Medical Association', *British Medical Journal* (hereafter *BMJ*), no. 3 (1930): 19-24.
11. The therapeutic properties of tea were widely recognized in France where tea was believed to be a preventive against cholera and its moderation in England to 'the extended use of that aromatic leaf which in reality possesses more virtues than are generally accorded to it'. *Report from the Select Committee on the Trade with China*, London: House of Commons, 1840.
12. By 1813, Britain was buying about 32 million pounds (14.5 million kgs) of tea.
13. D. Flynn and A. Giraldez, 'Cycles of Silver: Global Economic Unity through the Mid-eighteenth Century', *Journal of World History*, 2(2002): 391-427. During the first decade of the nineteenth century, China gained about $26,000,000 in her world balance of payments. See, D. Twichett and

J. Fairbank (eds.), *Cambridge History of China*, vol. 10: *Late Ching, 1800-1911*, Cambridge: Cambridge University Press, 1978.

14. A partial solution to the problem was found by bringing Spice Islands cloves and Japanese copper to India and China, and Indian cotton textiles to South-East Asia.
15. In Montogomery Martin's work entitled *Colonies of Great Britain*, it appears that the East India Company alone sold the following quantity of opium:
    - In the year ending 1800: 4,054 chests for 3,142,591 *Sicca Rupees* (hereafter s)
    - In 1810: 4,561 chests for 8,070,955 s.
    - In 1820: 4,006 chests for 8,255,403 s.
    - In 1830: 8,778 chests for 11,255,767 s.
    - In 1837: 16,916 chests for 25,395,300 s.
16. A passage cited in the *Report of the Select Committee of the House of Commons* in 1830 reads: 'sugar possesses in a most concentrated form a large portion of alimentary matter, capable not merely of supporting but of strengthening life.' Contemporary medical journals such as the *BMJ* carried articles which hailed sugar as a 'muscular food', a nerve restorative; a most valuable article of diet, while pamphlets as the *Christian Philanthropist* called sugar a nourishing and heat giving and sugar was one of the four foods, which 'God has given for the support of heat.' Tea was regarded as a preventive against cholera; its simulative properties being upheld all over Europe. The protagonists of the Temperance Societies in England even urged people to replace drinking gin and whisky with tea. Opium also went from being a medicine to mass drug food.
17. It is recorded that sugar was the first luxury indulged in – 'next to the actual necessaries of life'; its use being limited by the price.
18. The medical concept of addiction was developed by German psychologists in the 1870s. To these, criminologists such as Cesare Lombroso added the notion of degeneration, hereditary biological disposition towards crime and decadence, which was also linked to drug use.
19. Jonathan Goodman, Paul Lovejoy and Andrew Sherrat, *Consuming Habits: Global and Historical Perspectives on How Cultures Define Drugs*, New York: Routledge, 1995, pp. 121-41.
20. The English had after a slight skirmish managed to establish a small base at Canton in 1637, and continued so for 150 years till 1664.
21. Solomon Bard, 'Tea and Opium' (paper presented at the International Conference on Lin Zexu: The Opium War and Hong Kong, held at Hong Kong Museum of History, December 1998).
22. Prior to 1796, opium was admitted into China on payment of a duty when a few hundred chests were imported. Yet clandestine sales of 20,000 chests imported towards the latter half of the nineteenth century, cost the

Chinese 40,00,000 pound sterling every year. See N. Allen, *The Opium Trade with China and its Effects*, 1839, Massachusetts: J.P. Walker, 1853.

23. Carl Trocki, *Opium, Empire and the Global Political Economy*, New York: Routledge, 1999.
24. Following the discovery of tea plants, the East India Company decided in 1836 to embark on experimental tea cultivation with plant and labour imported from China. It was planned that the tea plants from China would finally replace the wild tea plants growing in Upper Assam. The first box of tea leaves from Assam to London sold at a 'record price of 21 to 38 shillings a pound'. This 'cautiously positive verdict' led to the beginning of the 'commercial life' of Assam tea. In 1839, a provisional committee of the Assam Tea Association met in London, which was followed by the setting up of the Assam Company, which included wealthy and influential Bengali entrepreneurs including the famous Tagore family of Bengal. In 1840, the Assam Company formally began cultivation and production of tea in Assam. Jayeeta Sharma, *Empire's Garden: Assam and the Making of India*, Duke: Duke University Press, 2011, pp. 31-2.
25. Chatterjee, *A Time for Tea*, p. 22.
26. Robert Mudie, *China and its Resources and Peculiarities, Physical, Social and Commercial: With a View of the Opium Question and a Notice of Assam*, London: Grattan and Gilbert, 1840, p. 190.
27. Amalendu Guha, *Planter-Raj to Swaraj: Freedom Struggle and Electoral Politics in Assam, 1826-1947*, New Delhi: Indian Council of Historical Research, 1977, p. 2.
28. Francis Hamilton, *An Account of Assam*, ed. S.K. Bhuyan, Guwahati: Department of Historical and Antiquarian Studies, 1963.
29. 'Transactions of the Agricultural and the Horticultural Society 1859', *Calcutta Review* 34-5(1860).
30. 'Minutes of evidence before the Select Committee appointed to inquire into the progress and prospect and the best means to be adopted for promotion of European colonisation settlement in India', *Calcutta Review*, vol. 34(1860).
31. Rajen Saikia, *Social and Economic History of Assam, 1853-1921*, Delhi: Manohar, 2001, p. 214.
32. Mirza Nathan, *Baharistan-i-Ghaibi*, tr. Moidul Islam Bora, Guwahati: Department of Historical and Antiquarian Studies, 1992
33. Heramba K. Barpujari, *Comprehensive History of Assam*, vol. III, Guwahati: Publication Board Assam, 1994, p. 110.
34. Suryya K. Bhuyan, *Asamar Buranji Katha*, Guwahati: Department of Historical and Antiquarian Studies, 1989 (rpt.).
35. In Arabic, opium is referred to as *afing* or *afiyun*. The Sanskrit term for opium is *Ahiphena* or *Nagaphena*. See, Moraes, *Opium*, p. 84.

36. Suryya K. Bhuyan, 'Asamat Kani', in Birinchi K. Baruah (ed.), *Arunodoi Sambadpatrat Nagaonar Batori* (News on Nagaon in *Orunodoi* Magazine), Nagaon: Assam Shaitya Sabha, 1856.
37. Satyendranath Sarma, *The Neo-Vaishnavite Movement and the Satra Institutions of Assam*, Guwahati: Lawyers Book Stall, 1977, pp. 150–1.
38. Edward Gait, *A History of Assam*, Calcutta: Thacker, Spink and Co., 1906, p. 362.
39. Saikia, *Social and Economic History of Assam*, p. 214.
40. *ACOECR*, 1925, p. 37.
41. *Committee Appointed to Enquire into Certain Aspects of Opium and Ganja*, 1913, ASA.
42. Evidence of E.R.R. Gilman, a tea planter at Sonapur, Assam, who had been a resident in Assam since 1872. As per his evidence, the opium eaters were 'healthiest and best workers and live longer than the non-opium eaters. If it (opium) is stopped, one might as well shut up all the tea gardens in Assam, employing local labour.' A native tea planter from Sibsagar, Jagoonath Darogah, upheld that opium was used as a palliative by the 'working classes who labour on the rice fields'. *Minutes of Evidence: Royal Commission on Opium*, 1893, vol. II, p. 285.
43. In his testimony before the Assam Congress Opium Enquiry Committee 1925, Story, the manager of Dejoo Tea Garden in Lakhimpur district [opium addiction estimated at 98 per cent (including adults and children), attribute the use of opium – 'the garden had in former days been particularly subject to dysentery and cholera ... the large extent of the vice of opium having been distributed years ago as a remedy'], *ACOECR*, 1925, p. 33.
44. Interestingly, the highest concentration of opium shops were in those *mehals* which were in the vicinity of the tea gardens in Darrang, Mangaldoi, Nowgong, Golaghat and Kamrup, where the number of opium shops in a *mehal* always exceeded the number of shops sanctioned by the committee of mauzadars and Deputy Commissioners. In Mogulbasa mouza of Darrang, for a population of 3,783, as against 3 shops recommended, there were around 13. In Mangaldoi, the number was 27 shops against 18 recommended, in Hadirgaon of Nowgong, 11 shops against 6 notified. Certain tea planters held licenses for the sale of opium to the workers in his employment, in violation of the rules prescribed. However, in 1877, the planters were prohibited to take up separate licenses for opium shops. They were asked to bid for opium *mehals* and also forbidden to supply opium to their workers as wages except as a 'present'. From Deputy Commissioner, Nowgong to Secretary to the Chief Commissioner of Nowgong, 1877, ASA Opium must have been used as a tool to induce and enhance labour productivity, apart from pacifying hostile recruits and for retaining them. *Minutes of Evidence. Royal Commission on Opium,* vol. II (1895). He held

opium *mehals* at Panbari, Kharija Domuria and Domuria where the number of shops was 11, 22 and 9 against 4, 4 and 2 that were sanctioned by the *mauzadars* and deputy commissioner. Studies conducted on the conjunction of the use of drug foods with the rise of capitalist world market have revealed a vital link between the Introduction of drug foods and the rise of capitalist economies' close relationship has been revealed between the type of subsistence and the stimulants used. W. Jankowiah and D. Bradburd, 'Using Drug Foods to Capture and Enhance Labour Performance: A Cross Cultural Perspective', *Current Anthropology* 4(1996): 717-20.

CHAPTER 3

Thinking Imperially: Intertwined Interests of Colonial Science, Medicine and Opium

> Assam is a melancholy picture of a rich and wonderful fertile garden turned into a wild waste of jungle. The people of Assam seem to be still suffering from a rapid decay, they are idle and vicious, in the excessive use of opium and utterly indifferent to all that goes around them so long as they have their daily food and hours of deadly intoxication (*Washington Express*, 6 January 1870).

By THE 1830S, the fertile valley of Assam by the Brahmaputra became the most valuable of the acquisitions of the colonial empire in India. Assam's portrayal as the land of abundance and one of great geographical and commercial importance followed the discovery of tea plants and minerals as coal and petroleum. These discoveries directed the attention of the colonial administration to Assam and in 1833, the then Governor-General Sir John Shore ordered for an extensive survey into the administrative structure, commercial and agricultural resources of Assam. This led to a series of cartographic and botanical surveys that served to illustrate the enormous potentiality of the newfound frontier province.[1] However, following the experience of the Burma war of 1824-6 which precipitated an 'Imperial crisis' with a huge mortality rate suffered by the British and the Indian troops as they fell prey to climate and diseases, whereby arose a penchant for an identification of diseases. The vulnerability of existence in tropical lands and the implicit threat of disease and death necessitated the accumulation and classification of knowledge on the 'medico-geographic zones'. This was linked to the imperatives of colonial rule and domination. It was here, as Kumar believes, that colonial expansion forged an alliance between science and medicine.[2] Science became the 'sanctioning authority'; in investigating and supervising of colonies.

It will be interesting here, to understand as to how science and medicine facilitated the study of colonies which was significant to the evolution of the British colonial enterprise. It will also be attempted to analyse opium in context of the narrative of the science of addiction that certainly touched areas of imperial concern.

Colonial Medical Surveillance

Discourse on 'How to rule India and how to survive in the Tropics?' accelerated attempts to compose a general geography of health and disease proper to each physical environment that was encountered in India along with the probable causes of their development and methods of treating them. It was here, as Kumar observes that the interaction of circumstances of material life, considerations of the political economy and the extraction of new knowledge about the physical and social milieu facilitated the emergence of the novel domain of tropical medicine, which he refers to as, the 'scientific step-child of colonial domination and control'.[3] The determining factors were climate, race, geography or all of these taken together.

Indeed, from the early nineteenth century, there was a constant and increasingly urgent search for a greater understanding of the idea that people living in certain areas of the country are more susceptible to particular diseases. This influence of external nature and surrounding circumstances on the living body became an important field of investigation in around the second half of the sixteenth century. By the 1800s it was one of the most highly cultivated disciplines of medical topography. By medical topography is meant everything connected with a locality, which is based upon health preservation and disease prevention. This discipline sought to investigate the complexity of the causes and circumstances, which influence health. *Medical topography* also entailed the study of the 'epidemic constitutions' and therapeutic concerns of the surroundings on human health. Embracing military, commercial and ethnographic concerns, medical topography was one of the largest scientific enterprises in British India during the first half of the nineteenth century.[4] Encouraged by neo-Hippocratic traditions and following a strong impulse in Europe to the study of medical topography,[5] a multitude of research was embarked upon, following which every important province and city in Europe had a topographical monograph. Similarly, the East India Company surgeons also embarked on attempts to compose a general geography of health and disease proper to each physical environment that they encountered in India along with the probable causes of their development and the methods of treating them.

Forwarding a proposal to the Medical Board of Calcutta in the 1830s, James Ranald Martin, Surgeon of the Bengal Army [6] proposed an exclusive list of incidental observations, which were as likely to influence, as he suggested,

> (i) the population within the range of inquiry, with description of the dwellings in common use, the clothing, bedding and furniture, fuel, diet, etc., the peculiar modes of cure adopted by the inhabitants, the state of poor and mode of rearing children, (ii) tables of marriages, births, deaths and diseases, (iii) the diseases of plants and other articles used as food by the people, (iv) longevity with a general view of mortality among all ages and sexes and (v) states of the thermometer, barometer and hydrometer.[7]

Accepting his line of argument on the need to medically survey the regions and populations, the Bengal Government instructed all the officers of the medical service – whether in the civil or military branches – to furnish information on the medical topography of their respective stations. This spawned a series of works such as John M'Cosh's *Topography of Assam* (1833), and Robert Rankine's *Notes on the Medical Topography of the District of Sarun*.[8] Practicing medical topographers tried to record any environmental factor that might affect health in a particular place such as temperature, altitude, water quality and amount of rainfall, wind direction, electrical air currents, soil types, thunderstorms, hailstorms, etc., to ascertain the influence of external conditions on the health and duration of life.[9] Any form of natural landscape as rivers, mountains, marshes, etc., which had significant influence on the physical constitution of man were places of observation and investigations by medical topographers. Following the *Hippocratic* tradition,[10] the physicians believed the danger came from the formation of 'miasma' or 'marsh poison' which occurred when vapour rose from rotting vegetation, stagnant water and the soil itself. *Miasma* was held responsible for many different diseases such as malarial fevers, diarrhoea, dysentery, diphtheria and yellow fever. Descriptions of climate were themselves also evaluations of the social or political status of a place or of its inhabitants. It was also an attempt at understanding geographic locations through the diseases they produced.

Indeed the travel accounts of the eighteenth and nineteenth centuries defined a new region for settlement by its medical geography which were increasingly specific in their details of the climate, the quality of water and food, altitude and prevalent diseases. Such accounts were part of the genre of medical topography that arose out of an increasing interest in documenting and measuring the relationship between the disease and the environment in seventeenth century Europe. The association of climate, habitability and European adaptation was morally important as a mark of their rationality and politically important as a sign of their fitness to rule other nations.[11]

Technologies of Rule

Medicine and geography along with science, emerged as 'technologies of rule', playing a crucial role in imperial expansion; enabling colonisers to map their new domains and to exploit more effectively their human and material resources. They were 'tools' through which colonialism was endorsed, sustained and empowered. Indeed as David Arnold remarks, '[...] medicine was a conspicuous element in the process of European exploration and colonization virtually from the outset – in the search for medical herbs and spices, in the struggle to stay alive in new lands, in the manner in which the newcommers exchanged or extracted knowledge'.[12]

A number of authors writing on the etiology and treatment of diseases found in the tropical lands also underlined the imperatives of epidemiology of disease and the fragility of 'European' existence in India. William Falconer was the first who published a work of this character, entitled, *Remarks on the Influence of Climate, Geographical Situation, Nature of the Soil, Inhabitants, Quality of Food, and Mode of Living, Dispositions, Temperaments, Manners of the People, Intelligence, Laws and Customs, Forms of Governments and the Religion of the Human Race.* James Lind wrote an excellent treatise on the *Diseases of Europeans in Hot Climates and on the Means of Preserving the Health of Sea-faring Men during Long Voyages.* James Johnson propounded the idea that different races have evolved slowly to fit in their environment. He became one of the foremost authorities on the diseases of the tropical climate.[13] In 1816, he founded the *Medico-Chirurgical Review*, a journal that he edited until shortly before his death. In 1835, James Ranald Martin persuaded the Government of India to authorize a series of medico-topographical reports by medical officers on the various stations and districts where they were stationed. His *Notes on the Medical Topography of Calcutta* published in 1837, presents the earliest attempts at a colonial scrutiny of Indian terrain as an urgent and practical necessity.

These works came to play a larger role in the consolidation of the colonial role. Recent scholarship strongly argues that surveys and reports were part of the 'documentation project' that were both 'totalizing and individualizing'. 'Investigative modalities' in Cohn's usage not only had economic and military utility but it also performed an important function in legitimizing British rule.[14] Medicine had utilitarian propensity. It reflected and produced structures of European dominance. It was important in securing the consent of the governed to imperial rule – consent being the essence of Gramsci's notion of hegemony,[15] valuable in imperial propaganda. It manifested the benevolent intentions of India's rulers and stemmed the tide of increasing criticism of colonial rule in Britain itself. In addition to these overtly propagandist functions, medicine also played a more subtle role in the advancing 'project modernity'.[16]

As has already been mentioned, the 'medicalization of colonial power' arose out of a crisis, 'demonstrating feelings of vulnerability and superiority' as Arnold argues and which had powerful political connotation. Mark Harrison asserts that it was a reflection of the 'reformist nature of the colonial state in India'.[17] This highlights the late nineteenth century policy of 'Constructive Imperialism'[18] with embedded notions of concern for public health and the globalization of International Health Diplomacy.[19] For instance, the first International Sanitary Conference organized in 1851 marked an important step towards the crystallization of health diplomacy, which emerged because of a concern about infectious diseases. Indeed, it was one of the duties of the local sanitary commissioners to prepare a medical topography of their respective province or presidency. The *Report of the Royal Sanitary Commissioner of India* shows that the average mortality of European soldiers in India during the first half of the nineteenth century was 69 per cent per 1,000.[20]

The public health risks that acquired global significance during this period was associated with infectious diseases – opium and alcohol, occupational hazards and trans-boundary pollution. This 'threat of infectious diseases' gained prominence following the development of the germ theory of disease and the professionalization of medical science. Doctors, surgeons and medical men evaluated the threat and risks of infection and this discourse produced processes, rules and institutions for global health governance. Colonial medicine, through it's topographical surveys and discourse on the physiological and pathological effects of 'warm climates' defined India – as an exotic space, a dangerous and unfamiliar environment. By 1830, it became fashionable to explain all attributes, physical and otherwise to the 'pathogenic climate' and the 'miseries of tropical life'. Thus, for instance, James Ranald Martin writing on 'The Physical Climate of Calcutta in Bengal', remarked on the geological nature of the soil as one of the most important causes of physical climate.[21]

To the medical topographer, a minute enquiry of the above would lead to acknowledge interesting and important information regarding the causes and cure of diseases as far as they may be connected with the climate. By locating disease within a landscape, they suggested practical measures to avoid the worst effects of disease.[22] It was one of the tasks of medical topography, using the health of the civilian population as well as the army's own records as a guide, to locate the safe and avoid the sickly places. Such entrenched anxieties about an encounter with a landscape 'terra incognita' with scores of

Europeans falling prey to 'a perilous climate', the entire north-eastern frontier was to be subjected to medical exploratory surveys. Such investigations revealed a different imagery of the 'romantic east' with 'a melancholy picture of a rich and wonderful fertile garden turned into a wild waste of jungle'.[23]

With the intention of opening of an unknown frontier for the Europeans, following Ranald's medico-geographic survey of Calcutta, John M'Cosh, Assistant Surgeon General of New Medical College, Calcutta in 1837, was instructed to investigate and surmise the topography of Goalpara and Guwahati, which were under his medical charge. In the meanwhile, Captain Thomas Welsh's *Report on Assam* (1796), enumerating the agricultural and commercial resources of Assam had evinced great interest among the colonial administrators. Since the mid-nineteenth century, the European officers in-charge of the different districts of Assam were obliged to send detailed reports along with the statistics to the Governor-General in Council, to ascertain whether it would be habitable. Such surveys were extensive, elaborate and assiduous, yet regional and authoritative in nature.

Aura Morphinia

EXPERIENCE AND RESPONSE TO OPIUM 'USE AND ABUSE'

Whether incidental or accidental, opium abuse had become a scourge of the nineteenth century society, so much so that the century was dubbed as 'the age of intoxication'.[24] Recreational indulgence in stimulants was regarded as a 'morbid appetite, a habit or a vice' until at least the end of the nineteenth century. It was only by the turn of the century – the period of the so-called 'age of medical reform',[25] which conjured up images of 'opium epidemics'[26] and 'drug plagues'.[27] The medical theory of humoralism[28] was replaced by the germ theory of disease around the 1860, which attributed opiates with producing a specific 'medical' syndrome, reinforced as a 'disease' – that came to be termed as 'opium inebriety'.[29] This was to lead to the foundation for a more general disease model of addiction. Certain contemporary scientific developments were highly influential in shaping the notion of addiction. The emerging specialism of toxicology that resulted in degrading of opium was an important one. Opium was pushed out from the list of pharmaceuticals and labelled as a poison.[30] Again, the emergence of the class of professional medical fraternity greatly facilitated altered perceptions of opiate use.[31] They were motivated to intensify their experimental and observational investigations for a comprehensive understanding of the drug and its properties. In 1877, Edward Levenstein, a German physician, wrote the first detailed description of opium addiction. The development of the modern pharmacological concept of opium addiction as disease was by the German psychologists in the last quarter of the nineteenth century, which greatly strengthened the medical profession's vociferous campaign against the use/abuse of opiates.

As Virginia Berridge remarks, the disease theories were part of late Victorian progress, a step forward from the moral condemnation of opium eating to the scientific elaboration of disease views. The drug user was assumed to be a victim of 'toxic psycho-neurosis' and he became a specific type of personality, a 'toxcimane' or a drug addict.[32] Opium was publicized as a disease of the nervous system and not subject to control by will. The condition developed as an 'opium diathesis' or a special inherited tendency to use opium or other narcotics. Italian criminologist Cesare Lombroso's notion of 'degeneration', a hereditary biological inclination towards crime, which was linked to drug abuse, further intensified the stigmatization of the opium addict. Following his exposition of the 'etiology of crime', the notion of 'degeneration' came to be regarded as a hereditary and progressive disease.

Since the 1820s, pharmacologists began to use the term for what is currently called 'physical dependence', namely the acquired physical need for drugs.[33] It was believed that while the habit is forming and before indulgence became a necessity to the system, 'The effect of opium is peculiarly soothing and tranquilizing, the stimulation reaching a certain point and remaining stationary for many hours. The habit holds the system in shackles as of steel. The patient finds it impossible to abstain from the poison beyond a fixed time.'[34]

The symptoms of the opium disease were stated as instability, low vitality, fatigue and increased sensitivity to pain and diminishing powers of restoration. Medical intervention was validated and the disease theory had it's effect on the methods of treatment. Berridge, again highlights a significant facet – that the disease theory of addiction 'was never an autonomous, scientifically elaborated entity; it was always accompanied by a strong moral overlay'. In the latter part of the nineteenth century, a 'hybrid theory of disease' incorporating both medical and moral formulations emerged. Addiction was both disease and vice, a form of 'moral bankruptcy', 'disease of the will', or a 'form of moral insanity'. Opium was destructive to the faculties of the body and the mind. Startling revelations on the relation between opium and suicides further accentuated the move towards denunciation of opium use. Opium use and its user were viewed as vectors of an infectious disease and hence were required to be quarantined to prevent the dissemination of the infection. Such an undertone of threat had permeated the psyche of the Victorian society that had already witnessed the prolific destruction wrought by 'opium poisoning' to the individual and the society.

In a similar tone, the physical 'degeneration' and mental 'enervation' that the 'opium plague' wrought in Assam was highlighted in official reports and extensively reported in the print media of the nineteenth century. Such reporting depicted opium as a tropical predator whose extinction was essential to the survival of temperate civilization. As Louise Foxcroft remarks, the genre of social investigation not only reported on difficult issues but also provided the public with unfamiliar perspectives from which to view society. From the 1840s various medical journals, like the *Lancet*, *British Medical Journal* and *Edinburgh Medical Surgical Journal* and the *Medico-Chirurgical Review and Journal*, were carrying accounts of and opinions on opium smoking; opinions which were undoubtedly intended to widen and inform both the medical and the political debate. Articles written were intended to engage the moral sensibilities and anxieties of the reader by exposing the many dangers of addiction and by suggesting the possibility that the condition could spread, like a noxious contagion. This stirred up an intense intellectual debate and had great influence on public perception and political action. The defined attempts to control and regulate opiate use were part of this process and stimulated series of attempts of the international community to regulate international trade in narcotics and strengthen domestic enforcement regime. Indeed, medical reforms were part of the wider reformatory politics that characterized nineteenth century Britain. The *laissez faire* approach to government that characterized Britain in the eighteenth century was increasingly challenged in the nineteenth century by a more centralized and interventionist view of government.[35]

Opium was a fatal epidemic, destructive to the powers and faculty of the mind. It was an 'addictive and debilitating disease' and many such similar accounts which appeared in popular newspapers with increasing regularity elucidated the emerging awareness and response of a concerted anti-opium movement, influenced by the Opium Wars of 1839-42 and 1856-8. By the formation of the Anti-opium Society (1840),The Edinburgh Committee for the Suppression of the Indo-Chinese trade (1859) and significantly, the 'Anglo-Oriental Society for the Suppression of the Opium Trade' (1874) and its official mouthpiece the *Friend of China* effectively launched an intense intellectual debate over what it termed as unjustifiable and immoral. The *Friend of India* took up the mantle of responsibility of advocating for the abolition of the 'poppy plague' in India. In 1839, it published a series of critiques including a number of monographs and pamphlets on the British opium policy and its consequences, such as – the *Consequences of the Use of Opium*, and *Use of Opium in Assam*, advocating prohibition of the use of intoxicants and stimulants. Toeing a moderate path, the SSOT believed that the law should not put down the use of stimulants. It called for moral restraint as much effective as attempts at suppression. Interestingly, they ascribe the use of opium to the system of bondage prevalent in Assam,[36] which the missionaries mentioned in their memoirs and journals as a reason for excessive indulgence in opium taking. This view found adherents and was extensively debated in the *Bengal Hurkaru* and *The Englishman* that held that slavery and opium taking produces enervation, want of industry and poverty and poverty produces bondage and slavery. Slavery again produces further opium taking, death and thus is the population kept down. It is the absence of all wholesome and profitable industry that gives rise to addiction of 'gin-drinking' or 'opium-taking'. Such views did not go unchallenged though. The case for prohibition of opium in Assam was openly debated in the House of Commons where the opposition asserted that opium for the Assamese who are deprived of any other luxuries of life was a boon for the labouring populace.[37]

Opium Mania, that Dreadful Plague

CONSTRUCTION OF OPIUM AS AN 'IMPERIAL PROBLEM' IN NINETEENTH CENTURY ASSAM

To the Mughal mansabdar Shehabuddin Talish reporting on the topography and climate of Assam in the year 1662-3, Assam was a 'dangerous, horrible, self-confined gloomy country'. Such a climate harboured the cause of many diseases. Nevertheless, he acknowledged the strength and courage of the people.[38] Centuries later, in 1808, Francis Hamilton, found it 'as a very poor place'.[39] An enthusiastic European writer in the year 1839, describing Assam as he saw it, eulogized it as 'a paradise, with numerous crystal streams and atmosphere perfumed with the fragrant weed'.[40] Ironically, by 1876, Assam represented 'a melancholy picture of a rich and wonderful fertile garden turned into a wild waste of jungle'. This was attributed to the utter 'indifference' of the people of Assam rendered 'idle by hours of deadly intoxication'. Haliram Dhekial Phukan's note, *Of the Air and Water of Assam* lends veracity to the views expressed by the Persian chronicles and the European observers who claimed that it is the topography that has rendered Assam prone to diseases. He writes,

> I have discovered that the water of the Brahmapootra in Assam greatly assists digestion and promotes health. Of this, there is no doubt. The water of many other mountain streams seems only to create diseases. Ghahattee is surrounded with hills hence a great deal of putrid vegetation and many decayed bodies produce a fetid smell which renders the people of this place both weak and diseased. Of late, many have died of dysenteries, the cause of which appears to be that those who accustom themselves to the 'use of opium', are scarcely seized by any other disease but the dysentery, when it seizes such a man, it generally carries him off. Very few men in this country attain a greater age than fifty or sixty.[41]

Captain John M'Cosh, Assistant Surgeon of the East India Company in Assam, in his *Topography of Assam*[42] reiterated the implicit threat posed by the pestilential climate of Assam. His report is impregnated with descriptions of the unhealthy miasmatic state of the province with marshy jungles, multitude of old tanks which were the hotspots of diseases as malaria and kala-azar.[43] John Leslie's *A Sketch of the Medical Topography of Gowhattee with an Account of the Prevailing Diseases*,[44] D.A. Macleod's *Medical Topography of Bishenath*,[45] and John Butler's *Travels in Assam: During a Residence of Fourteen Years*[46] account for the insalubrious climate of *Gowhattee, Bishenath, Jorehauth, Nowgong* and *Sadiya*. Official reports as the *Physical and Political Geography of Assam*[47] refer to the climate in the Assam province, both in the Brahmaputra and the Surma valleys, as marked by extreme humidity where kala-azar, malaria and cholera are the most prevalent forms of diseases. Opium, under such conditions was a panacea for the diseases of the tropical climate. Such climate, it was held, had made the Assamese to be opium eaters and unproductive.[48]

This metropolitan discourse on the landscape of Assam was necessitated by a most important discovery of tea, which had brought Assam within the configurations of imperialism. Hence, the approach of the medico-topographical surveys reflected the broad range of intertwined interests of imperial science and medicine in their understanding and investigation of the environment. For as Arnold remarks, climate was an important determinant not only of health but also of commercial and agricultural prosperity as well as moral and physical characteristic.[49] Hence, observations on climate were subjected to such 'scientific and geographical gaze', which also reflects their natural anxiety about their fragility in an alien landscape.

Abundant land availability in Assam came as a great boon for the British tea enterprise.[50] The Governmental legislation that created the Wasteland Settlement Rules of 1838 and 1854 emanating from Jenkins 'Scheme of Colonisation of Assam 1833',[51] addressed one of the two essential requirements of a plantation settlement: land. An adequate and consistent supply of workers to clear jungles, build bungalows and plant nurseries, however, remained a critical issue. In 1859, only 10,000 workers were available for employment against a requirement of 20,000. Initially, a few Chinese growers were imported,[52] followed by the employment of the Bodo-Kacharis,[53] a plains tribe in the Brahmaputra valley, who were regarded as of physically superior, industrious and not given to the use of opium habits. In the labour discourse as Jayeeta Sharma[54] asserts, the local indolence was blamed on the habit of opium consumption. In 1829, C.A. Bruce[55] regarded the consumption of opium as a subject to be one of great importance that could affect the cultivation of tea and he wished timely intervention by the colonial authorities to use effective means of prevention. The European tea-planters seemed to have an aversion towards 'the lazy opium-eating' native Assamese who were described as physically effeminate and unproductive. Lieutenant Colonel Hamilton Vetch in his testimony to the Select Committee[56] testified to the Assamese as being 'listless' and suffering from 'great want of energy' because of indulging to a vicious extent in opium eating. Initial unsuccessful attempts to grow tea were ascribed to the 'lethargic' workers 'all debilitated by opium and in no condition to perform the complex tasks of tea production'. Warning that opium was destroying his 'tea harvester's work ethic', Bruce, in an ardent request delivered to the *Agricultural and Horticultural Society of India* suggested that,

> [...] the opium mania, that dreadful plague which has depopulated this beautiful country, turned it into a land of wild beasts, with which it is overrun and has degenerated the Assamese from a fine race of people to the most abject, servile, crafty and demoralized race in India... Would it not be the highest of blessings, if our humane and enlightened government would stop these evils by a single dash of the pen and save Assam and all those who are about to emigrate into it as tea-cultivators, from the dreadful results attendant on the habitual use of opium. We should in the end be, richly rewarded by having a fine healthy race of men growing up for our plantations, to fell our forests, to clear the land from jungle and wild beasts, and to plant and cultivate the luxury of the world. This can never be effected by the enfeebled opium-eaters of Assam, who are more effeminate than women. [57]

Bruce's plea for the prohibition of opium reflects, however, the colonial unease over the lack of local labour for working in the tea gardens. It was the tea enterprise that led to the evolution of, to quote Jayeeta Sharma, 'socially exclusionist policies'[58] which perpetrated the myth of the effeminate and indolent Assamese peasant.

They failed to be productive subjects – the consequence of relentless use of opium.

Was opium a baneful luxury or an innocent indulgence? Questions such as these were debated in the House of Commons and in the contemporary newspapers. British and American newspapers as *Daily Evening Bulletin* (15 August 1889), *Daily National Intelligence* and *Washington Express* (6 January 1870), *St. Louis Globe Democrat* (2 July 1876), *The North American* (19 May 1840)[59] carried vivid descriptions of the terrible consequences that opium eating had wrought in. The missionary mouthpiece *Friend of India* carried articles in its various issues, as the *Consequences of the Use of Opium* (20 August 1840), *Use of Opium in Assam* (3 September 1840), etc., depicting a picture of destruction that the opium evil had wrought in Assam, all of which had assisted in the emergence of a consensus against the use of opium. The early Baptist missionaries in Assam, through articles in their missionary journal, the *Orunodoi* (meaning new dawn) like, 'Evils of Opium' (January 1846), 'Death of an Opium-Eater' (May 1846), 'Kani Erabar Katha' (June 1861), made an attempt at addressing the evils consequent upon indulgence in opium. Opium was a fatal epidemic, destructive to the powers and faculty of the mind. It was an 'addictive and debilitating disease' and many such similar accounts of the physical ruin which appeared in popular newspapers and medical journals such the *Edinburgh Medical and Surgical Journal* (1835)[60] with increasing regularity significantly perpetrated the myth of opium as a tropical predator whose extinction was essential to the survival of temperate civilization.

Most of these accounts elucidated the emerging awareness and response of a concerted anti-opium movement, influenced by the Opium wars of 1839-42 and 1856-8. The anti-opium propaganda embarked upon an agenda well drafted by the medical professions. With the formation of the Anti-opium Society (1840), The Edinburgh Committee for the Suppression of the Indo-Chinese trade (1859) and significantly, the Anglo-Oriental Society for the Suppression of the Opium Trade (1874) which through its official mouthpiece the *Friend of China* effectively launched an intense intellectual debate over the opium trade as unjustifiable and immoral. The *Friend of India* took up the mantle of responsibility of advocating for the abolition of the 'poppy plague' in India. In 1839, it published a series of critiques including a number of monographs and pamphlets on the British opium policy, as *Consequences of the Use of Opium*, and *Use of Opium in Assam*, advocating prohibition. The *Morning Contemporary* adopted the same reasoning and maintained that it would be cruel to deprive the Assamese 'of their only comfort and enjoyment amid a whole life of unmitigated wretchedness', which found support from a section in the House of Commons. There were also instances of individuals ascertaining the reasons for a situation of what they considered as 'opium mania' in Assam. In a private letter to a friend, an official of the East India Company writing from Assam mentions, 'the cultivation of opium is free in Assam – the fearful results from it's use, which every day present themselves to notice, are very painful to witness'.[61] Opium was not only scandalizing the 'religion of the gospel', but also came to be regarded as prejudicial to the interests of legitimate commerce.[62]Along with the anti-opium pamphlets, the medical journals also conjured up images of the terrible physical and mental suffering consequent upon the use of opium. The missionary rhetoric fuelled by the medical propaganda on the 'use and abuse of opium' challenging the libertarian approach of minimum interference translated into investigations into the causes and effects of opium consumption.

In 1853, an official investigation into the administration of the province of Assam, publicized a totally denunciatory view of opium consumption, as a social evil which 'destroys the constitution, enfeebles the mind and paralyses industry'.[63] Subscribing to the official opinion, Anandaram Dhekial Phukan, among the first few English educated Assamese intellectuals, regretted that 'The universal use of opium has converted the Assamese, once a hardy, industrious and enterprising race into an effeminate, and weak, indolent and degraded people.'[64] Opium eating was 'barriers to improvement', as A.J. Moffat Mills clearly mentioned, and agreed with Colonel Matthie that 'something must be done to check the immoderate use of the drug'.[65]

Such an undertone of threat had permeated the psyche of the Victorian society that had already witnessed the prolific destruction wrought by 'opium poisoning' to the individual and the society. In a letter to the American Baptist Board of Foreign Missions, Miles Bronson lamented thus,

> [...] the universal practice of using opium is most discouraging circumstance. Its effects are so deadly, stupefying every power and faculty and rendering its victims little less than dozing brutes. It destroys all ambition or desire to excel in anything, and is the most prolific source of crime in the country. Multitudes of person I daily see going almost naked and without any single comfort of life, who, if they get a piece or two, will immediately expend it in the noxious drug.[66]

Criminalization of Opiate Use and Policing of Users

The 'criminalization' of opium use and user spawned up a series of debates on whether it was a habit or disease. While this was certainly a manifestation of the prevalent views with inherent interests, the evolving concept of addiction, which followed the ascendancy of the germ theory, was certainly a catalyst. If the opium user was a moral degenerate, his deviant behaviour could be corrected through punitive measures. The focus here is on the politics of deviance as an 'imperial problem'[67] as seen in actions by Parliament, published research reports, official investigations and propagandist appeals. Tough laws were thus enacted to correct and reform the opium eater. Opium use was stigmatized. The opium eater was an 'endangered individual', which made him a coherent object of social intervention, and this gave rise to a system of 'behavioural accountancy'.[68] In the *Statistics of Civil and Criminal Justice in the Extra Regulation Province of Assam,* for the year 1844, it was recorded that Assam had a high number of litigation cases. Crimes such as murders, rapes, and suicides were presumed to be registering an upward trend in the 'opium districts' – districts earmarked for their distinct opium usages. This was held to be particularly true for Assam, where opium was cultivated and consumed by almost every individual, the results it was claimed, were turning out be disastrous to the body and psyche of the individual consumers. Thus, it had earned for itself the infamy of being the 'most unspirited, unimpressible and most litigious population among the Extra Regulation Province –

such being the consequence of unmindful indulgence in opium smoking'.[69] Various treatment approaches were devised including detoxification and where total abstinence was deemed unachievable, as in Assam, medically supervised maintenance was stressed. It is here, interestingly, that an intersection of the medical and criminal discourses is noted. In Assam, the method of confinement of opium users, led to a special investigation by the Government following the deaths of 'opium shattered paupers' following the withdrawal of the drug from those long addicts to its use. The investigations led to a Government circular in 1851, which enforced certain regulations regarding opium eaters in jails. They were to be exempted from labour[70] and were made to undergo a course of preparatory treatment in the jail hospital.

In the reports of the jail administration, the medical men have hinted at the irreversible harm that opium does to the mental and physical health of an individual. Such information was instrumental in presenting a case for interference in the general habits of the people. Assistant Surgeon A. McLean, in medical charge of Gowhatty (Guwahati), in his remarks relative to the public health of Gowhatty station, held the habit of opium eating as practiced by men, women and children 'to an excessive and injurious degree'. To him, opium eating was the cause of sickness and mortality and suggested the immediate suppression of poppy cultivation throughout the province.[71] Dr. John Barry, civil surgeon of Goalpara district, in his report lamented that the people are addicted to the use of opium, which commits ravages everywhere and is responsible for the 'piteous and deplorable' condition of Assam. Dr. W.B. Long, civil surgeon of Sibsagar, deciphering the physiology of the opium eating habit, he commented, 'The habit renders them listless and apathetic; weakens their digestive system and produces congestion of the brain and other organs particularly of the liver and kidneys. There has been noticed the liability to severe congestive inflammation of the lungs, to which opium eaters are liable after slight labour.... The offspring of such a race is degenerate, weak and sickly.'[72]

The officer in civil charge of Nowgong in reporting the state of the district hinted on the link between crime and opium eating.[73] Major J.F. Butler, principal assistant to the Commissioner of Assam, also expressed his consensus with the former opinion on proliferation of crime involving those addicted to opium.

The only way to control and prevention of epidemic diseases was thought to be sequestration. This was one of the major aims of the public health movement that emerged in Britain in mid-nineteenth century. The quarantine of opium users was to be effective in institutions where they could be corrected and reformed. In India, it was believed that this purpose would be best served in a jail. The jail as a correctional home for social deviants was a 'tool' of the overall civilizing mission. This implied a 'paternalistic British view' of an ideal colonial society as jails were viewed as 'correctional institutions', which endeavoured to modify inmate behaviour through a series of coercive and corrective practices.

Towards the closing decades of the nineteenth century, the civil surgeons of the jails in Assam were instructed to maintain a detailed record of the history of opium consumers admitted. The steps taken to record a history of opium consuming inmates have revealed interesting insights into the British approaches to treatment of opiate addicts in the nineteenth and early twentieth centuries. The Following four points were sought to be investigated by the civil surgeon in-charge of the jails: (i) What number of convicts assert themselves be habitual opium consumers? (ii) What quantities do they say they consume ordinarily? (iii) What treatment do the doctors approve in their case? (iv) What is the effect on them of stopping their supply of opium?

Recognizing the need for treatment including identifying patterns of drug consumption and consequent problems, the available modalities of drug treatment and working out the cost-benefit analysis of the various treatment programmes including organization of treatment was high on the agenda of the jail authorities. It follows that the treatment of inmates used to opium was very much a personal decision of the civil surgeon in-charge, based on his levels of experience and on whether the inmate was a habitual or casual consumer of the drug. Certain prisoners denied the habit through fear or suspicion as to the motives of the enquiry. Observation became an investigative tool for those in the habit of consuming different quantities of opium responded to effects of totally or gradually discontinuing the supply and this affected the relative health of them and of non-consumers during their prison life and their stamina to perform the allotted tasks. Although as a rule, opium was not given in jails in Assam, yet the surgeons were instructed to observe special care in the course of the treatment to ensure that the cessation of the drug did not in any way prove detrimental to the health of the prisoner.[74] Under the orders of the Chief Commissioner, the surgeon was to particularly report on the stoppage of opium to the opium consumers under detention and to record the responses. The body of the opium consumer thus became a site of experimentation with varying doses of opium to be allowed, depending on whether the consumer was a habitual or an occasional user.[75]

A scale of diet was prescribed with 'various articles of food of a stimulating and easily digested nature', as spices of sorts, *tyre* (a preparation of milk, which was regarded nourishing) moderate quantity of spices, milk and sugar. This was regarded essential as it was found that lack of a balanced and nourishing diet led to the onslaught of 'dyspeptic symptoms', which increased the vulnerability of future attacks of diarrhoea, dysentery or cholera. Although tobacco and opium were prohibited inside the jail compound,[76] yet the Magistrate on the suggestion of the medical officer recommended that a certain quantity of opium could be allowed to the opium eaters' initially. The dose was, however, to be gradually withdrawn. Maintaining opiate addicts on medically monitored daily doses of narcotics was first introduced as a treatment for addiction following as its stoppage was found to be prejudicial to the health of a large number of opium eaters who were admitted into the jails for various crime. The diminishing death rates, as available for Kamrup jail,[77] was ascribed to the effective implementation of the suggested prison reforms. Initially the Government was reluctant to admit the deaths of prisoners due to withdrawal. Yet the contemporary official investigation reports of the gaols of Kamrup, Dibrugarh, Sibsagar and Darrang, for the years 1861-7, revealed large-scale sickness and high mortality rates to be common amongst the opium eaters. Certain general traits of the conditions of opium eaters before and after admissions and the result of the stoppage of the drug on their physical and mental well-being were areas of special investigation. The general health of the opium eaters on admission into jails was found to be very poor. They were always regarded as 'a sickly set.' It was discovered that most of the opium eaters suffered from dysentery, which was attributed principally to the sudden stoppage of opium following their conviction. The Jail Administration Report remarked, 'A large percentage of the Assamese consume about 100 to 150 grains daily of solid opium and its sudden discontinuance, coupled with the complete change of diet, affects the digestive organs materially.' It regarded the stoppage of opium as 'injudicious' and 'improperly managed', while deploring the total absence of aftercare facilities. It lamented also on the lack of basic amenities including provision of safe drinking water, sanitation and proper diet, all of which were found to be in a state of utter neglect. Regarding withholding of opium and its consequences, the medical officer of Kamrup jail, G. Simons, remarked as follows, 'the sudden stoppage of opium appears not only to have been unattended with injury but to have diminished bowel affections among those previously addicted to the use of the drug'. He held that the health of the prisoners had decidedly improved following the withholding of opium, which had been launched as an 'experimental measure'. Relying on the data submitted and recommendations made thereof, a series of reforms in the prison administration were adopted with reference to those addicted to the habit.

While the Superintendent of Gauhati jail was in favour of an allowance of five to eight grains of opium, in some cases the allowance could be as high as ten grains. In Silchar jail, for those particularly in bad state of health and unable to bear the withdrawals, the dosage was to be diminishing daily down to nothing in twenty to forty days. Although in a few cases, it was felt necessary to continue small doses for a longer period, especially during illness such as chronic dysentery. Dr. Warburton in the Sanitary Report on Tezpur jail revealed that when any treatment was necessary, adopted in the case of opium eaters was the same as is in former years, namely, deprivation of opium followed by a light nourishing diet and in some cases stimulants in small quantities. The medical officer at Dibrugarh allowed no opium to any prisoner. Opium varying from six to sixteen grains and in one instance dosage of

1 *anna* weight of opium daily was permitted by the hospital assistant only to those prisoners suffering from dysentery and diarrhoea owing to the stoppage of the drug at Lakhimpur, but subsequently the allowance was discontinued. The same was the case at Sibsagar where in no case the civil surgeon, who treated all such cases with milk diet, allowed opium while at Mangaldai, tincture of opium was administered to those confirmed opium eaters who suffered from diarrhoea owing to deprivation of the drug. The medical officer at Goalpara allowed three grains of tincture of opium each for a few days only. At Hailakandi, only those opium eaters were allowed five and six grains of opium respectively where the inmates were attacked with diarrhoea and dysentery on stoppage of the allowance of opium. One grain each of opium was given to prisoners at Barpeta jail for a few years before complete cessation of the dose. Most of the reports were unanimous on initial discomfort following diminishing dosage of the drug. The treatment of opium eaters varied considerably and the results were unequal. While a few of them, it was observed, complained of indigestion and diarrhoea, a few experienced restlessness for a couple of days or so following deprivation. There were also instances of prisoners showing signs of depression following withdrawal. Recovery was, however, reported to be quick in a majority of cases. Most of the opium eaters discharged during the year had gained in weight. The extracts of medical reports of jail hospitals clearly showed that in the majority of cases, the effect of stopping the supply of opium was not injurious to the health of the opium eater.

Whereas the 'pharmacological manipulation' of replacing the opium with another drug for safe withdrawal was replaced in the mid-nineteenth century, there now emerged a belief in 'total care' following detoxification of the addict. Although there was lack of unanimity on the techniques to be employed, whether, it was to be a long-term reduction procedure or a rapid withdrawal method, the centrality of treatment in shaping the principles of effective drug policies was slowly beginning to be realized.[78]

The issue of the treatment of addicts was taken up as an 'important point to be practically considered by the Assam Congress Opium Enquiry Committee' appointed in 1925. A great majority of the witnesses pointed to the fact that 'in most cases – there is no very great hardship with regard to the final extinction of the opium habit'. It recommended that all opium addicts under the age of forty years should be dealt with as medical patients.[79] The 'pharmacological manipulation' which I have referred to in the preceding paragraph offers an interesting perspective to the intertwined interests of colonial science and medicine. In associating opium with degeneracy, science and medicine were potential allies. The colonial science looked with disapproval to indigenous notions of opium use as a medicine. The use of opium (papaver somniferum), indigenous system of medications in China, Persia and India where opium was cultivated and used by the people is a rejoinder to the fact that opium use was an accepted part of the popular culture in these places. Opium use in Assam originated with its ability to relieve fatigue, stress and the most common affliction of the valley – dysentry. It is not improbable that they use continued well after the medical condition was relieved owing to its soporific effects, which served to allay the exertions and drudgery of the daily life.

A Virtuous Gratification: A Baneful Luxury

POPULAR USE OF OPIUM IN ASSAM

Sources, mostly in the nature of memoirs informs us that during *Kani Seva*, a ceremony – of a semi-religious nature practiced during the nineteenth century – the offering of opium for consumption in assemblies. It had been introduced amongst the more ignorant classes at which opium consumers assembled and opium was distributed. It was believed that such ceremonies could help avert sickness or other impending trouble. The distribution and consumption of opium was regarded as common at *Namgoa* – religious services held at the *Sattras* (Vaishnavite monastery). Astrologers also suggested – entertaining four or five *bhakats* (disciples) with opium for the cure of the diseases.[80] Even the women folk who gathered in the *Gopini Sabhas* (secret assemblies of women) were in the habit of consuming opium. These semi-religious uses of opium appear to be purely the invention of interested opium consumers and to have no authority in the *shastras* (religious texts) of Assam.[81] Although the existence of regular opium dens was denied by the colonial administration, yet in sources available, there are references to *kanikholas*, which meant a house where opium was sold and where the opium-eaters frequently met, probably in the house of one or other of their number and smoked together.[82] There is also a good deal of evidence, which indicates the societal abhorrence of opium smoking parties. Such meetings were not viewed with favour in the society, as it was a commonly held belief that at such meetings young men were lured into the opium habit by the *Bor-kaniyas* (mature opium eaters). In addition, the *kaniyas* were accused of organizing petty thefts in the village in order to get the means for indulging in intoxication.[83] The habit was increasingly common at such social gatherings as marriages and funerals at which opium was used. In cases of damage for breach of promise of marriage, it was not unusual to find an item like 'opium 5 tolas' said to have been offered as a gift, along with trinkets and other items by the parents of the bridegroom to the party of the bride before marriage.[84]

If this was the social image of opium consumption, there were again, varying opinions on the habitual and excessive use of opium in Assam as has already been referred. The Miris, Deoris, Ahoms, Mataks, Chutias were identified as the chief consumers of opium in Assam with Barpeta, Darrang, Nowgong, Gowalpara as the worst affected districts.[85] It was used by all classes of population and it was freely administered to infants and children. Despite uncertainties prevailing within the colonial administration, late nineteenth century official reports began to highlight the critical use of opium amongst the Assamese consumers. Such official accounts suggested that people in Assam were using opium as a medicine and that it was used to cure common diseases like stomach pain, headache, gynecological disorders and various other diseases common to small children. The Royal Commission on Opium of 1893 agreed that opium was a 'safe stimulant', efficacious in malarial tracts and relatively harmless. When documenting and investigating the use of opium in Assam, the Commission, called forth testimony from several government and non-government officials, landowners and opium consumers. Many of them deposed that opium did no harm and that any kind of prohibition of opium use would lead to popular disturbances.[86]

Many witnesses advocated its use under special circumstances, citing it as a stimulant under conditions of severe exertion. For instance, Upendranath Barooah, headmaster of the Jorhat Seminary, answered in affirmative, 'if they (the workers) did not eat opium, they would die from diseases, malarial fevers and bowel complaints'. Opium was believed to increase the power of exertion and benefit 'hard workers on a short diet'.[87] Many upheld that opium served as a preventive against dysentery, asthma, rheumatism, fatigue and was also consumed for pleasure.

In his written evidence to the Commission, planter J.P. Gilman, cited the instance of, '[...] a native who was the largest employer of labour in Assam and held a large contract for earth work, who lamented that not more than 10 per cent of the Assamese could be employed simply because they were the first to sicken and die from fever through opium eating' and how 'the use of opium made them so stupid and sleepy – that they were not worth employing'.[88]

Viewed in this context, is worthy of mention, a memorandum signed by around three hundred members of the Jorhat Sarbajanik Sabha led by eminent trader Jagannath Baruah.[89] The memorandum was forwarded to the Assam Chief Commissioner, against the proposal of prohibition of opium,

> People of Assam have been in the habit of using opium and other narcotics, from the remotest times. Opium is an invaluable medicine in any disorders of the stomach; it alleviates pain and possesses sedative power of restoring health. It is useful after forty years of age in prolonging life and is an undoubted preventive against malaria. The hard-working classes in the malarious plains of Assam require some stimulant to keep up their power. Opium taken in a moderate quantity is beneficial and positively necessary for a large number of people, earning their livelihood by manual labour in the swampy fields and in the gardens of Assam and of boatmen and others. There is very little abuse of opium....[90]

Echoing a similar opinion, another well-known Assamese entrepreneur Harbilas Agarwalla, in his testimony opined against the prevalent view of linking opium eating with increase of crime in the province.[91] He cited the instance of Sylhet and Cachar, which had high crime rate as compared to the Brahmaputra valley, which had the highest opium consuming populations. He, however, was, against the government policy of periodic raise in the price of opium that he held was detrimental to the health of the peasants who used it as a stimulant. William Roberts, the sole medical member of the Royal Commission on Opium, 1893 had considered both the 'Medicinal side' and the 'Euphoric side' of opium.[92] He noted the habit of opium consumption in excess among the peasantry in 'low-lying, damp and malarious' districts of Assam, Bengal and Bihar. He traced such a situation to the present or past cultivation of opium in that province or district. Roberts explains and defends the beneficial effects, which he maintains the 'starving ryots' of Assam and Orissa derive from the use of 'opium as an economiser of food'.[93]

J.J.S. Driberg, the Commissioner of Excise in Assam, was of the view that the present use of opium is a 'vice' and in most cases, a 'necessity'. He opines,

> [...] the inhabitants of low-lying swampy and damp use opium to counteract the damp and malaria. They themselves say that they would die from fevers if they did not use opium and known medical men hold the same view. These people are opium eaters but not of the class described in the papers. They are good agriculturists; good subjects and good fathers of families. They take their opium just as a good Englishman could take his peg. Of course there are Assamese who take too much opium just as there are Englishmen who take too much liquor but that opium eating is always a vice.[94]

Opium as Medicine in Assam

Unlike in China, where there existed a long convention of the use of opiates as medicine, in Assam it was not a favourite with the Assamese physicians, although it was suggested as a remedy in cases of insomnia, cold and coughs, fevers, lockjaw and dysentry.[95] They likewise recommended it in rheumatic affections but at the same time, maintained that opium, could provide only temporary relief and cautioned against excessive and long-term use, which certainly had addictive properties. Recipes for the use of opium medicinally, prescribed by the *kaviraj*, particularly for diarrhoea and dysentery do occur in *vaidya*, the indigenous system of medicine in Assam. Instances of the following prescriptions in the treatment of diseases find mentioned in the pharmacopeia:

(i) Diarrhoea – nutmegs, borax, *ambhora* and *dhutura* seeds, opium reduced to powder and then made into a pill mass with the juice of *bhaboli lata*, of which 5 *rati* weight to be given twice daily.
(ii) Dysentery – nutmeg, cloves, *pupri*, opium, powdered and mixed to the consistency of a pill mass with the juice of *naghumala* leaves and 2 *rati* weight given once a day.
(iii) Another prescription in cases of dysentery is the following – asafotida, opium, capsicum, camphor, nutmeg, powdered and mixed up with water in the consistency of a pill mass; dose 2 *rati* weights once a day.[96]

The names of some of the most important indigenous medicines found mentioned in the *Materia Medica* of the region include, *Jamalgota* (*Croton tiglium*), Madar (*Calotropisgigantea*), Bagbharendra (*Jatrophacurcas*), Hara (*Terminiliachebula*), Somdal (*Gynocardia cassiafistula*), Mishmiteeta (*Coptisteeta*), Afeem (*Papaver somniferum*), Kot Karanja (*Caesalpina guilandina*), Katbis (*Acontium napelius*), Bel (*Egle marmelos*).[97]

Conclusion

The transition of opium from a 'panacea' to a 'problem' is reflective of the change in perception of the use of opiate use. It is this transition that is problematic and beset with ambiguity. In England, opium was labelled a poison as early as 1828. But in India, till the end of the nineteenth century, opium as RCO claimed was a safe stimulant. The demonization of opium preceded a significant development – the professionalization of medical science. As Levine rightly argues, medicine and medical doctors were facilitators in the 'modernity project'. Colonial medicine perpetrated the myth of the colonial subjects as prone to infectious diseases was the marker of difference between the 'savage' and the 'civilized'; the 'primitive' and the 'modern'. The control and prevention of epidemic diseases was possible only by sequestration as Peiris remarks, 'casting deviance outside spaces of enlightenment'.[98] This was replaced towards the beginning of the twentieth century when opium users were to be treated not in jails but in hospitals embodying 'total care'. This was also emblematic of the shifts in colonial policy which post mutiny (of 1857) was inclined more towards utilitarianism and reformism.

Notes

1. The existence of gold-dust mines, salt brines, and platinum deposits in the north-east frontier was revealed by the geographical surveys carried from the beginning till the mid-nineteenth century. Large deposits of iron ore, coal limestone, and petroleum as revealed in subsequent surveys had pronounced Assam a valuable colonial acquisition. Apart from that, the flourishing external trade links with adjoining regions as Bengal, Bhutan, Nepal and China was alluring to the British mercantile interests. Barpujari, *The Comprehensive History of Assam,* pp. 75-93.
2. Deepak Kumar, 'Developing a History of Science and Technology in South Asia', *Economic and Political Weekly* 28(2003): 2248-51.
3. Ibid.
4. Mark Harrison, 'Difference of Degree: Representations of India in British Medical Topography, 1820-1870', *Medical History Supplement* 20(2000): 51-69.
5. Prosper Alpin was one of the first to occupy himself with topography from a medical point of view. He wrote a book on the natural history of Egypt – the diseases of its inhabitants; the ancient and modern medicine of the country. It is full of judicious and erudite reflections in which the good taste of the author is prominent. James Bontius collected interesting observations on the natural productions of the West Indies and of the diseases, which habitually prevail there. William Pison wrote a similar work on Brazil and united afterwards, in the same edition, his work with that of Bontius, under the title of *Historia Naturalis et Medica India Orientalis.* The celebrated traveller Koempfer collected a mass of excellent observations in medicine and botany, during the ten years he was employed in travels in Persia, Armenia, Japan, the kingdom of Siam and other parts of Eastern Asia. Refer, Pierre Victor and Renonuard, *History of Medicine: From its Origin to the Nineteenth Century*, Cincinnati: Moore, Wilstach, Keys & Co., 1856, p. 482.
6. James Ranald Martin (1796-1874) served as Surgeon of the Bengal Army and was appointed as the Physician to the Council of India. He had also served as a member of the Royal Commission on Army sanitation. His studies and reports on medical and topographical relationships defined the genre and inspired further medical topographical investigations elsewhere

in India. Among his major studies are, *Notes on the Medical Topography of Calcutta* (1837) and *The Influence of Tropical Climates on European Constitutions, including Practical Observations on the Nature and Treatment of the Diseases of the Europeans on their Return from Tropical Climates* (1856).

7. *Sixth Report of the Select Committee on Indian Territories, Together with the Proceedings of the Committee*, Minutes of Evidences and Appendix, vol. 29, London: House of Commons, 1853, pp. 1-76.
8. David Arnold, *Science, Technology and Medicine in Colonial India*, pt. 3, vol. 5, Cambridge: Cambridge University Press, 2000.
9. 'Review of the Progress of Sanitation in India', *Calcutta Review*, XCIX (1858): 93.
10. Hippocrates is regarded as the 'father of medicine'. His *De Aere Locis et Aquis* is a wonderful and innovative exposition of the relationship between climate, landscape and diseases.
11. Elizabeth M. Collingham, *Imperial Bodies: The Physical Experience of the Raj, c. 1800-1947*, Cambridge: Polity Press, 2001, p. 280.
12. Arnold, *Warm Climates and Western Medicine*, p. 5.
13. Mark Harrison, 'Racial Pathologies: Morbid Anatomy in India, 1770-1850', in Biswamoy Pati and Mark Harrison (eds.), *Social History of Health and Medicine in Colonial India*, London: Routledge, 2009, pp. 173-94.
14. Bernard Cohn, *Colonialism and its Forms of Knowledge: The British in India*, Princeton: Princeton University Press, 1996.
15. Walter L. Adamson, *Hegemony and Revolution: A Study of Antonio Gramsci's Political and Cultural Theory*, California: University of California Press, 1980.
16. Levine argues that Western science and medicine was synonymous to progress and dynamism and symbolized 'modernity', and colonies were the antithesis of the idea of anything modern; they were 'backward', breeding ground for diseases and inhabited by the 'savage', Phillippa Levine, *Prostitution, Race and Politics: Policing Venereal Diseases in the British Empire*, New York: Routledge, 2003.
17. Pati and Harrison (eds.), *The Social History of Health and Medicine in Colonial India*, op. cit.
18. The Colonial Secretary Joseph Chamberlain was a leading proponent of the policy of constructive imperialism. Douglas M. Haynes, *Imperial Medicine: Patrick Manson and the Conquest of Tropical Disease*, Pennsylvania: University of Pennsylvania, 2001, pp. 6-10.
19. David P. Fidlern, 'The Globalization of Public Health: The First Hundred Years of International Health Diplomacy', *Bulletin of World Health Organisation,* 79(2001): 842-49.
20. 'Review of the Medical and Physical Society's Transactions', *Oriental Observer*, 24(1833): 287.
21. James R. Martin, 'The Physical Climate of Calcutta in Bengal', in his *The*

Influence of Tropical Climates on European Constitutions Including Practical Observations on the Nature and Treatment of the Diseases of Europeans on their Return from Tropical Climates, London: John Churchill, 1856.

22. The theory of humoralism and the 'environmental paradigm' of understanding of diseases was, interestingly also echoed in the indigenous system of medicine – the Ayurvedic and the Unani system. The 'tridosh' theory of diseases, formulated in the middle of the first millennium BC, is very much similar to the humor theory of Hippocrates. It ascribes the origin of diseases to the disturbances in the equilibrium of the three cosmic elements – airs; fire and water. The theoretical base of the Unani system is also derived from the teachings of Hippocrates and is also based on the Humoral theory. Ram D. Varma, *The Art and Science of Healing Since Antiquity*, Bloomington, Indiana: Xlibris Corporation, 2011.
23. *Washington Express*, 6 January 1870.
24. John F. Logan, 'Age of Intoxication', *Yale French Studies: Intoxication and Literature* 50(1974): 81-94.
25. It refers to the period stretching from the late seventeenth to the early twentieth century. Medical reform was part of the wider reform movement that characterized post-enlightenment England. This witnessed an evident shift from unregulated open market in the eighteenth century to increasingly regulate medical education and practice and the emergence of scientific and utilitarian medicine. Roger K. French and Andrew Wear, *British Medicine in an Age of Reform*, Abingdon: Routledge, 1991.
26. The period beginning around AD 1500 is believed to have witnessed the world's first widespread psychoactive substance abuse which appeared as the 'opium epidemic', which followed the 'gin epidemic' in England, beginning in the 1600s and declining by the 1800s. Opium epidemic, they asserted, occurred primarily in Asia, which began by the 1600s. See, William K. Bichel and J.R. Dhume Grandpe, *Drug Policy and Human Nature: Psychological Perspectives on the Prevention and Management*, Germany: Springer, 1996.
27. Carl Trocki, *Opium, Empire and Global Political Economy: A Study of the Asian Opium Trade – 1750-1950*, Abingdon: Routledge, 1999.
28. The medical theory of humouralism, belonged to the classical antiquity of Galen and was a qualitative system based on four causes: hot, dry, cold and moist. Ill health would result when the humours were imbalanced and out of harmony. The 'principle of Individual Humouralism' held that everyone possessed their own peculiar and innate crisis and it was acknowledged that one drug remedy might suit some but harm others. Louise Foxcroft, *The Making of Addiction: The 'Use and Abuse' of Opium in Nineteenth Century Britain*, Farnham: Ashgate Publishing, 2007.
29. The concept of 'inebriety' was in the early part of the nineteenth century

developed by Norman Kerr to address the undesirable patterns of alcohol use. Kerr was a leading English advocate of the disease position. Norman Kerr described the condition as a disease of the nervous system allied to insanity and characterized by an overpowering impulse of craving for the oblivion of narcotism. He recognized the physical dimensions in 1880, distinguishing the predisposing and existing causes of inebriety. Heredity, together with sex, age, climate, marriage relations and temperament were grouped as predisposing characteristics.

30. The Pharmacy Act of 1868 placed 'opium and all preparations of opium or of poppies' in Part Two of the 'poisons schedule'. The control of poisons was paramount to the medical profession and its consolidation.
31. Early 'disease concept' advocates did not regard intoxication as a disease but rather the symptom of a disease. The disease was portrayed as (a) the cluster of physical and social problems produced by indulgence and (b) 'ungovernable appetite' that overwhelms wilful choice and control of intoxicants. White, 'Addiction as a Disease: Birth of a Concept', *Counselor*, 1(2000): 46-51.
32. Virginia Berridge and Griffith Edwards, *Opium and the People: Opiate use in Nineteenth-century England*, London: A. Lane, 1981.
33. Hanan Frenk and D. Reuven, *A Critique of Narcotine Addiction*, Massachusetts: Kluwer Academic Publishers, 2000, pp. 13-15.
34. Fred H. Hubbard, *The Opium Habit and Alcoholism*, New York: A.S. Barnes, 1981 (rpt.), pp. 15-42.
35. French and Wear, *British Medicine in an Age of Reform*, pp. 1-8.
36. Slavery was a recognized institution in the society of medieval Assam. The royal family including members of the nobility and the religious institution (*Sattras*) employed a large number of people, both male and female, to cultivate their farms and also work as domestic servants, variously referred to as *Das*, *Dasi*, *Golam* or *Bandi*, *Beti* (male and female slaves) for whom the state had no obligation. Although as is attested to by contemporary sources, both literary and official, that the life of slaves in Assam was comparatively trouble-free. Apart from being provided with daily necessities, a bondsman could buy liberty by repaying their debt. Slaves could also marry although children born out of wedlock were considered to be their master's property. In general, they were treated as members of the family, although eventually slavery did have a demoralizing impact on the society. The deterioration in their condition post-Burmese invasions of Assam had bred great discontentment amongst their kind. Jahnabi Gogoi, *Agrarian System of Medieval Assam*, New Delhi: Concept Publishing Company, 2002, pp. 118-43.
37. British Parliamentary Debates, 'Suppression of the Opium Trade', 1843, accessed from hansard.millbanksystems.com/commons/ on 11 December 2008.

38. Shehabuddin Talish was the official reporter of Mughal commander Mir Jumla when he raided Koch Behar and Assam in 1663. His *Fatiyyah-i-Ibriyyah* is a first hand account of Assam in the later half of the seventeenth century and hence regarded as authentic. Shehabuddin Talesh, *Tarikh-e-Aasham*, tr. A. Mazhar, Guwahati: Department of Historical and Antiquarian Studies, 2009.
39. Francis Hamilton, *An Account of Assam*, ed. Surrya K. Bhuyan, Guwahati: Department of Historical and Antiquarian Studies, 1987.
40. 'Idea of Assam', the North American, Philadelphia, 14 September 1839 (accessed from Gale Digital Library).
41. *Oriental Observer*, 5(1832): 37.
42. Towards the mid-nineteenth century, the Governor-General in Council, directed the medical officers, whether in the civil or military branches to furnish, through the Superintending surgeons or physicians information with reference to the medical topography of the district, station and cantonment area, etc. This spawned a series of works on medical topography and M'Cosh's work was a part of the genre that arose out of measuring the relationship between disease and environment in seventeenth century Europe, which was transplanted into Indian colonies.
43. John M. Cosh, *Topography of Assam*, New Delhi: Logos Press, 2000 (rpt.), pp. 98-101.
44. John Leslie, 'Sketch of the Medical Topography of Gowhattee with an Account of the Prevailing Diseases', *Medico-Chirurgical Review and Journal of Practical Medicine*, 20(1833): 363-7.
45. Letter from 'Assistant Surgeon Macleod, Assam Light Infantry to Major White, Commanding Assam Light Infantry, Jorehauth, Assam, 4 April 1833', Appendix B (IV), in Francis Jenkins, *Report on the North-East Frontier of Assam*, ed. H.K. Barpujari, New Delhi: Spectrum Publications, 1995.
46. John Butler, *Travels in Assam: During a Residence of Fourteen Years*, Guwahati: Manas Publications, 2004 (rpt.).
47. Government of Assam, *Physical and Political Geography of the Province of Assam*, Shillong: Assam Secretariat Printing, 1896, p. 18.
48. Extract from the *Report of the Commissioner of the Dacca Division (Eastern Bengal) for 1894-95 Contrasting the Dacca Division with Assam Shows, as by a Sidelight the Fiscal and Commercial Blight Produced by the Opium Habit in Assam*, Calcutta, 1895. Appended to the Final report of the Royal Commission on Opium 1893-4 in a report titled, William Roberts. 'Memorandum on the General Features and the Medical Aspects of the Opium Habit in India', *Indian Medical Record,* pp. 107-9.
49. David Arnold, *Colonizing the Body: State, Medicine and Epidemic Disease in Nineteenth-Century India*, California: University of California Press, 1993.
50. The importance of tea as an imperial taste can hardly be underestimated. Following the losses incurred with China because of the opium wars, the

discovery of tea in Assam caught the fascination of the British. The Charter Act of 1833 was amended to facilitate import of British capital, subsequent legislations facilitated the emergence the tea capitalists in Assam. With the formation of a Tea Committee in 1834, in subsequent years all developments were centred around tea and the Assam Company.

51. It was Jenkins, the Commissioner of Assam (1834-66) who in his report, following the grant of the Charter Act of 1833 (which marked the final ascendancy of the British industrial interests over the mercantile interests and had it's full impact on the settlement of Assam), he advocated grants of wastelands to Europeans. His policy aimed at attracting European capital, while following a discriminatory land revenue policy-exorbitant land revenue rates and granting substantial revenue concessions to the planters, to 'produce sugarcane, indigo and such other plantation crops'. Amalendu Guha, *Planter-Raj to Swaraj: Freedom Struggle and Electoral Politics in Assam 1826-1947*, New Delhi: ICHR, 1977.
52. H.A. Antrobus, *A History of the Assam Company, 1839-1953*, T.&A., Edinburgh: Constable, 1957.
53. They were tribes who were willing to work in the tea gardens.
54. She remarks on the differences constructed and perpetrated in colonial Assam of the 'diligent' Kachari tea labour and the 'indolent' Assamese peasant. Those unwilling to facilitate in the colonial tea enterprise were marked out as unproductive, uncivilized and not amenable to labour. Thus the need for reform and improvement. Jayeeta Sharma, *Empire's Garden: Assam and the Making of India*, Duke: Duke University Press, 2011.
55. One of the pioneers of the propagation of tea cultivation in Assam.
56. *Report from Committee on Colonization and Settlement (India)*, Great Britain Parliament: House of Commons, 1859, pp. 185-438.
57. 'Baneful Effects of Opium on the Assamese', *Transactions of the Agricultural and Horticultural Society of India*, Calcutta: Baptist Mission Press, 1840, p. 34.
58. Sharma, *Empire's Garden*, pp. 62-71.
59. In 'Assam and Chinese Teas', *Daily Evening Bulletin*, San Francisco, 1882, 'Idea of Assam', *The North American and Daily Advertiser*, Philadelphia, 1840.
60. 'Transactions of the Medical and Physical Society of Calcutta', *Edinburgh Medical and Surgical Journal*, 44, Edinburgh: Adam & Charles Black, 1835.
61. W. Ball, *The Eclectic Review*, vol. II, Arnold & Co., 1840, p. 719.
62. In a letter dated '26 October 1839, Hong Kong bay off Canton', a group of influential merchants from Britain, complained of how, 'the mischievous effects of this traffic in interfering with the importation of British manufacturers as well as of all descriptions of Indian produce, other than the forbidden drug, in absorbing the attention and capital of both native and foreign merchants and in subjecting the whole foreign commerce to a

system of jealous and vexatious restrictions, can hardly be overrated and are most palpable to anyone on the spot whose powers of observation are not impaired by prejudice or interest.' *The Eclectic Review*, p. 720.

63. Letter from Lieut. Col. F. Jenkins, Governor-General North-East Frontier; Appendix 'D' Memorandum by Lieut. Colonel Matthie, Appendix B No. 275 of 1853, in A.J.M. Mills, *Report on the Province of Assam*, Guwahati: Publication Board Assam, 1984.
64. 'Observations on the Administration of the Province of Assam by Anandaram Dhekial Phukan', Appendix J, in Mills, *Report on the Province of Assam*.
65. Mills, *Report on the Province of Assam*, p. 19.
66. See, 'Assam: Letter of Mr. Bronson', *Baptist Missionary Magazine*, vols. 25-6, Calcutta: American Baptist Foreign Mission Society, 1845, p. 122.
67. Ewen Green, *Ideals of Empire: Political and Economic Thought: 1903-1915*, London: Routledge, 1998.
68. P.P. Purpura, *Criminal Justice: An Introduction*, Boston: Butterworth-Heinemann, 1997.
69. 'Administration of Civil and Criminal Justice in the Extra Regulation Province 1864' (accessed from Gale Digital Collections).
70. Assistant Surgeon McLean, recommended against the indiscriminate employment of convicts who eat opium in digging tanks should be discontinued. See, remarks by A.J.M. Mills, Officiating Judge of the Sadr Dewani Adalat, in Mills, *Report on the Province of Assam*, 22 May 1853, pp. 330-1.
71. 'Letter from Assistant Surgeon, A. McLean, in Medical Charge, Gowhatty to A.J.M. Mills, Judge of the Sudder Court, on Special Deputation to Assam, Gowhatty, 17 May 1853', Appendix J, No. 397, *Report of the Province of Assam*, pp. 377-90.
72. *ACOECR*, 1925, 19-22.
73. 'Contemporary Opinion', *Friend of India*, Calcutta: Calcutta University Press, 1840, p. 568.
74. Extract from the Proceedings of the Chief Commissioner of Assam, in the Judicial Department, No. 1061(1882), ASA.
75. A habitual consumer found to be consuming around 10 to 20 grains of opium. No uniformity is noticed in this instance for it was laid down that, 'The question of treatment is not one in regard to which a hard and fast rule can be followed', Dr. Russell at Gauhati jail recommended small and slowly diminishing doses; Dr. Warburton at Tezpur, rarely allowed opium, depending on nourishing diet and stimulants. At Silchar, it was reported that the Civil Surgeon allowed the habitual consumers 5 or 6 grains a day at first and lowered the supply by a grain a month, until it was withdrawn to help the consumer in adjusting to the deprivation. Tezpur jail authorities

allowed opium to under-trials while the Civil Surgeon of Silchar subsidiary jail notes that some prisoners improved in health under the treatment adopted, that of gradually stopping the supply of opium although a few deaths were reported owing to a complication of diseases and emaciation. *Annual Reports of the Jail Administration of the Province of Assam*, Shillong: Assam Secretariat Press, ASA.

76. The connivance of the jail authorities in supplying opium to the prisoners in lieu of bribes is echoed in the administrative reports. Dr. Mouat, in his report in 1867, under the head 'Conduct of the Civil Constabulary Guard', refers to the 'delinquencies' of the constables who were accepting bribes from the relatives of the prisoners to supply the addicted inmates, their regular dose of the drug. This was regarded as a serious offence, as it seriously affected the successful operation of the treatment in the jail hospitals. Those found guilty were terminated from their offices. R. Pringle, *Reply to Dr. Mouat's Rejoinder on the Ethics of Opium and Alcohol*, Anerley: J. Nicholas Press Office, 1892.
77. The following is the death rate for five years in the Kamrup jail for five years: 1851-2: 12.60 per cent, 1852-3: 10.90 per cent, 1853-4: 10.37 per cent, 1854-5: 8.10 per cent, 1855-6: 7.60 per cent. *Annual Reports of the Jail Administration of the Province of Assam.*
78. Bary Stimmel, *Evaluation of Drug Treatment Programs*, New York: Haworth Press, 1983, pp. 33-5.
79. *Assam Congress Opium Enquiry Report*, p. 46.
80. Hemchandra Barua, *Kaniyar Kirtan: A Play in Assamese on the Evils of Opium-Eating*, Guwahati: Hem Chandra Prakashan, 2003 (rpt.).
81. *Report of the Committee to Enquire into Certain Aspects of Opium and Ganja Consumption, 1912*, Shillong: Assam Secretariat Press, ASA.
82. Benudhar Kalita, *Phulagurir Dhewa*, Nagaon: Krantiklal Prakashan, 1994 (rpt.).
83. *Minutes of Evidence Taken Before the Royal Commission on Opium*, 1893.
84. Ibid.
85. 'Consumption of Opium in Assam by Persons of Different Castes and Tribes', Appendix XXXV, *Minutes of Evidence Taken Before the Royal Commission on Opium*, 1893.
86. *Indo-European Telegraph*, 1893.
87. Joshua Rowntree, *The Opium Habit in the East*, Scarborough: The Bar Library Press, 1895.
88. *Minutes of Evidence Taken before the Royal Commission on Opium between 18 November-29 December 1893*, vol. II.
89. Jagannath Barua was a wealthy tea planter of Assam who owned six tea estates, viz., Letekujan, Bessabari, Tirual, Tipomia, Bahani and Rawraiyah. The tea planting community was usually regarded as collaborators of the

colonial administrators and hence the stand of the Jorhat Sarvbajanik Sabha is reflective of this attitude. Ramesh C. Kalita, 'Opium Prohibition and Rai Jagannath Baruah Bahadur', *Proceedings of North East India History Association* 16(1995): 182-91.

90. Jorhat Sarbajanik Sabha, Memorial submitted to Chief Commissioner on Opium, 1893. Appendix XXXVI, *Royal Commission on Opium*, p. 462.
91. Harbilas Agarwala owned opium *mehals*; hence his statement. Nevertheless, he had expresed the opinion that it was only through a stringent excise system that the abuse of intoxicants including opium could be curbed. *Minutes of Evidence taken before the Royal Commission on Opium*.
92. See, William Roberts, *Memorandum on the General Features and the Medical aspects of the Opium Habit in India*, Appended to the *Final Report of the Royal Commission on Opium*, pp. 107-9.
93. *Assam Congress Opium Enquiry Report*, p. 36.
94. Driberg's statement was in response to a Government of India letter in 1890, forwarding a memorial from the Society of the Suppression of the Opium Trade, on opium and opium dens in the provinces of India. Refer, 'Letter from J.J.S. Driberg Commissioner of Excise, Assam to the Secretary to the Chief Commissioner of Assam (1891)', ASA.
95. Jorhat Sarbajanik Sabha, Memorial submitted to Chief Commissioner on Opium, 1893. Appendix XXXVI, *Royal Commission on Opium*.
96. William W. Hunter, *A Statistical Account of Assam*, vol. I, New Delhi: Spectrum Publications, 1990 (rpt.).
97. Ibid.
98. Anoma Peiris, *Hidden Lands and Divided Landscapes: A Penal History of Singapore's Plural Society*, Hawaii: University of Hawaii, 2009.

CHAPTER 4

On a Route Laced with Opium: Networks of Commerce and Consumption in a Colonial Hinterland

> It's climate is cold, healthy and congenial to European constitutions; its numerous crystal streams abound in gold, dust and masses of the solid metal, its mountains are pregnant with precious stones and silver, it's atmosphere is perfumed with tea growing wild and luxuriantly, and its soil is so well adapted to all kinds of agricultural purposes, that it might be converted into one continued garden of silk and cotton and coffee and sugar and tea over an extent of many hundred miles (M'Cosh, *Topography of Assam*).

Introduction

'THE GREAT OBJECT of the Government in every quarter of the world is to extend the commerce of the country', Lord Palmerstone[1] told Parliament in 1839. In Palmerstone's stance, was a certain 'geopolitical logic'. Such underpinnings of developing British 'spheres of rule', hinged on 'unlimited commerce', which assumed strength by the 1830s and 1840s. Such visualization of 'Empire' – 'with a Stuart monarchy pursuing an equally bold and authoritarian imperial policy around the globe'[2] aimed to embark on an 'Imperial Grand Strategy'. This dictated and influenced a subtle shift from mere mercantilist concerns to the larger visions of British Empire building. Darwin identifies certain imperatives, which led the British to expand with a 'new urgency' towards Asia and the Near East. According to him, it was a way of relieving the economic distress and restoring domestic tranquility.[3] The need for revenue resources for financing England's growth in internal and overseas trade which created an impulse for conquest, were involved in determining a specific course of territorial expansion in South Asia. To Bernard Cohn, 'the state building process in Great Britain was a cultural project, closely linked with its emergence as an imperial power and India was its largest and most important colony'.[4] It needs no reiteration that the British Empire was built on commerce and finance. The representatives of the British East India Company were keenly observant of all that might offer commercial opportunities.[5] Thus, effective control over the productive resources was deemed imperative to ensure financial vibrancy. Their concentration on ensuring economic dominance enabled the buildup of a complex system of 'trade, diplomacy and war'. A growing crisis with Burma in the north-eastern borders of Bengal became an argument justifying further imperial expansion on the north-eastern part of their possessions in India.[6] A major concern with locating routes of communication was ensuring lines of defence in case of the Burmese aggrandisement.[7] Such security concerns were undoubtedly enmeshed with the commercial intentions of the British East India Company.

Mapping a Frontier Landscape

Exploring the unknown was not only a curiosity but also a challenge given the imperatives of the process of colonial state building in India. The fluidity of the frontier of the north-eastern part of its colonial possessions presented innumerable economic and political possibilities. Nonetheless, there were myriad factors that dictated and influenced the process of territorial conquest of the fertile valley of Assam.

A careful examination of the epigraphic and literary sources would reveal that from the early times, the kingdom of Kamrupa was noted for her textiles and invaluable forest and mineral produce. It carried on a brisk internal and external trade both by land and by water. Marketable commodities were exported not only to the neighbouring provinces but also to adjacent countries: Burma, Tibet,

China – by mountain passes, land and water routes. Persian chronicles and accounts left by early European travellers in Assam like Tavernier, Bernier, Manucci and Glanius speak of Assam as a very fertile country with trading links across Burma into China. Indeed, it was the lucrative trade with Tibet and China passing through Assam that had invited the aggression of the Turko-Afghan and the Tai-Shans, which was certainly a vital factor in efforts to capture the Brahmaputra valley.[8] Assam's strategic location at the crisscross of commerce with China and Ava (present day Myanmar) enhanced colonial interest in the region. That apart, the expansion of riverine trade with Bengal was found to offer innumerable possibilities. In his narratives, Captain Bogle, pointed out the superior advantages of the Assam trade, as compared with that of Bhutan, Nepal and Lhasa and was in favour of 'an open and unrestricted trade with Assam'.[9] Under such circumstances, the British Government readily responded to Raja Gaurinath Singha's appeal for military aid against the Moamariya rebels. The Anglo-Burmese war of 1826 afforded a well-intentioned pretext of intervention and subsequent conquest of Assam. Lord Cornwallis, Governer-General, deputed six companies of troops to Assam under Captain Thomas Welsh. The extensive report, which the latter submitted under the orders of the Government of Bengal, furnished a graphic account of not only the internal condition of the country but also its administrative structure, state of commerce and resources – agricultural, mineral and forest products. John Peter Wade who had accompanied the troops under Welsh as Medical Assistant compiled the earliest *Sketch of the Geography of Assam* and Buchanan Hamilton published the results of his survey in 1809. In 1832 under orders of Lord William Bentick, Francis Jenkins and R.B. Pemberton conducted a survey of the entire north-eastern frontier. Their reports were replete with accounts of Assam as a possible 'great entrepôt for commerce'. As one of the earliest of the East India Company's officials, Captain Thomas Welsh, comments in his *Report on Assam*,

The country of Assam is represented as abounding in the most valuable products and it were therefore an object of public interest to take measures for restoring peace and quiet with a view to promote the intercourse of commerce, now so much impeded by the depredations that the defenseless state of the inhabitants and the barbarism of the Government subject it to. By all accounts they are a very peaceable and an industrious people, and if not molested by these annual marauders would in a short time bring the country into a flourishing state, whilst the trade, if laid under proper restrictions which should secure them from imposition and violence, would in all probability, become very extensive and beneficial by creating a demand for articles, the produce of Europe and Bengal and supplying this country and Europe with a valuable return in bullion and other products of the country.[10]

A contemporary account by a Persian translator on the extent and the probable state of commerce corroborates the observations made by Captain Welsh in his *Report on Assam* and throws much light on the flourishing state of both inter-provincial and international trade including the means of transport. It also laments on the *policy of isolation* of the ruling Ahom monarchs, which according to it had resulted in the economic stagnation of Assam,

Commerce could never have been very considerable in Assam under the discouraging restraints imposed by a Government particularly jealous of strangers. The subversion of all regular government and the desolation of the country reduced it to nothing. The actual commerce is therefore very inconsiderable though reviving and it would be unreasonable to doubt, that it might in time, under the influence of the British Government be rendered extremely beneficial to both states.[11]

These reports foreshadow the growing importance of the region as central to the imperial strategy of opening up communications. In 1793, a commercial treaty was concluded by Captain Thomas Welsh at the behest of the East India Company officials with the Ahom king Gaurinath Singha. As per the terms of the treaty, trade restrictions between Bengal and Assam were done away with.[12] A major part of Upper Assam, with the exception of the tracts of Sadiya and Muttock, were restored as legal possessions to the successor, Raja Purandhar Singha in 1832. Of the many injunctions that the colonial government obligated the Raja was to stop poppy cultivation and use of opium in his territory.[13] In 1834, Colonel Jenkins proposed a policy of active encouragement to expand the commercial relations between the Singphos and the Shan and Chinese of Yunnan.[14]

Seizure of commercial privileges was followed by political man-eouvres for territorial control as had ensued in Siam and Burma and thence in Assam. Fear of increasing disruptive activities of the Chinese following the opium *imbroglio*, had prompted the British pragmatic policy to anchor its interests on the north-eastern frontier of India, which could be developed into a stronghold to pursue its economic and political agenda in the entire East Asian region. Imperialistic ambitions were further fuelled by the rising wave of Russian expansionist spree in East Asia. As Eric Tagliacozzo rightly remarks, aggressive imperialist tendencies were veiled as missions to 'modernize an endangered kingdom'.[15] In 1838, Purandhar Singha was accused of mismanagement and de-throned. Assam thus passed under the direct management of the Company's officers as a Non-Regulation Province of the British Empire.

A Route from Assam to Yunnan

It was both economic causations and political imperatives that guided British policy considerations in mapping the commercial viability of the north-east frontier. Cold statistics and correspondence from the personal papers of leading British firms of the time, Jardine Matheson and Baring Brothers, the debates in the British press and parliament reveal how the issue of opening up of trade with China was intensely pursued. The existence of trade links between eastern Assam and Upper Burma into the southern part of China across the hills throughout the thirteenth and fifteenth century is well documented.[16] Emdad-ul-Haq illustrates a range of issues that are pertinent to the understanding of the origins and development of drug abuse and illicit trafficking in Pakistan, India and Bangladesh.[17] Richards' work on opium trade in India in the latter decades of the nineteenth century also agrees on it.[18] Interestingly, not much scholarship has been directed towards investigating the lure of the opium trade through Assam into China in the latter half of the nineteenth century, particularly into Yunnan which was one of the most important opium-producing province of China. It is important to mention here that as early as the 1830s, poppy cultivation in

Yunnan had to face the onslaught of the Qing prohibitory decree cultivation of poppy consumed after 1917.[19]

A focus on the direction of trade and traffic of commodities passing through Assam around 1833 reveals the stimulus arisen for trade through Shan provinces into China. At the crossroads of consumption and commerce, opium was the 'perfect modern commodity of exchange'. It had great value in small portions. The East India Company wanted to reclaim the West Yunnan trade, which had been seriously threatened by the Qing prohibitory decrees. This had rendered it imperative to explore possibilities of reclaiming the monopoly trade in opium, which they had to forsake. The centralized control of the land routes through which opium was being poured into Yunnan (south-west China) was considered as a possible alternative. By the year 1839, the Company had strangled the Pali-Karachi route to redirect the Malwa opium trade through Bombay and thence into China.[20] They now sought control of the opium traffic, which they discovered, laced the north-eastern frontier of India.[21] As early as 1826, Captain David Scott, the then agent to the Governor-General in Assam, had with much foresight, tried at opening up of a direct trade route between China and India through Assam.[22]

The history of the north-east frontier in the mid and late nineteenth century is enlivened by travel accounts focusing on identifying – (a) new and rare plants and (b) search for trade routes to Central Asia, Tibet and China. The Christian missionaries were also interested in opening missionary routes and were toying with the ideas of accessing Tibet and China through Assam via Burma.[23] The topographical surveys of the region had assured Captain Jenkins of the strategic importance of the Sadiya frontier in Assam, with geo-political implications. It was established that Sadiya carried on an extensive trade with Tibet, Ava and through Shan province into the south-western province of Yunnan in China,[24] in musk, amber, ivory, gold, silver, lead, Burmese silks, variety of narcotic substances and cotton. There are references to the *mela* or annual fair at Sadiya, which was thronged by the hill tribes – Mishimis, Singphos, Khamtis and the Miris. The Mishimis would throng the tea gardens of Sadiya for work during the winter months carrying of musk, skins and roots along with considerable quantities of opium.

Around five trade routes from Sadiya and Upper Assam leading to Tibet and China proper had been identified. From Sadiya, they had surveyed three possible routes to Tibet, the most practicable being the Lohit valley route which would lead into Zayul, the south-eastern province of Tibet.[25] The Lohit valley, inhabited by the Mishimi clans – Digaru and Miju, was famed as the 'Opium Valley'. Cultivation of opium was a lucrative indulgence, both as a valuable commodity and a wonder stimulant. Mention is made of the overland route to China via Assam, Tenga Pani River, Khamti and Singpho country across the Irrawaddy River into Yunnan (Map 4.1).[26] The most important and the easy route were on the

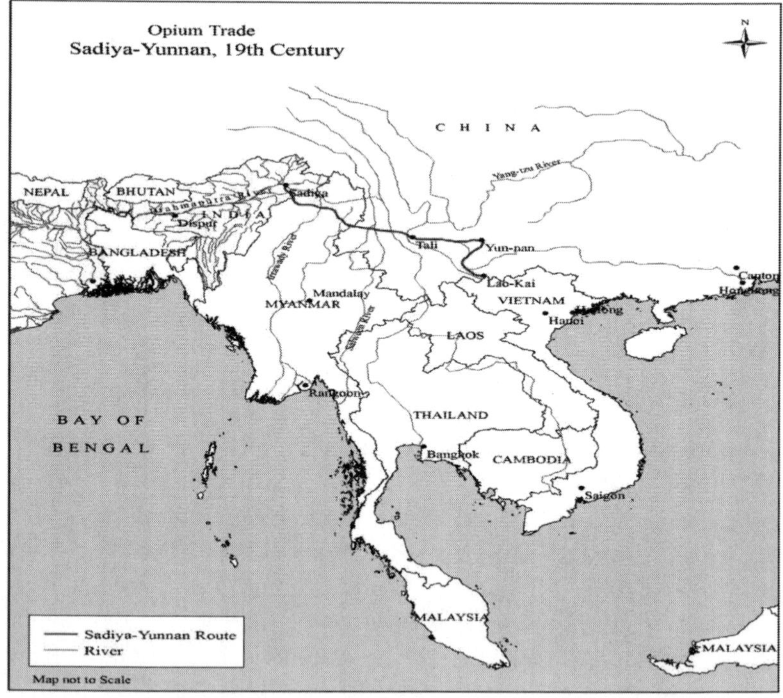

Courtesy: E.C. Young, 'A Journey from Yun-Nan to Assam', The *Geographical Journal,* 30 (1907): 18

MAP 4.1: ROUTE-MAP FROM SADIYA (UPPER ASSAM) TO YUNNAN (CHINA)

north-eastern side over the Patkai to the upper districts of Burma and thence to China.[27]

Mention is made of the Borkhamti country at close proximity to the Chinese province of Yunnan and Schezwan. It has been ascertained that a large amount of goods were traded through Margherita and other bordering villages to the Khampti and Singpho country. The transborder tribesmen from Borkhamti and from the Hukong (Burma) valley similarly carried large quantities via Margherita and even as far as Titabar in Assam. It was therefore considered that the opening of the Khamti and the Borkhamti country would uncover tremendous possibilities of Assam-China trade being conducted through the river routes – Irrawady-Salwin (then Burma) and thence into Yang-tse-kiang (region of China).

Surveying the region in 1826, Captain Wilcox in his memoirs had taken incidental note of the great demand for opium, apart from salt 'amongst all Indo-Chinese nations'.[28] He mentions the drug selling at '4 or 5 rupees a seer only, while I was at Sadiya'. Even though the Khamtis and the Singpho villages had large extants of land devoted to poppy cultivation,[29] there are interesting references to Khamti traders making purchases of China opium at the rate of 10 seers 6 chattaks a pound though they are said to have a great preference for the Assam opium, which, however, cost them about 30 seers a pound.[30] Captain Francis Jenkins in his surveys had also referred to the colonial commercial projects to China from the Borkhamti country, 'that is so near the Chinese province of Yunnan and Schezwan and the Shan tribes to which the Khamtis belonged compose a large segment of the population of these provinces'.[31]

The Digaru and the Miju tribes inhabiting the Lohit valley 'where the loveliest white poppies were flourishing', were also notorious as 'opium smugglers'. In the cold weather, a number of them would come down into Sadiya to find work in the tea gardens of Assam, bringing goods to trade in the market such as musk, skins, roots and certainly quantities of opium. Besides selling the opium, they also used it largely as a stimulant themselves.[32] That the Digarus maintained trade relations with the Chinese provinces is evident from the coins, metal smoking pipes and other Chinese goods that were found in their possession.[33] The land to the north of Sadiya, and the south-east of Mishimis, was inhabited by the Khamtis – who extensively cultivated opium poppy. Their neighbours, the Singphos described by Robinson as powerful and numerous were also 'great opium eaters'; every Singhpo village also had a certain amount of poppy cultivation.[34]

Opium, salt, betel nut, tobacco, and silks of Assam were articles in great demand. The Tibetans also figure as trade partners bartering rubber, ivory, beeswax and ginger for salt, opium and clothing with the inhabitants of Assam. In 1862, the Secretary of State for India, Charles Wood, directed the attention of the Government to the numerous memorials received from commercial associations of England[35] for opening up of commerce with the Shans and the Western Chinese. Each of these memorials suggested that the trade should be opened by the 'only practicable way for continuous commerce – by land route, direct from the port of Rangoon across Eastern Pegu to the Upper Kamboja or Mekong River in the direction of the Chinese south-western frontier city in this country'. He also cited a dispatch from the Government of India, '[...] that the Chief Commissioner of British Burma has been desired to keep his attention directed to the prospects of trade with Western China and to avail himself of every favourable opportunity to obtain a knowledge of the different routes, which have been suggested for tapping the commerce of China at that quarter.'[36]

The Government was keen on exploring the possibilities of opium trade into China through Assam via Burma which is evident from the dispatch sent by the Viceroy and Governor-General of India, Lord Elgin in 1862. There were clear instructions for the Chief Commissioner of British Burma for securing the route to Burma by which 'opium should be conveyed – either duty free or on payment of a moderate transit duty' – from Indian territory (Assam) to the extreme north of Yunnan, and by which Chinese coolies should also travel from Yunnan to the unpeopled districts of Assam, granted by the Bengal Government to be cleared for tea plantations.[37]

It is also apparent from the correspondences that the colonial government was contemplating the possibilities of setting up a direct rail link between India and China. It was opium, which was meant to be carried on to China along with tea and general merchandise. Among the major lines proposed was – through Assam, which was strongly advocated by M.A. Purcell, Chief Engineer and Lieutenant-Colonel D. Briggs, then Superintending Engineer of Assam. It was proposed to run through Assam, cross a small portion of Tibet and form its junction with the Yang-tse-kiang.[38] Correspondences between Bengal Government and the Political Agent deputed at Burma refer to the instructions to the Agent to ensure a safe passage to the Chinese labourers to clear ground for tea plantations in Assam and also of conveying the opium of India to Yunnan at the insistence of the British merchants following the Chinese hostility.

We also come across references to the commercial pursuits of the Assamese and the Marwari merchants undertaking arduous journey from Sadiya and thence across the Patkai via Burma into the south-western province of Yunnan in China, famed as the prime region for the cultivation of poppy.[39] References abound on the track of the *beparies* (Assamese merchants) from the Muttock country in Upper Assam. The Assamese merchants followed the overland routes through the villages about Jorhat and Rungpore carrying with them rice and *kanee* and bartered their articles for salt, depending on the market being cheap or dear.[40] The Marwari merchants had their establishments at Beesa and were actively involved in trading activities into the valley of Hukwang.[41] It needs to be mentioned here that the Marwari traders had great interests in the opium traffic in Assam and the north-east frontier.[42] Even in the absence of any reliable statistics, their involvement in the trade of opium cannot be completely ruled out, as by the end of the nineteenth century, they were fairly established as owners of opium *mehals* and later as owners of large number of retail outlets and very often as opium smugglers.

Opium in Assam

Though certainly not central to the local economy, opium undeniably weaved the politics and commerce of the north-east frontier of British India into a story of surveillance and control. Opium was all over the frontier. This led to a series of attempts at centralized control over the flow of an 'ambiguous commodity', where control was both difficult to implement and enforce. It may be said that the attempt to modulate and influence the flow of an addictive consumable reflects the British imperative to control the flow and exchange of 'illicit' commodities across frontiers that helped in identifying certain landscapes as ambiguous – desirable yet dangerous. Alongside there was an understanding of the subtle relationships between the intertwined interests of commerce and anthropology of consumption with the 'drug cultures' in context. This also explains the identification of the indigenous Assamese population as 'the opium consuming – timid, apathetic, effeminate' and hence unproductive subjects.

To the British, the racial factor was an important ingredient in formulation of policies of regulation and intervention. The quantification of the Assamese and their 'licentious habits' apparently referring to their excessive use of opium – as comprised of chiefly the people who live in the Brahmaputra valley – the northern part of Assam. The districts of Kamrup, Nowgong, Darrang, Lakhimpur including those of Balipara Frontier Tract and the Sadiya Frontier Tract (which form part of the Darrang and Lakhimpur districts, respectively) claimed to have been inhabited by the indigenous Assamese were also those, which had a history of extensive poppy cultivation and intense consumption.[43] 'It is among the indigenous Assamese race that the opium habit chiefly prevails and especially among the hill tribes as they come down and settle in the plains. Of the districts, it was the districts of Nowgong, Sibsagar and Lakhimpur, which were the worst affected and Kamrup and Darrang were the least infected regions.'

The report of RCO 1893 estimated the percentage of population accustomed to opium use as – Kamrup 53.38 per cent, Darrang 46.41 per cent, Nowgong 76.37 per cent, Sibsagar 63.76 per cent and Lakhimpur 47.13 per cent of the total population were estimated at being addicted to opium. Most ethnic and caste groups like the Chutiya, Hojai, Maria, Matak, Dom, Ahom, Ganak, Kalita, Keot, Lalung, Mikir, Miri, Salai, Jugi, Koch, Rajbongsi, Tanti, Mira, Kumar, Moran, Phakial, Hari and Teli were mentioned in the official records as the principal opium eating races and castes.[44] Like the peasants, the hill tribes, chief among them being the Abors, Miris, Mishimis, Khamtis, Singphos and the Daflas, inhabiting the borderlands of the frontiers of Assam also took opium. The indexes of consumption for the Sadiya Frontier Tract as mentioned in the official records were as high as 237.029 seers for each 10,000 population, which was the highest on record in British India.[45]

The 1893 Royal Commission on Opium, usually considered the first authoritative statement on the opium problem, contained references to the large extant of opium cultivation[46] being a potent factor in the proliferation of opium consumption in the province before 1860, the year private cultivation of poppy was prohibited in Assam. However, nowhere do we come across references of opium being raised as a commercial crop; colonial accounts of the early and mid-nineteenth century, however, reveal references to poppy being raised as a homestead crop.

Assam is a Great Opium Field

In Assamese, poppy is referred to as *afu* or *afing*. References available claim of every Assamese homestead cultivating poppy plants for private consumption. It is, however, difficult to ascertain as to how much land from one's total landed property was used for opium due to lack of any available statistics. Though a small amount did find its way to the nearby market, it was certainly not meant for export. The *ryot* had no tax to pay for his opium field, no restrictions were placed on him.[47] As in other parts of India, it was the white variety of poppy that was exclusively brought under cultivation. The necessary pre-requisites for a successful culture of opium were claimed to be a mild climate, plentiful irrigation, a rich soil and diligent husbandry.[48] The lands selected for poppy cultivation were generally situated near villages where the facilities for manuring and irrigation were present. Robinson, in his *Descriptive Account of Assam* mentions as to how the poppy plant was the only crop regularly and constantly watered. Describing what he terms as a 'remarkably primitive' mode of irrigation with a small wicker basket tied to the end of a bamboo and with this instrument, a man bailed up water from small reservoirs for this purpose that was used to water the poppy field.[49] Poppy was chiefly cultivated in the *char*[50]areas, along with the mustard crop.[51] It was estimated that in Assam, prior to the prohibition of the private cultivation of poppy, around 12,500 acres of land in the five districts taken together were under poppy cultivation.[52] The districts of Nowgong, Sibsagar and Lakhimpur were the principal poppy growing areas in the province. A survey of Nowgong put up the total area under poppy cultivation before the ban on private cultivation as 2,650 acres.[53] The quantity grown in the district was estimated to be about 400 maunds.[54] In 1875-6, the total area of in Sibsagar around 18,27,995 acres or 2,855 square miles was cultivated area as per an estimate of 1875-6.[55] Opium figured as a prominent import of the district apart from salt, oil, brass, and utensils [56]which in 1852-3, was cultivated on around 1,550 acres of land. *Kanee* was sold in the markets at rates varying between fifteen and twenty rupees per seer. [57]

Captain Welsh's *Report on Assam* (1793), furnishes one of the earliest accounts of large quantities of poppy being raised in the homestead. It was not an article of merchandise as yet. He had referred to the prospects of its being cultivated as an article of commerce. Francis Hamilton's *Account of Assam* (1809) also takes notice of opium poppy as one of the agricultural products of Assam. Assistant Surgeon John M'Cosh reported on the principal articles of cultivation in Assam as rice, mustard seed, opium and cotton. Leslie in his *Medical Sketch of Gowhatty* also mentions poppy as among the cultivated plants of Assam apart from rice, pulse, Indian corn, mustard seed, sugar cane, cotton, tobacco and some ordinary vegetables.[58] To Major Butler, opium was valuable and mentions how in Assam, 10 maunds of poppy seed could be bartered for 1 maund of salt, implying both salt and poppy seeds as valuable commodities. In his *Travels in Assam*, he mentions opium among the staple products of the districts. It had entered the peasant production cycle. As per his estimate, around 2,426 *poorahs* of land was cultivated with opium in 1847 in the district of Nowgong. Major Butler had calculated that around 3 acres of land sowed with poppy could produce an annual yield of 606 maunds 20 seers of raw opium. When sold at an average rate of Rs. 5 per seer, the *ryots* seem to have realized from the sale of opium around Rs. 1,21,300.[59]

In Nowgong district, the land stretching in between the river Kolong and the Brahmaputra, the *chaparee mahals*, was regarded as ideal for poppy cultivation and was referred to as the *afu-toli*. Poppy crop was cultivated in the river islands surrounded by deep channels and covered with reed and grass jungle, with minimum labour for the floodwaters of the Kolong and the Brahmaputra, which aided in the luxuriant growth of the plant and yielded flowers in plenty. The inhabitants of Barpathar were claimed to cultivate small patches of ground for opium and mustard seed on the right bank of the Dhanseri and the inhabitants of Nagarah and Jamguri in like manner cultivated land on the left bank of the Doyang River.[60]

Mid-nineteenth century colonial accounts on Assam are saturated with descriptions of the cultivation of the poppy plant and the mode of extraction of the juice of the plant, which was processed into *kanee*. G.R. Barry's *Report on the North-East Frontier* presents a vivid description of the cultivation of poppy plant in Assam along with the mode of consumption,

> Of poppy, the white variety is generally cultivated. The plant is cultivated in little patches of ground around the cottages of the villagers and its round white flowers during the rise of the year, give the face of the country a simple and pretty appearance. In March, the plains are full of parties of men, women and children engaged in wounding the heads of the poppies with knives and steeping rags with the juice issuing forth. A portion of the cloth so dipped being soaked in a vessel of water forms a sort of infusion for drinking. Most of the people used this mode, while others mix up a preparation of the deleterious drug with tobacco of their 'hookahs'. As taken by the poor classes without or instead of, nutritious food, and the effects of opium become manifested by withering the skin and flesh of the eaters, impairing their faculties and inducing premature old age. As used however in moderation by the richer classes, together with wholesome and abundant diet, the eating of this, is not considered by some professional judges to be so pernicious a habit as the indulgence in ardent spirits, which too often follows in the track of European civilization.[61]

Following the ripening of the plant in February, the juice oozing from the poppy buds was absorbed by a piece of old rag, which when saturated, was rolled up and enlarged by the addition of successive layers till a mass of about a seer in weight was obtained.

It was in this state, when it was denominated as *kanee*. It was consumed by drinking a watery solution of the impregnated rag or smoking the extract obtained by evaporation. *Kanee* soon after harvest, was sold for Rs. 8 per seer but at a later period fetched double the price.[62]

With much foresight, David Scott, the first Agent to the Governor-General in Assam had proposed the setting up of opium farms.[63] He had ordered experiments to be conducted to ascertain whether opium could be grown into Assam with a view to high revenues. However, a careful investigation of the relative value of Assam opium revealed that it could not be delivered at anything like the price at which the Government would receive it. The prime cost of pure opium was estimated at around Rs. 9 or 10 a seer. Moreover, the climate was unfavourable for the large-scale cultivation of poppy. Major Butler informed Captain Jenkins, '[...] the time and labour the Assamese now bestow on its culture, if devoted to other products fit for export, such as *sursoo*, jute, *reah,* cotton, *mogah*, etc., would not only enable them to purchase all the opium they require cheaper than they grow it but afford a handsome profit, bring a greater breadth of land under cultivation and conduce to the general prosperity of the Province.'[64]

Experiments in commercial poppy plantation for opium production at Kamrup had also been unsuccessful. Reports of soil sample analysis by H. Piddington, done in the 1830s revealed that the soil was unproductive for the growth of the poppy plant.[65] Hence the scheme of setting up an opium agency was given up. By the mid-nineteenth century, following the rapid growth of tea plantations and reports of destruction of valuable timber[66] it was suggested that the use of forest lands by the opium cultivators should no longer be allowed.[67]

> Indeed, it is painful to contrast the active industry of the former population as evidenced by the gigantic ruins to be met with in the country with the listless apathy of their descendants who spend most of their time under the influence of opium, caring little for anything else after they have satisfied the cravings of hunger. Men, women and even children indulged in opium, which they prepare for use in a somewhat novel manner. Dissolving the opium in water they soak in the solution long strips of

cotton cloth about two inches wide, these when saturated are dried in the sun and used as occasion requires, a small piece of cloth being torn off and chewed or the rag soaked in water which is then drunk as a potion. The opium drinker becomes stupefied and intoxicated.[68]

A Practice of Opium Consumption and Experience

An aristocratic luxury during the period of the Ahoms; towards the mid-nineteenth century, opium eating had visibly become an integral part of the daily life of the Assamese. Memoirs and accounts of travellers into Assam, apart from official reports, have documented the standard of living of the people.[69] To the list of requirements of an Assamese household – rice, salt, oil, betel nut, a cooking utensil, a cotton cloth for a garment or an ornament for his wife, opium consumption was to join the list as a necessity. This metamorphosis of opium from luxury to necessity was attended with social, economic, and later on political ramifications.

When did opium become a visible social problem? Why did it become a social problem at all? How did it affect the Assamese society? What was its influence on the behaviour, in short the all-encompassing influence of opium on the Assamese society? What did it mean to the ordinary folk who were its mass consumers? It is in this context that an analysis of the prevalent 'sister cultures' – which facilitated opium's easy infiltration into the physical, social and cultural life of the people of Assam would enable an understanding of 'the type of soil on which opium was to grow'.[70] Assam has been a home to various racial groups – the Miris, Mishimis, Kacharis, Ahoms, Koch, Mech and Lalungs, etc. Each group has its own characteristic social outlook, mannerisms and its traditional stimulants like *laopani* (rice beer), *mod*, *phatika* (type of beer/wine prepared from rice), *dhapat* (tobacco) and *pan tamul* (betel nut chewing). Travellers to Assam, as early as 1752, mentioned about a 'local drink – a kind of wine or liquor made with pounded rice'. Every community that Tavernier came across in Assam savoured its local drink. He informs us also of its mode of preparation, '[...] they leave it (rice) in the sun and then ferment it with some water, then put some honey to soften the intolerable sourness of this drink; once fully prepared in this manner, it is not absolutely bad. They make it in their delight; it intoxicates like wine, when consumed in excess.'[71]

Of the variety of preparations from rice, were *mod*, *phatika*, and *laopani*, while Hunter in his *Gazetteer* also refers to a kind of 'rum' which was distilled from sugar. The Census also reveals the specific castes that were given to manufacture and selling of spirituous liquor, those belonging to the Sunri caste[72] along with the Pasi caste that were toddy manufacturers. The local preparation *mod* was available in the market for half a penny a quart while *phatika* was sold at the rate of a little over a penny.[73] W.W. Hunter was fascinated by the mode of preparation of the *laopani*, a favourite drink of the Ahoms, Mikirs, Kacharis, and the Lalungs, which he describes thus:

> The liquor made from the *bora* rice which is grown in the marshes is said to be of the finer quality than that made from any other. The grain is first boiled and certain intoxicating drugs are infused with it; the mixture is then kept closed in an earthen pitcher for five days in the cold season and for three days in the hot weather for the purpose of allowing it to ferment. Another preparation is made in this way, a small quantity of water is mixed with boiled rice in which certain drugs are mixed, the mixture is then left for seven or eight days in an earthen pot until fermentation has set in, when the contents are taken out, filtered and diluted with boiling water in the proportion of eight to one. These intoxicating preparations are mainly consumed by the hill tribes.[74]

It was allowed to be manufactured for home consumption but certainly not for sale upto the limit of 4 seers in the plains district and 12 seers in the hills district.[75] Drink apart, the use of tobacco smoking as a mode of recreation is well documented. In China as Zheng Yangwen makes us believe, the 'naturalisation' of tobacco smoking assisted the transition to taste and experience of opium smoking. In her memoir, Susan Ward tells us that *mixed smoking* (opium paste mixed with tobacco) was prevalent in Assam in the eighteenth century, 'Can any one reasonably expect that this true-born freeman, upon whom Nature has set the seal of perfect independence, will work for the planters on their gardens? Saving money has no charm for him. While there is a sufficiency of rice, salt and vegetables to eat, a bit of opium or the hubble-bubble in the house, he is happy and cares not for the future.'[76]

Tobacco was an important agricultural crop[77]along with betel nut (areca catechu) and the plantain. It was to be found universally in every Assamese homestead. Unlike opium, significant amount of tobacco was exported.[78] When required for chewing the tobacco leaves were dried under a shed or else pressed into a hollow bamboo (*chunga*) and allowed to ferment. When used with the pipe, the tobacco leaves were piled up until they ferment, then cut, mixed with molasses and made ready for the hookah.[79] Tobacco smoking pipes and apparatus were imported from China. Tufted bamboo trees were also used to make hookah pipes.

From Betel-chewing and Tobacco Smoking to Opium Eating

While tobacco smoking was an 'intellectual recreation',[80] the 'romance of betel-chewing' was a favourite indulgence prevalent in Assam. The habit is regarded to have been imported into Assam by the Khasis.[81] In Assam, it was a popularly held belief that no one could properly speak Assamese until he began chewing betel. It implied that chewing betel nut and *paan* facilitated social interactions, as was the case with chewing of betel in Indonesia and chewing *khat* in Yemen. Specially processed chewing tobacco with betel was also a favourite with the Assamese.[82] Every person carried a small towel called *tamol-gamocha* (towel for carrying betel nut) in which he packed areca nut, *pan* and lime. Indeed, an ideal Assamese homestead was described by a proverbial saying: *puve hanh* [ducks i.e. pond to the east] *paschime banh* [bamboo to the west], *dakshine dhuwa* [open to the south] and *uttare guwa* [betel to the north].[83]

It reveals how integral was betel chewing to the social, religious, and cultural life of the Assamese.[84] The *Yoginitantra* attests to the love of betel chewing among the Assamese women.[85] Constant chewing of betel would defile the normal appearance of the teeth into short square little blocks of ivory and of a brick-dusty red colour; as Susan Ward remarks, 'an Assamese with his mouth open conjures up visions of Dante's entrance to the infernal regions'.[86]

Further the use of *tema* (silver box), *bata* (plate) or *batti* (bowl)[87] as the betel chewing paraphernalia resembles closely to the fashionable opium smoking pipes, etc., which became the basis of the culture of opium consumption in China. *Tamul* was the first thing offered a visitor to an Assamese home and is a routine item after every meal. In certain religious ceremonies, elders are offered respect by youngsters with a bow and a *bata* or *sarai* with *paan* and *tamul* in it. At times, the village council absolved a culprit of his guilt if he bowed before it with a *paan* and *tamul* in a *bata*; confessed his guilt and sought forgiveness. In an Assamese marriage, *tamul* plays an important part. It is used as a sacred item in religious functions. *Tamul-paan* also forms an important component of the religious and social ceremonies of the Khasis and the Bodos.[88]

Betel leaf was cultivated extensively in the entire Brahmaputra valley and all places along the foothills. Shehabuddin Talish has mentioned of innumerable *paan* sellers in the Ahom capital Garhgaon.[89] The Ahom court had a highly designated Tamuli Phukan who looked after the regular supply of areca nut and betel leaf to the royal palace. *Paan* was an important ingredient in the preparation of opium for smoking; the opium decoction was mixed with dried betel leaves. *Paan* was also chewed after eating opium to reduce the bitter taste of the opium preparation. Stale betel leaves were beaten into a paste and then mixed with raw opium. The opium paste was then inserted in a pipe, which was then lighted and smoked.

There are two modes of consumption of opium popular among users – (1) opium eating and (2) opium smoking. Opium smoking was viewed with disfavour in Rajasthan and Punjab. Opium-eating was the popular and accepted mode of consumption of opium. Exactly when the habit of opium smoking first obtained a foothold in Assam or when the preparations made for smoking were first introduced, is not quite clear. Assam apart, up to the beginning of the nineteenth century, no writer had recorded the smoking of opium in India, although it prevailed in China. A highly interesting and intriguing reference contained in Don Simibaldo's account puts forth the argument that the 'habit of opium smoking was communicated to the Chinese by a neighbouring people, the inhabitants of Assam, where it had prevailed from time immemorial'.[90]

Available data reveal the habit of opium eating as a favourite indulgence of the royal clans in Assam. In his *Report on Assam*, Captain Thomas Welsh has mentioned about opium as a taste of the elite, its use by the Ahom kings, including Raja Gaurinath Singha whom Welsh found to be always 'in an intoxicated state'. A chronicle records that sometimes criminals were compelled to swallow opium tablets as a sort of punishment during the rule of the Ahoms. Maniram Dewan records that it was during the reign of Lakshmi Singha, that the poppy seeds were introduced from Bengal and cultivated at Beltola, near Gauhati. It was believed to be consumed only by the royal house and the aristocratic families.[91] Small and long strips of narrow rags on which the fresh opium after collection was smeared and the whole rolled up into a ball about the size of a small hen's egg and carried about for daily use or sold as merchandise in all the *bazaars* (market places) by the *ryots* of Assam for sale and common consumption. This had attracted much attention of the colonial administration. Opium was stated to be the most profitable crop raised by the cultivators.[92]

Ecstatic and Enfeebled

THE *KANIAS* (OPIUM-EATERS) OF ASSAM

There is a very suggestive adage in Assamese, which says: *Paankhowa Dhunia, Malikhowa Kania, Phata-kanikhowa Khekar-khowa.* It means that smoking opium is a kind of luxury; the real opium eater is one who takes opium dissolved in water and he is the worst sinner who smokes opium in rags contracting afflictions of the lungs.

M'Cosh in his *Topography of Assam* mentions the method of preparing opium by absorbing the fresh juice of the poppy with a strip of cotton cloth till it is saturated. When dry, it was tied up in rolls for the market and called *kauni/kanee.* In using it about two square inches of cloth was dipped into the boiling water and drunk. In the year 1835 in a set of reports sent to the Government by the European officers in-charge to different districts of Assam, the mode of collecting and consuming opium was detailed. It referred to the 'unique practice' of collecting opium in Assam, 'When the flower of the poppy pods fall off, the cultivators make diagnosed incisions in them with a knife and as the juice exudes, it is wiped off with shreds of cotton cloth, about an inch broad which when well saturated is rolled up into balls, the shape and size of a pigeon's egg, in which form, it is sold by weight. When used, portions of cloth are cut or torn off and soaked in a cup of water.[93]

Available literature illustrates the forms of opium consumption in Assam as *kanimolikhowa*, *kanipaan* or *kanipankhowa* and *lodakani*. When opium is eaten in small pills or made into a decoction by mixing it with water, the process is known as *kanikhowa* or *kanimolikhowa*. When the opium decoction is mixed with a paste of dried betel leaves, then it is called as *kanipankhowa*. The preparation of opium decoction for smoking was time consuming as well as expensive.[94] The quantity of opium to be prepared depended on individual preferences. The opium decoction was boiled for about thirty minutes to a required consistency to remove the impurities in a spoon called *heta*. The decoction was cleaned and set for cooking until it was transformed into a paste. The paste was then cooked with finely cut betel leaves, stirred until dry. The fried betel leaves were mixed up together, heated until the leaves showed a greenish brown tint. The mixture was then poured inside a bamboo pipe called the hookah, made up of one wider piece of bamboo and one much narrower piece stuck into the broader piece in the shape of the letter V with one arm extending downwards. The narrower piece is much shorter and into this the prepared opium is placed for smoking, the mouth of the smoker is put to the top of the broader piece. As soon as one part of the mixture was smoked through, another is put in and so the process goes on through the night until the consumers have smoked to the required depth of intoxication. After each pull at the hookah, sweet things were consumed as plantains, sugar cane or sweet tea possibly to get rid of the bitter taste. It was believed that this form of smoking was alluring and most of the new addicts began their habit by smoking. *Lodakani* was prepared from the cakes that were issued at the government retail outlets. Raw opium was mashed into a thick paste, which was then savoured along with betelnut, curd, banana or sugar cane to ease off the bitter taste of opium.[95]

Accounts of colonial officers are also interesting insights into the mode of consumption of opium in Assam. *The Botham Committee Report of 1913-14* hinted at the prevalence of the form of opium smoking prevalent everywhere in Assam, which is known in other parts of India as *madak*.[96]

In Assam, as was the case with other parts of India, the *madak* form of opium smoking was prevalent. Raw opium was mixed with water, which was then heated to boiling point. The boiling was continued, and the impurities that formed as a scum on the surface of the boiling fluid were gradually removed. The heating was continued until a thick suspension was formed. This was then strained through a piece of cloth and charred leaves of *babul* (*Acacia arabica*) were gradually mixed with it until it assumed the consistency of a thick, stiff paste. This mass was then rolled into small balls called *madak golis*, which were available for smoking purposes. As a rule, two and a half ounces of *madak* were prepared from one ounce of opium. Sometimes, instead of *babul* leaves, leaves of *amla* (*Phylanthus emblica*), safed *babul* (*Acacia leucophloea*) and *paan* (*Piper betel linn*) are used. When used by the elite and the aristocracy, *kalabatoo* (burnt gold or silver threads) were sometimes added to the mass, as it was supposed that these imparted to the mixture aphrodisiac and tonic properties.[97] The other form of opium, *chandu/chandul*, or clarified opium was a stronger preparation, and was regarded to be in use in India by persons who were heavy smokers. The *chandu* form of opium was prepared by boiling a strained solution of opium in water until it became thick in consistency. As the concentration proceeds, crusts form on the surface of the simmering mass. These were then removed as they formed, until finally a thick mass of the consistency and appearance of coaltar was obtained. This was the 'smokable extract', and was the *chandu* or *chandul* of opium smokers. The *chandu* commonly smoked was often adulterated by addition of dross scraped from *chandu* pipes, which had high morphine content.[98] In Assam, it was regarded as a favourite mode of smoking opium amongst the Kachari population of Mangaldai in Darrang district.[99]

The introduction of opium in cake form was said to have greatly facilitated the habit of opium smoking. Addressing this important issue in the Council, an Assamese member of the Council, Nilmoni

Phukan told the Council that on being questioned the Nagas informed that they had relaxed the cultivation of poppy since the introduction of 'shining cakes' of opium, *Aito Hole Bhaal; Atai Pabo, Amato Hole Eh-Bo-Tan, Aloop Sakoo Panito Ase* (these cakes are shining and attractive and can easily be got in prepared form, but our process is very tedious, the juice oozes out in small drops like drops of tear).[100] Interestingly, the opium eaters had different appellations for the *abkaree* opium, which they classed as *Sorkari kani* (Treasury opium), *Mohaldaror kani* (that is opium derived out of shortweight by the mahaldars), *Sorai kani* (smuggled opium) and *Adhi kani* (when an opium eater cannot afford to buy his opium, he arranged with another opium eater to pay for it and he takes half of it).[101]

Opium smoking was a ritualistic act in China. In Assam, we are yet to come across any account to reveal that opium smoking was considered a sign of refinement and status. This is evident from the consumers being termed as *kania,* an appellation by which they were designated, in consequence of their being indolent and irregular characters. Although there was nothing of the sort of opium den like in China, there were certainly *kholas* where the opium smokers would gather and smoke in company. Such *kholas* were certainly looked down with great disfavour and regarded to be assisting the proliferation of the habit. To the author of *Rasik Puran,*[102] the *Kanias* revere the poppy plant and attribute divine origins to the *afu* (poppy plant). The reason as the *kania* extols it is its association with the Hindu God, Lord Indra. It is a belief among the opium eaters that in his moment of revelry, Lord Indra, is said to have blowed his mouth at the *afu* plant which then descended from the heavenly palace to the earth. The *a* in *afu*-stands for the *aakash* (the heaven) and *fu* (act of blowing air from the mouth). Its heavenly association as per the belief of the *kanias* makes it highly sacred and no 'pure' *kania* would ever perform his *kanipan* (opium eating) ceremony without taking his daily bath. As a 'new-born' into the Kania community, he slowly moves up the hierarchy by gradually increasing his regular dosage, he is then assigned the nomenclature of the *Borkania* (elder opium eater). As per the rules of the Kania community, he was duty bound to consume opium worth Rs. 5

every month. He occupied a highly respectable stature among the *kanias* of the place. He was served by an entourage of atleast twenty *kanias*, who were on ready attendance in the *kani seva* to serve him with all the paraphernalia of consuming opium on his slight gesture with the chants of *O Rama! O Krishno*! (Hail Rama! Hail Krishna). A category called the *Borola Kanias*, i.e. widowed or jilted opium eaters, more often than not jilted, were to be found in almost every village. They were regarded as the most notorious among the *kanias*, many of whom carried also out the petty pilfering business in the locality.

> When they would finish drinking opium to its last dreg, when satiety begins, when they begin to drag on a miserable existence when times seem hanging heavily on them, they again feel tempted to smoke away the little vitality that is still left in them. Now they can afford the time but not the money required for smoking. They would then lure the young men of the village to their private opium den and thereto teach them the luxury of smoking. The tempting manner in which they sit round the *Khola*, the idle gossip that goes merrily round the hearth, the *Tita-mora*, which gives zest at every puff are enough temptations to entrap these youths who at their age are more prone to play the part of a rake than to learn the lesson of sobriety.[103]

The *1893 Report of the Royal Commission on Opium* and the *1913 Botham Committee Report* had remarked that, 'young men commonly acquire the opium habit in the company of smoking parties'. This was also attested to by Colonel Chopra of the Calcutta Tropical School of Medicine in 1928, in his study of the habit of the opium in India. In his study, he cited that smoking opium in company was certainly inducing and leading to the proliferation of the opium habit. He concluded that, in many cases the habit was contracted through smoking opium in company or through eating opium at social gatherings like marriage and funerals or at ceremonies or a semi-religious nature-customs, which were prevalent. A few witnesses also cited the aphrodisiac properties of the drug as an important reason for taking opium. He, however, found no evidence of opium being used as a substitute for alcohol.[104] We also come across references to the many ways, including religious, which was believed to have facilitated the spread of the habit. During the *Bhakat*

Khowa puja opium was offered as part of the rituals. They would burn the opium and get the opium eaters to pray for their good health.[105] It is interesting to note that there was a widely prevalent belief that it was greatly fostered by the worship of Kamakhya temple and encouraged to 'intensify the vile orgies of Kamakhya'. The use of opium for 'unholy excitements of worship' were believed to have spread the habit and 'brings with it its own retribution in the form of early physical decay and decrease of population'.[106] Rai Bahadur A.C. Agarwalla, in his testimony before the Assam Opium Enquiry Committee 1933, disclosed how *kanias* were once considered as honourable persons and in certain places, it was a privilege to give girls in marriage to *kanias*.[107]

In a memorandum presented by William Roberts, the sole member of the 1893 RCO articulated his views on the 'Opium Habit in India'.[108] In his study, he classified the highlighted 'Medicinal side' and the 'Euphoric side' of opium. The 'Medicinal' or 'anti-periodic' use prevailed in excess of the average among the peasantry in low-lying, damp and malarious districts, as found in Bengal, Bihar and Orissa. Roberts upheld the view that opium had a 'close relationship to the greater or less prevalence of malaria in the localities'. Moreover, the origin of the present excessive use of opium was the reason for the prevalence of opium cultivation in that province or district. In addition, in Assam, prior to 1860, poppy cultivation was rampant in upper districts of the province. The Medical Memorandum confirmed that moderate consumers of opium were protected against recurrent attacks of malarial 'poison'. Colonial officials maintained the validity of the argument that 'opium was an invaluable prophylactic against malaria and used as a household remedy'. Interestingly, this was when it's medicinal properties had been seriously challenged in the metropolis.

J.J. Driberg, in his testimony before the 1893 RCO claimed that opium was a preventive to counteract bowel complaints, rheumatism, diabetes and malarial fever.[109] Most of the European tea planters who testified before the Commission, believed that opium eaters were 'amongst the healthiest and the best of workers. If it is stopped, one might as well shut up all the tea gardens in Assam employing local labour'.[110] However, the Assamese intelligentsia was divided in their opinion on the use of opium as a medicine. Gunabhiram Barooah denied that opium had any medicinal value, while Madhav Chandra Bardoloi informed the Commission that it was the absence of medical facilities and 'fear' of allopathic medicines that opium was looked upon as a 'panacea'.[111] William Roberts defended the therapeutic properties of opium, as a remedy and prophylactic against malaria,[112] while also eulogizing its immense benefits as 'economiser of food'.[113] The investigations of the Assam Congress Opium Enquiry Committee were a clear refutation of the medical properties of opium. Almost all the native medical practitioners were unanimous against opium possessing curative properties in malaria and kala-azar. Contrarily, it had a depressive effect on the immune system.[114] One of them even expressed that 'opium will reduce the sensibility and make them sleep without any mosquito curtains in insanitary surroundings full of mosquitoes'.[115]

Opium smoking and eating was frowned upon in the society, as an addict's pernicious influence was felt in many ways on both the familial peace and societal harmony. They were viewed as deviant characters given to the use of crime for money to satisfy their craving for the drug. Those under the influence of the drug were prone to 'altered behavioural patterns' and were regarded as posing threats to family solidarity and societal harmony. The most noxious effect of opium on families was the degradation of morality. In memoirs and interviews, there are descriptions of people who wilfully sold their wives and children to others for money to satisfy their cravings. 'Almost all opium eaters are reduced to paupers. Many of them have parted with their landed properties and are reduced to a state of destitution'.[116] This was a typical situation as per the 1925 Assam Congress Opium Enquiry Committee Report. While inspecting Tinsukia, Nadial and Barpathar villages, mostly inhabited by the Muttock community, the Committee members were confronted with families of opium eaters. 'Almost all the villagers are day labourers. They earn only to buy their dose of opium.' The dose varied from half a *tola* to one *tola* of opium daily. Most of them confessed that they would like to give up the habit and wanted medicine to be cured of the habit. In their testimony before the Committee, many of the opium eaters informed about their personal experiences following the intake of opium and the repercussions as also their intention to rid themselves of the habit. As regards the reason for taking to opium, they used it initially as a medicine and later became addicted to it. Most of them believed they had contracted the habit in the company of those who were used to the habit of taking opium. Almost all of them confessed to have suffered terribly, physically, mentally as well as it had brought upon the family economic ruin and social wrath. 'I have been using opium for 10 years and I started the practice when I came to Timon. I was ill and my husband who is an opium eater advised me to take opium. I have only one sari and I wear torn clothes at home. I shall not allow my son to take opium. [Premia, wife of Kartick – a garden labourer, Timon Tea Estate, age 40 years (ACOER, 1925)]

The opium eater was regarded as a deviant character, a social wreck, given to crimes for money. He was untrustworthy, unproductive and hence unreliable.[117] An opium eater was always distrusted and especially in courts of law, an opium eater witness was nicknamed *kani to kia sakhi* meaning 'a tola worth of opium', and his evidence was generally discredited.[118] As to why was opium smoking so widespread; contemporary documentary evidence seems to suggest a basic answer to the question – that (i) it was a cure for physical ailments and mental suffering and (ii) Lack of proper medical facilities, unhygienic living conditions with no proper sanitation and fear of Western medicine. 'I was advised by a fakir to use opium as a medicine for cough' [Sondar Ahom, Cherekapar, Seebsagar, age 65 years (ACOER, 1925)]; 'I had some illness and one Mohora who is himself an opium-eater advised me to take opium and from that time onward I have been using it' [Pokhon Borai, Chapmora, Mahmora, ex-tea garden labourer, age 63 years (ACOER, 1925)].

Opium eaters confessed having incurred debt and sold a greater portion of the valuables to the Marwari merchants. Generally they pledged utensils, ornaments, etc., for their drug. Here are some illustrative examples: 'I have spent more than forty thousand rupees and I have ruined myself during this period' [Manik Chandra Hazarika, Landholder, Tinsukia, age 40 years]; 'I spent about 6/8 rupees per month on opium. I earn daily about 10 *annas* as a day-labourer' [Madharam Koch, Noali Christiangaon, age 54, Seebsagar (ACOER, 1925)].

Almost all the opium eaters admitted that the use of opium had rendered them physically incapacitated.

I have become weak and emaciated and suffered the consequences of the habit. I think it is a great evil. I would not allow my son to eat opium. [Minaram Ahom, Koerpur, Seebsagar, age 44 years]; I spend about rupees 6-8 per month for my opium. I earn daily about ten *annas* as a day labourer with a little extra. I shall not allow my sons and daughters to contract the habit, as I have become a wreck myself. I have no lands at all, neither do I cultivate any land on rent. I am living on the land of my father-in-law. [Madharam Koch, Noali Christiangaon, Seebsagar, age 54 years]; Opium eaters are physically weak and inactive. They look thin and hungry. With swollen eyes, black lips and dark appearance, they are not capable of any work and can work only under the influence of the drug. [Tirtheswar Buragohain Phukan, Landholder, President of the Ahom Association, Sibsagar (ACOER, 1925)].

Conclusion

Initially confined to the upper echelons of the society, opium was a status marker. Tobacco smoking and betel-chewing cultures had assisted opium's favourable acceptance into the Assamese way of life, very much by the beginnings of the nineteenth century.[119] It certainly was a favourite indulgence, which was cherished by the users, as is evidenced by the distinctive mode of preparation, which imparted to it a distinctive characteristic, if it can possibly be referred to as 'Assamization of opium'. The Assamese were accustomed to tobacco smoking, which later was experimented with opium (*kani-paankhowa*). Similar was the use of *tamul* and *paan* in the preparation of opium for eating (*kanimolikhowa*). Whether to them it was a favourite pastime, an aphrodisiac or a panacea is yet to be ascertained with certainty.[120] However, it was the proliferation among the lower strata, the 'downward diffusion', as Yangwen makes us believe, as was the case with tea and opium in China, along with 'deference of the community'[121] that is, the participation of the lower classes made opium visible as a socio-economic problem by the beginning of the nineteenth century. The imageries of 'opium intoxicated, effeminate and indolent Assamese' was attended by a host of economic, social, administrative and legal ramifications for the province. Imperial concerns were quick to identify a culture of consumption with commercial significance in a colonial frontier. The nineteenth century witnessed the entrenchment of colonial interests in Assam and it's integration within the configurations of opium imperialism of the East India Company. The variant patterns of usage enabled in exploring the 'indigenous usage of psychoactive' alongside mirroring the society's level of political complexity. They were 'great opium eaters' – such identification spawned up the propaganda of the 'civilizing mission' ushering in a new era of material exploitation and political domination. This identification was also to have a significant impact on the development of regulation of opium and its use.

Notes

1. Henry John Temple, 3rd Viscount Palmerstone (1784-1865), popularly called Lord Palmerstone, was a British statesman who served twice as the Prime Minister of Great Britain in the mid-nineteenth century.
2. Shekhar Bandyopadhyay, *From Plassey to Partition: A History of Modern India*, New Delhi: Orient Longman, 2004, p. 39.
3. John Darwin, *The Empire Project: The Rise and Fall of the British World System*, Cambridge: Cambridge University Press, 2009.
4. Bernard Cohn, *Colonialism and its Forms of Knowledge*, New Gersey: Princeton University Press, 1996 (rpt.), p. 3.
5. Robin W. Winks and Wm. R. Louis, *The Oxford History of the British Empire: Historiography*, Oxford: Oxford University Press, 1999, pp. 403-6.
6. The Burmese monarch had shown expansionist tendencies since the second half of the eighteenth century when it subjugated Peru, Tenasserim and Arakan and then in the early years of the nineteenth century extended his influence in Manipur, Cachar and finally Assam. Bandyopadhyay, *From Plassey to Partition*, p. 59.
7. Following the knowledge of communication routes in the north-east frontier, the British had decided to ward off any future Burmese depredations by any of the four lines, namely by Assam, Manipur, Arakan or Rangoon. 'Military and Commercial Routes', in Capt. R. Boileau Pemberton, *Report on the Eastern Frontier of British India*, Guwahati: Department of Historical and Antiquarian Studies, 1991, p. 153.

8. Nisar Ahmed, 'Assam-Bengal Trade in the Medieval Period: A Numismatic Perspective', *Journal of the Economic and Social History of the Orient*, 33(1990): 169-98.
9. British diplomat George Bogle (1747-81) and scholar Thomas Manning (1772-1840) in the seventeenth and eighteenth centuries headed the British diplomatic mission into Tibet. Thomas Manning became the first English national to enter the city of Lhasa and secure attendance upon the Dalai Lama in 1811. Clements R. Markham, George Bogle and Thomas Manning, *Narratives of the Mission of George Bogle to Tibet: And the Journey of Thomas Manning to Lhasa*, Cambridge: Cambridge University Press, 2010 (rpt.), pp. 58-60.
10. 'Report on Assam, 1794: From Captain Welsh to Edward Hay, Esq., Secretary to Government, dated 6 February 1794.' Nagendra N. Acharya, *Historical Documents on Assam and Neighbouring States*, New Delhi: Omsons Publications, 1983, pp. 8-14.
11. Neil B. Edmonstone, 'Report Related to Assam in 1797 Made by the Persian Translater', *Asiatic Journal and Monthly Miscellany* 19(1825): 125.
12. Suresh K. Sharma, 'Commercial Treaty Concluded by Captain Welsh with Gaurinath Singha (28 February 1793)', in *Documents on North East India: Assam (1664-1935)*, New Delhi: Mittal Publication, 2006, pp. 13-16.
13. Sharma, *Documents on North East India: Assam (1664-1935)*, 'Treaty between T.C. Robertson and Purandhar Singha, Raja of Assam 1833', which specifically states, 'It being notorious that the quantity of opium produced in Assam is the cause of many miseries to the inhabitants, the Rajah binds himself that, whatever measures may be determined on with a view to checking this source of mischief in the territory of the Honourable Company, corresponding measures shall be adopted in the territory made over to him.'
14. Refer letter/correspondence from Captain Jenkins to W.H. Macnaghton Esquire, Secretary to the Government, Calcutta, 22 July 1833, Political Department, in Francis Jenkins, *Report of the Northeast Frontier of India*, ed. Heramba K. Barpujari, New Delhi: Spectrum, 1995, pp. 1-82.
15. Eric Tagliacozzo, 'Ambiguous Commodities, Unstable Frontiers: The Case of Burma, Siam and Imperial Britain, 1800-1900', *Comparative Studies in History and Society*, 46(2004): 354-77.
16. Dharma Kumar (ed.), *The Cambridge Economic History of India*, vol. II: *1757-2003*, Cambridge: Cambridge University Press, 1983.
17. Emdad ul Haq, *Drugs in South Asia: From the Opium Trade to the Present Day*, London: Macmillan, 2000.
18. John F. Richards, 'Indian Empire and the Peasant Production of Opium', 15(1981): 59-82; 'Opium and the British Indian Empire: The Royal Commission of 1895', *Modern Asian Studies* 36(2002): 375-420. Richards

suggests that from 1842-80, opium revenue was on an average around 15 per cent of India's total revenues. Indeed by 1843, opium had become the second largest source of revenue for India. Opium revenues contributed more than customs and stamp duties combined which was the fourth and fifth largest source of revenue.

19. Alan Baumler, *The Chinese and the Opium under the Republic: Worse than Floods and Wild Beasts*, Albany: State University of New York Press, 2007, pp. 94-101.
20. Claude Markovits, *The Global World of Indian Merchants 1750-1947: Traders of Sind from Bukhara to Panama*, Cambridge: Cambridge University Press, 2000.
21. By 1858, all trade in Central Asia had passed into the hands of the Russians and British exploratory surveys had confirmed that 'the whole of our frontier was shut against us for commercial purposes'. Hansard (House of Commons Daily Debate) Archive, 16 March 1858.
22. The possibilities of opening up a direct trade route between India and China through Assam were also visualized by a prominent member of the Governor-General's Council who in the course of a minute observed as early as 1826. 'We may expect to open new roads for commerce with Yunnan and other southwestern Provinces of the Celestial Empire through Assam and Munipore', S.C., 12 May 1826 (minutes on the treaty of Yandaboo), Rebati M. Lahiri, *The Annexation of Assam*, Calcutta: Firma KLM, 1954, pp. 44-50.
23. B.N. Mukherjee in a study, mentions the existence of a regular and brisk trade and the involvement of local states in the early period. He had cited the discovery of the *Harikela* coinage, the *Paglatekh* hoard and the *Paschimbagh Copper Plate* (tenth century AD) of the existence of a thriving commercial contact between the north-eastern region of India with China and the countries of Southeast Asia and Bengal respectively. B.N. Mukherjee, *External Trade of Early North-Eastern India*, New Delhi: Har-Anand, 1992, pp. 17-29.
24. Yunnan was the primary production site as also the supply depot for opium, which flowed into Guandong, Shannxi and Beijing. This alarmed the Chinese authorities who clamped down prohibition decrees upon Yunnan in 1831. See, David Bello, 'The Venomous Course of Southwestern Opium: Qing Prohibition in Yunnan, Sichuan and Guizhou in the Early Nineteenth Century', *Journal of Asian Studies*, 62(2003): 1109-42.
25. The other being through the valleys Dihang or Tsang-po (the streams of the Brahmaputra River) had been rendered intractable due to the hostile attitude of the Abors and Dibang valley. Ronald Kaulback, 'The Assam Border of Tibet', *Geographical Journal*, 83(1934): 177-90.
26. Henry Cottam, 'Overland Route to China via Assam, Tenga Pani River,

Khamti and Singpho Country across the Irawaddi River into Yunnan', *Proceedings of the Royal Geographical Society of London*, 21(1877): 590-5.

27. The capital of Bor Khampti, Manchee, was visited by Captain Wilcox in 1826 who reported that it is at a close proximity, about 150 miles from the borders of the frontier province of 'China-Yunnan' and Szechwan with great commercial prospects. The province of Szechwan was stated to be one of the largest and finest of the Chinese empire, more than 2,00,000 sq. miles or nearly as large as Bengal or France. Yunnan was assumed to be about 2/3rd of that size. The population of both the provinces was estimated to be around 11 million. Francis Jenkins, *Report on the Northeast Frontier of India,* ed. Heramba K. Barpujari, New Delhi: Spectrum Publications, 1995.
28. John Anderson, *A Report on the Expedition to Western Yunnan via Bhamo*, Calcutta: Office of the Superintendent of Government Printing, 1871, 50.
29. Gray, 'Journey from Assam to the Sources of Irrawady', 224.
30. C.R. MacGregor, 'Journey of the Expedition under Colonel Woodthorpe, R.E. from Upper Assam to the Irawadi, and Return over the Patkoi Range', *Proceedings of the Royal Geographical Society and Monthly Record of Geography*, 9(1887): 19-42.
31. 'Jenkins to W.H. Macnaughton, 22 July 1833. The Khamtis and the Singphos', Francis Jenkins, *Report on the North Eastern Frontier of India*, ed. H.K. Barpujari, New Delhi: Spectrum, 1995, pp. 3-19.
32. Kaulback, *The Assam Border of Tibet*, p. 181.
33. Birendra C. Chakravarty, *British Relations with the Hill Tribes of Assam since 1858*, Calcutta: Firma KLM, 1981, pp. 4-23.
34. William Robinson, *A Descriptive Account of Assam*, Delhi: Sanskaran Prakashak, 1975 (rpt.), p. 326.
35. In the year 1860, seven memorials were sent up to His Majesty's Government – the Chambers of Commerce of Manchester, Huddersfield, Leeds, Bradford and Halifax, Liverpool and the Salt proprietors of Cheshire and Worcestershire. *Parliamentary Papers*, vol. 52, Great Britain Parliament: H.M. Stationery Office, 1862, pp. 97-112.
36. 'Burma Commercial Treaty', in Correspondence between Captain Richard Spyne and Hon. William-Ewart Gladstone on the commercial opening of the Shan states and Western Inland China 1853', *Accounts and Papers of the House of Commons Reprint*, Great Britain: LLC, 2009.
37. *Accounts and Papers of the House of Commons.*
38. *The Railway News and Joint-Stock Journal*, vol. X, 1868.
39. Suryya K. Bhuyan, *Anglo-Assamese Relations 1771-1826*, Guwahati: Lawyers Book Stall, 1990 (rpt.).
40. 'From C.A. Bruce to Captain Jenkins, Upper Assam 12 February 1833', in Francis Jenkins, pp. 60-76.

41. John M'Cosh, *Topography of Assam*, Calcutta: G.H. Huttmann, Bengal Military Orphan Press, 1837.
42. Ibid., p. 63.
43. *Statement Showing the Population, Consumption of Opium and the Chief Opium Eating Races in Assam, 1893*. Great Britain Parliament, Royal Commission on Opium 1893, vol. II (henceforth RCO 1893, vol. II), Great Britain Parliament: H.M. Stationery Office, 1895, ASA.
44. Ibid.
45. *Assam Opium Enquiry Committee Report 1933* (henceforth *AOECR 1933*), Shillong: Assam Secretariat Press, 1933, ASA, pp. 9-11.
46. In Assam, private cultivation of poppy was banned in 1860, although it continued to be cultivated in other parts of the north-east frontier until well into the early years of the twentieth century.
47. 'Tea and Opium Trade', *Asiatic Journal,* 1(1837): 15.
48. It was basically a winter crop, cultivated in the *chapari* (inferior) lands along with mustard seed.
49. Robinson, *Descriptive Account of Assam*, p. 272.
50. Sand banks on the river Brahmaputra were rendered fertile with silt deposition after the flood waters had receded and was extensively cultivated during the winter months with mustard and before anti-cultivation measures mustard and poppy were the crops, which grew luxuriantly in the char areas.
51. A.J. Moffat Mills, *Report on the Province of Assam*, 'From Major Vetch, Officiating Commissioner of Revenue, Assam to Colonel Francis Jenkins, Commissioner of Revenue', Assam, 23 March 1853.
52. Kuladhar Chaliha, 'Opium in Assam', *Modern Review* (1937), NAI.
53. Out of a total area of 2,185,600 acres, 240,000 acres were under cultivation in 1875-6 in Nowgong. The area under cultivation as rice 1,16,876 acres, food grains 36,000 acres, oil seeds 73,700 acres, tea 2,600 acres, opium 2,650 acres, sugar cane 1,600 acres, tobacco 1,950 acres, fibres 500 acres, other crops 1,700 acres. William W. Hunter, *A Statistical Account of Assam,* vol. II, Delhi: Spectrum, 1990 (rpt.).
54. B.C. Allen, *Assam District Gazetteers,* Nowgong, Allahabad: The Pioneer Press, 1905, p. 12.
55. Allen, *Assam District Gazetteers, Seebsagar*, pp. 11-12.
56. The estimated area under different crops in Sibsagar was estimated at – rice 2,10,140 acres, food grains 10,648 acres, oil seeds 6,948 acres, sugar cane 4,218 acres, fibres 15 acres, tobacco 298 acres, tea 19,585 acres, vegetables 11,826 acres and other crops 12,881 acres. Allen, *Assam District Gazetteers,* pp. 252-62.
57. Allen, *Assam District Gazetteers, Seebsagar*, p. 12.

58. *Transactions of the Agricultural and Horticultural Society of India*, vol. 3, Calcutta: Baptist Missions Press, 1839.
59. John Butler, *Travels in Assam: During a Residence of Fourteen Years*, New Delhi: Manas Publications, 2004 (rpt.), p. 244.
60. 'Letter from Captain E.P. Lloyd, Officiating Collector, Nowgong, Assam to the Commissioner of Revenue, Assam, Nowgong', *Separate Revenue,* no. 177, 8 November 1859, ASA.
61. G.R. Barry, *Memorandum on the Province of Assam*, Calcutta: Baptist Mission Press, 1858, p. vii.
62. 'Letter from Major Hamilton Vetch, Officiating Commissioner of Revenue, Assam to Colonel Jenkins', Commissioner of Revenue, 62(1853), pp. 73-4.
63. Nirode K. Barooah, *David Scott in North-East India, 1802-1831: A Study in British Paternalism,* New Delhi: Munshiram Manoharlal, 1969 (rpt.), p. 101.
64. Mills, *Report on the Province of Assam*, p. 70.
65. The soil investigation report revealed that it contained no carbonate of lime and only traces of phosphate and sulphate and that iron was almost wholly in the state of carbonate of iron, a widely different compound from the simple oxides. For 'poor yellow loams' would not be suitable for growing of cotton, tobacco, opium or sugar cane other but was utterly conducive to the growth of the tea plant.'On the Soil Suitable for Cotton, Tobacco, Sugar and the Tea Plant' by Mr. H. Piddington, *Transactions of the Agricultural and Horticultural Society of India*, vol. 3, Calcutta: Baptist Mission Press, 1839, pp. 31-6.
66. 'Letter from D. Reids, Executive Engineer in Assam, Dibrugarh to Col. F. Jenkins, agent to the Governor-General, North Frontier and Commissioner of Assam, Dibrugarh', *Separate Revenue,* 11 October 1859, ASA.
67. 'Letter from Lt. Col. David Reid, Officiating Executive Engineer, Upper Assam, Dibrugarh to Col. F. Jenkins', Commissioner of Assam, *Separate Revenue*, 27 March 1860, ASA.
68. T.T. Cooper, *The Mishimee Hills*, Delhi: Mittal Publications, 1971 (rpt.), pp. 102-3.
69. Assam's economy was essentially a subsistence one based on agricultural production. The standard of living was poor. Boiled rice, soup of pulses, vegetable curry, some milk curd and a little quantity of fish or meat of pigeon or duck constituted the usual menu for lunch and dinner. To quote Anandaram Dhekiyal Phukan, 'there is not a single family in Assam that is not engaged in the culture of lands. Every family provides itself by agriculture with almost all the necessities of life. They cultivate rice, pulses, fruits and vegetables to supply their table, mustard to light their houses,

and silk or cotton to provide their garments. The utensils were mainly earthen pots and pan and few brass and bell metal utensils, besides banana leaves. They slept on mats spread on the floor or on small bamboo platforms.' For details, refer, Jalad B. Ganguly, *An Economic History of North East India 1826-1947*, New Delhi: Akansha Publishing House, 2006, pp. 98-117.

70. Yangwen observes that it would be difficult to understand opium's assimilation into the Chinese social life without 'contextualising' it within the existing cultures of consumption in China as tea, tobacco and snuff including the culinary tradition involving the use of herbs, etc. See, Zheng Yangwen, *The Social Life of Opium in China*, London: Cambridge University Press, 2005.
71. Jean Baptiste Chevalier as the French governor of Chandernagore (1767-78) embarked on diplomatic pursuits to open up the remote corners of the country including Assam and Tibet. His memoir *Journal de mon voyage a Assem* (Journal of my travels in Assam) are a candid presentation of the economic and political conditions of 'a forbidden kingdom'. Although many European diplomatic and mercantile agents had visited Assam, Chevalier was the first ambassador of a European Company to make a request for establishing a factory in Assam. For details, see, Jean B. Chevalier, *Adventures of Jean-Baptiste Chevalier in Eastern India (1752-1765): Historical Memoirs and Journals of Travels in Assam, Bengal and Tibet*, tr. Caroline Dutta-Baruah and Jean Deloche, Guwahati: LBS Publications, 2008.
72. The Sunris however had taken to trade by the late nineteenth century abandoning their hereditary occupation as to them drinking liquor was deemed derogatory. Hunter, *Statistical Account of Assam*, vol. I, p. 185.
73. Hunter, *Statistical Account of Assam*, vol. I, p. 195.
74. Ibid., pp. 126-7.
75. Extract from the Proceedings of the Chief Commissioner of Assam in the Revenue Department, 1882, ASA.
76. Susan R. Ward, *A Glimpse of Assam*, Calcutta: Thomas S.S Mith, 1884, p. 51.
77. In 1874-5 in Darrang district around 852 acres of land under tobacco cultivation averaged an outturn of 3,084 in maunds. In 1872, in Nowgong, 1,950 acres of land was under tobacco cultivation. Although tobacco grown was of inferior quality, yet in Nowgong, it was the only crop, which was manured 'plentifully and regularly.' As per a survey in 1875-6 in Sibsagar, tobacco was cultivated at an estimated 298 acres of land. Hunter, *Statistical Account of Assam*, 86, 196, 254.
78. It is believed that the habit of tobacco smoking was spread from the Portuguese settlements at Rangamati in Goalpara. Jahnabi Gogoi, *Agrarian System of Medieval Assam*, New Delhi: Concept Publishing Company, 2002, pp. 72-3.

79. The Hookah or the Hubble Bubble was the native apparatus for smoking. The pipe had a long stem which carried the smoke through a coconut shell filled with water and as it was being drawn through it, it produced a bubbling sound, hence the name hubble-bubble. Susan R.Ward, *A Glimpse of Assam*, p. 133.
80. Ibid.
81. The Monkhmer speaking Khasis, the earliest tribes to migrate to Assam are believed to have introduced the habit of betel chewing in Assam.They called it *Kuai*. In Assamese, betel is *tamol*, the Sanskrit word is *tambula*. The Assamese also referred to *tamol* as *guo*. Indeed, Guwahati, the name of a major city in Assam, is supposed to have been derived from such formations as *gua* and *quak* meaning betel nuts. Jogesh Das, *Folklore of Assam*, New Delhi: NBT, 2005, pp. 55-7.
82. Profulla C. Borua, *Fundamentals of Assamese Culture*, Guwahati: The Author, 1965, p. 21.
83. Ibid., p. 13.
84. The custom of offering *paan-supari* to the guests and visitors is a common courtesy and has been prevalent in many parts of India from very ancient times and it exists amongst all sections of the society to the present day. It is a common custom to offer *paan-supari* before and after meals to guests and because of its carminative properties, it is a digestive when taken after a heavy meal. Ayurvedic physicians also recommend it as it contains aphrodisiac properties. Besides the active principle of the areca nut, the essential oil of the betel leaf also produces a kind of intoxication; it enhances the effects of the areca nut and acts synergistically upon the central nervous system. Ram N. Chopra and I.C. Chopra, *Indigenous Drugs of India*, Kolkata: Academic Publishers, 2006.
85. Gogoi, *The Agrarian System of Mediavel Assam*, p. 135.
86. George M. Barker, *Tea Planter's Life in Assam*, Calcutta: Thacker, Spink and Co., 1884, p. 73.
87. Henniker in his monograph appreciates the art of metal moulding in Assam. F.G. Henniker, *The Gold and Silver Wares of Assam: A Monograph*, Shillong: Assam Secretariat Printing Office, 1905.
88. Borua, *Fundamentals of Assamese Culture*, p. 15.
89. Shehabuddin Talesh, *Tarikh-e-Aasham*, tr. Mazhar Asif, Guwahati: Department of Historical and Antiquarian Studies, 2009, p. 101.
90. Don Sinibaldo De Mas, 'England, China and India', tr. Hartmann H. Sultzberger, *All about Opium*, England: Biblio Bazaar, LLC, 2009 (rpt.), p. 102.
91. Guha, *Medieval and Early Colonial Assam*, p. 281.
92. J. Owens representing Assam at a meeting of the Asiatic Society, presented apart from a variety of *ayeen abkarry*, two balls of the opium rags. Proceedings of the Asiatic Society, August 1844.

93. *Minutes and Evidence before the Select Committee 1859*, p. 196.
94. *ACOECR*, 1925, pp. 37-8.
95. Benudhar Sharma, *Majirpara Meijalai*, pt. 1, Guwahati: Assam Jyoti, 1985.
96. The opium is boiled down with a little water to the consistency of a paste and then mixed with the shredded and fried leaves of betel or less commonly, guava or other plants, *Bothan Committee Report*, 1913.
97. Chopra, *Indigenous Plants of India*, p. 377.
98. *ACOECR*, 1925, pp. 37-8.
99. Allen, *Assam District Gazetteers*, p. 45.
100. Assam Legislative Council (henceforth ALC) Proceedings 1934, ASA, pp. 600-1.
101. Testimony of Nilmoni Phukan, *AOECR*, 1933, pp. 141-59.
102. Dutiram Hazarika, *Rasik Puran* (unpublished), Guwahati: Department of Historical and Antiquarian Studies, 1877, folio I.
103. *The Assam Gazette*, August 1927, ASA, p. 967.
104. *AOECR*, 1933, p. 24.
105. Testimony of R.C. Haviland, Tea Planter, RCO, 1893, vol. II, p. 52.
106. 'Religious History of Assam', *Calcutta Review*, 52(1867), p. 77.
107. *AOECR*, 1933, p. 151.
108. In his 'Lectures on Dietetics and Dyspesia', he elaborates on the food customs of people as 'the outcome of profound instincts which correspond to important wants in the human economy'. Citing the progress and development of European nations, he observes that inspite of their use of alcoholic beverages; they have not witnessed any decline in productivity. Rather, they are amongst the prospering nations of the world. William Roberts, *Memorandum on the General Treatises and the Medical Aspects of the Opium Habit in India*, RCO, 1893.
109. Evidence before the RCO, 1893, vol. II, p. 262.
110. E.R.R.Gilman, Tea planter, in his evidence before the Royal Commission on Opium. He had purchased the opium mahals at *Panbari*, *Khas Domuria* and *Domuria Mahals*. Another planter Mr. Ernest Bridge, of Kopati Tea Estate, Mangaldai, also held that non-opium eaters frequently get fever, dysentry and bowel complaints when they work in the gardens during the rainy season and that had it not been for opium the fatal results from these ailments would be quite alarming. RCO, 1893, vol. II, p. 53.
111. Testimonies of Gunabhiram Barooah, who had retired as the Extra Assistant Commissioner and Madhav Chandra Bordoloi was the Extra Assistant Commissioner, Barpeta before RCO, 1893, vol. II, pp. 278, 340.
112. According to Roberts, the evidence presented before the Commission had revealed that local consumption of opium had a close relationship to the greater or less prevalence of malaria in the localities. For details, refer, Roberts, *The Consumption of Opium in India,* 24.

113. The RCO, 1893 Report revealed how during a famine in Orissa, the 'benign Government' ordered for free distribution of opium to alleviate the sufferings of the people. The Medical Memorandum declared, 'that opium ameliorated the lot of the underfed man and enabled him to live longer and better with a scanty diet'. This assertion though was severely criticized in a critique of the Medical Memorandum, which established that opium retards and does not aid in digestion (Dr. Cobbs. Theory of opium) and cited it as a possible source of gastritis (Dr. Burney Yeo's Manual of Medical Treatment). For details, refer, Roberts, *The Consumption of Opium in India,* p. 104.
114. Evidences of Dr. Umesh Chandra Mukherjee, Medical Practitioner for 39 years, Dibrugarh, Maulvi Tazuddin Bora (Medical practitioner), North Lakhimpur, Dr. Bepin Behari Bora (L.M.S. Government Pensioner), Officiating Civil Surgeon, Baroda, Charan Sen (Ayurvedic practitioner), Gauhati, Krishna Kanta Adhikari (Ayurvedic practitioner), Maulavi Abu Bokr Ayaz (Medical practitioner), Gauhati, Thanu Chandra Baruah, Kaviraj (Ayurvedic practitioner), Jorhat, Dr. Benode Behari Sen Gupta (Medical practitioner). All of them unanimously confirmed that opium has no prophylactic effect against malaria or kala-azar, *ACOECR*, 1925, pp. 98-113.
115. Evidence of Dr. Bepin Behari Bora, L.M.S., Government Pensioner, Officiating Civil Surgeon. *ACOECR*, 1925, p. 107.
116. *ACOECR*, 1925, p. 133.
117. Ibid., pp. 99-102.
118. Testimony of Radhanath Changkakati, RCO, 1893, vol. II, 83.
119. These were the socio-cultural forces at work, the leisure of tobacco smoking and the romance of betel chewing which led to the Assamese imbibe opium drinking as a favourite indulgence.
120. Colonial and native accounts and the various investigations conducted into the opium habit are all ambiguous in their opinion as regards the use of opium. Even medical opinion in the nineteenth century was divided in their opinion on the therapeutic effects of opium. While it is likely that its use by the royal clans in Assam might have been as a luxury, it appears that its proliferation among the lower strata was inspired by its analgesic properties, considering the absence of proper medical facilities in the province in the nineteenth century.
121. From being a royal leisurely pursuit, opium had by the eighteenth century filtered down from the mid-Ming Court to the upper and upper-middle class, in China, where it's aphrodisiac properties were hailed. Eighteenth century saw its use proliferate among the lower classes. See, Zheng Yangwen. 'The Social Life of Opium in China, 1483-1999', *Modern Asian Studies*, 37(2003): 1-39.

CHAPTER 5

From Assam *Kanee* to Behar *Abkaree*

THE TRANSITION OF the East India Company from a trading concern to an administrative power involved a paradigmatic shift from a 'let alone policy' to one of active intervention for the 'good of the greatest number'. Underlying such exposition of Victorian liberalism, however, was an active economic agenda, of which the opium monopoly was an important component. By the latter half of the nineteenth century, along with China, the chief battlefield of opinion and action gravitated heavily towards the British opium policy in India. It was designed to encompass all aspects of opium production, manufacture, distribution and consumption. Integral to this arrangement, was the general administrative structure designed and operated for the implementation of the opium policy. Following the initial success of the opium monopoly in Bengal, the colonial government in the aftermath of its conquest of Assam from the Burmese in 1826, embarked on attempts at establishing commercial plantations of opium poppy. It was suggested that a part of the Company's opium investment be allowed to be furnished from Assam, 'provided the locally manufactured drug was found to be of good quality'.[1] David Scott had attempted to induce the cultivators to grow poppy in Rungpore but he found that the cultivators preferred to consume it rather than engage in commercial production.[2] Unfortunately, for the Government, an analysis of soil samples established the soil as unfavourable for commercial cultivation of poppy.[3] The failure of the poppy crop in Kamrup led to the abandonment of the plan to establish an opium agency in Assam. A plausible alternative source of revenue was taxation. As Moffat Mills asserted, 'Opium they should have, but to get it they should be made to work for it'.[4] Scott had estimated that a minimum of two thousand *pooras* of land could be easily brought under this assessment and the net revenue was estimated at Rs. 25,000 a year. Such a move, as Scott held, would limit consumption and generate revenues. Unconvinced with Scott's proposition, the Bengal government was contented with securing a tacit approval from Purandhar Singha[5] in 1833, to implement measures to suppress poppy cultivation in parts of the province, which were under his suzerainty. Taking cue from a survey of the north-east frontier of Bengal province conducted by himself and Robert Pemberton under the instructions of Lord William Bentinck in 1832,[6] Jenkins during his tenure at Assam as the Chief Commissioner had warned against immediate suppression of the poppy cultivation. He believed that such a move would incite discontent among the populace who were much given to its use. Instead, he proposed to raise the taxes on the *bari* (homestead) and *chapari* (riverine) land[7] on which the crop was generally cultivated and which were being assessed at low rates.[8]

The government policy of drift followed until 1860 when several developments forced a total policy reversal. The decision to replace Assam *kanee* with Behar *abkaree* was followed by the total prohibition of the private cultivation of poppy. Anandaram Dhekial Phukan, in his memorandum to Moffat Mills, wondered, 'whether by interdicting the culture of the drug the Government contemplates to expel the general use of opium or proposes to substitute its own in lieu of the native opium'.[9] The government claimed that it was moved by considerations, '[…] to check the immoderate use of opium and rescue at least the rising generation from indulgence in a luxury which destroys the constitution, enfeebles the mind and paralyses industry'.[10]

The Company officials expected that local cultivation of opium could be restricted by the introduction of the *abkaree* opium (government-procured opium).[11] Since it was apparent that the local people were neither prepared to give up opium nor would they welcome a prohibition step, it was calculated that cultivation would rapidly decrease if *abkare*e opium could be bought cheaper, 'when people would have to pay a price to get the opium, it would reduce the ill effects for only those confirmed in the habit and who had the money to purchase would be able to get it. The Government would have the power to check the extension of this vice by increasing the price from time to time and thus placing it beyond the means of all but the most wealthy.'[12]

The influence of certain extraneous factors behind this policy must also not be lost sight of. Significant among these was the competition between Malwa opium[13] and Bengal opium and the notification of imposing a heavy export duty on opium in Burma, which would induce an extensive system of smuggling from Assam to the Burmese territory.[14] The government was highly apprehensive of the possibility of smuggling of cheap Assam opium into China where the drug was exorbitantly priced.[15] Moreover, as Townshed notes, how in tandem with the British government policy of free trade since 1860, revenue considerations coexisted with the desire to diminish the consumption of noxious commodities.[16] The tea planter's vociferous opposition to the cultivation of the poppy in Assam which threatened a prime commercial interest of the colonial power also should not be ignored. They regarded opium use as interfering with the supply of labour for the tea plantations.[17] All these collectively strengthened the case for an extension of the general system of taxing the consumption of opium in Assam as in Bengal Presidency. The tea-planters who had previously raised a voice against the use of this drug welcomed this move. For they believed that the introduction of excise opium in place of *kanee* would solve the problem of labour as to obtain the drug they would be required to work. After several consultations at various levels, engaging both official and non-official opinions, both of approval and dissent, Jenkins as early as 1844, advocated a prohibitory decree forbidding cultivation of opium throughout Assam.[18] The supply and consumption of *abkaree* opium only was held legal. 'There can be no doubt', the Board of Revenue agreed – 'that the use of opium as of all other stimulants is a legitimate subject of taxation in Assam as elsewhere...'.[19]

Excise in Assam, 1874-1928

The evolution of excise policies governing the production, consumption and distribution of opium ensured the security of control and revenue. In Assam, the 'Imperialism of Opium' as

Amalendu Guha asserts, was operated and maintained through a resilient excise system, under the pretext of ensuring *righteousness before revenue.*[20] The restriction on opium initiated by the prohibition of private cultivation and its manufacture was followed by a host of measures including surveillance to prevent smuggling.[21] The aim was to make it difficult and expensive for the consumer to purchase the drug. Notwithstanding its effects on curtailing consumption, there was a smooth flow of revenue into the Government coffers. Each of the provinces supplied with Bengal opium, viz., Bengal, north-west provinces and Oudh, the Central Provinces, Assam and Burma, derived large provincial revenues from the sale of opium, of which the Local Government was assigned three-fourths and the Imperial government received its share of one-fourth from the revenue proceeds.[22] The receipts from opium in Assam formed the bulk of the excise revenue (more than two-thirds of the total excise receipts). Indeed the Government's *policy of drift with trial and error* proved it at its ambiguous best – it was as Guha remarks a 'monopolist's profit maximising policy' in the garb of promoting collective good.[23]

Phase I: Profit Maximization while Restraining Consumption

Land formed as elsewhere, the main source of revenue in Assam in the nineteenth century. With the ever-increasing demands of the state, new avenues of taxation had to be explored. In considering opium as a financial resource, it appears that the practice of the Mughal government had been adopted under whom opium was farmed out on an exclusive privilege on annual payment in advance.[24] The colonial administration, however, adopted the declared intention in the Bengal Resolution (1813) that of 'maximum revenue and minimum consumption'. This ambiguity was in fact a characteristic of the British colonial policy and was well reflected in all its proclaimed attempts at 'righteousness before revenue', which merely served to disguise the commercial intentions of the British East India Company. A centralized system of distribution of excise opium was ensured under which: (i) provinces outside the Malwa system were coerced to prohibit the private cultivation of poppy and (ii) the sale of Bengal or Malwa opium at the excise shops.[25]

As a corollary to the restriction on cultivation and production, the trade in opium became a monopoly of the Government. And, henceforth, opium was to be issued from the local treasury at Rs. 14 a seer with effect from 1 May 1860. Anandaram Dhekial Phukan's forewarnings of refraining from such a drastic move to avoid 'the loss of numerous lives' and 'subject people to much calamity and unhappiness',[26] fell on deaf ears. In 1861, enraged against the Government policy of increasing taxation, *ryots* in Nowgong rose in revolt. Officially termed as *kania bidroh* (the opium eater's revolt), it is also referred to as the *Phulaguri Uprising*.[27] It caused consternation among the higher ranks of the British officials, still besieged with the livid memories of 1857. As H.K. Barpujari observes, 'already hard hit, the prohibitory order had shattered the domestic economy of the tribal areas where per capita consumption of opium was high'.[28] A realistic and concerted approach was therefore regarded as imperative. Accordingly, necessary administrative regulations were issued to the effect that the possession and sale of *kanee* in the province of Assam was punishable under Act XXI of 1856 from 1 January 1863.

The immediate result of the prohibition was encouraging for the Government. The colonial authorities observed a rapid increase of the opium revenue in Assam.[29] The selling price of opium had also been raised from Rs. 14 to 20 a seer in most of the districts, followed by an increase in the rates of assessment on non-*rupit* lands by 15 to 30 per cent in 1866. This caused a mild decline in opium revenue for the year to the extent of Rs. 32,529. Officials believed this to be the result of the introduction of the higher rates of assessment of land revenue and lower purchasing power of the people.[30] In Goalpara and Kamrup, the new rates were enforced but not in Upper Assam where the old rates were allowed to continue, until the discontent and restlessness caused by the stoppage of *kanee* cultivation had abated. In 1864-5, the gross receipts from opium were Rs. 16,45,662 and the net revenue estimated at about Rs. 11,21,078. The quantity consumed was about 2,044 maunds, which was estimated at about 57.7 per cent of the whole consumption in Bengal.[31] A part of the increase was due to the agricultural prosperity brought in by the growth of tea plantations in the province.[32]

The fixed license fee system was introduced in 1874 and this meant that any person could open any number of shops for the retail sale of the drug on payment of a fixed sum for each shop. The rates of fees were in the first instance, fixed in all districts where licenses were granted at Rs. 3 for half a year.[33] In January 1876, the Government of India proposed the system of *farming of opium mehals* thereby creating 'private monopolies' within fixed territories and limited number of shops for the retail sale of excise opium.[34] Each district was divided into a number of *mehals* (revenue divisions).[35] Under this system, the person/s who buy at auction the right to sell opium in the limits of a *mehal* had the exclusive right of sale in that *mehal* with permission to sub-let shops, subject to the sanction of the Deputy Commissioner. This system of selling licenses for the retail vend of opium by auction was followed with enhancements in the selling price of the drug corresponding with a decrease in the number of shops. The selling price of opium was raised from Rs. 23 to 24 per seer and the rate of license – fee for each shop was enhanced to Rs. 18 from 12 per annum. The Chief Commissioner fixed the number of shops permitted to be opened in each *mehal* on the recommendation of the Deputy Commissioner, based on the legitimate requirements of each locality.[36]

In 1873-5, there were as many as 5,137 opium shops while according to the Census of 1881, the number of villages in Assam valley was 6,776 – nearly the same number of shops as there were villages.[37] Nearly one person in every village held a government license.[38] Such high-density distribution of opium retail outlets came under strong criticism and it was alleged that the opium shops licensed by the Government were *kanikholas*[39] which were facilitating the spread of the opium habit. [40] The Government strongly denied the prevalence of such 'opium-dens' which 'are unsuited to the habits and ways of living of a sparse agricultural population such as that of Assam…'.[41] The Government maintained that the enhancement of the rates of revenue and stringency of the *abkaree* rules were a deterrent on the sales of the drug[42] though the continuance of 'illicit cultivation' was a cause of concern. The Board of Revenue in a report upheld the Government policy was a success, 'Considering the evil effects, physically and morally which the uncontrolled indulgence in the drug was only a few years ago producing among the Assamese, . . . that circumstances are now so much changed for the better, even though it be at a sacrifice of the Government revenue.'[43]

However, the fierce opposition to the continuance of monopolies by the anti-opium lobby forced a policy shift to licensing and regulation – which Baumler refers to as a 'legitimizing policy'.[44]

Phase II: From Farming to Licensing of Opium

When the Government of Assam decided to replace the monopoly vend of opium by the system of sale by auction in 1877, it had anticipated a considerable increase in the opium excise revenue. It expected a 'brisk competition' among the auction purchasers. Moreover, it was an inexpensive yet lucrative source of revenue and hence as Brook and Wakabayashi argue, 'opium farms for most part of the nineteenth century were major props of every colonial state'.[45] The system of *farming opium licenses* was initially claimed to be a financial success.

It was claimed that the farming system had resulted in better management of the opium excise revenue. There was a 35 per cent increase in the total revenue followed by a fall in the number of retail outlets with a corresponding decline in the general consumption of the drug. This was attributed to strict enforcement practices and gradual increase in the duties on excisable articles. Gradually, however, as the inefficiencies latent in the system began to reveal itself, it began to prove highly detrimental to the revenues. In the official circles there was wide apprehension that the increase in revenue was 'partly abnormal' as it had developed out of a gambling spirit developed by putting opium *mehals* to auction. It was evident that the increase of revenue was neither constant nor maintainable. The *keyas* and the tea planters had purchased the majority of the opium *mehals*.[46] This led to capital accumulation in the hands of few but could not lead to the emergence of a 'local capitalist class' unlike in China and other countries of South-East Asia where opium revenue farms were operating. Jalad Ganguly's remarks appear apt to describe the intent of the colonial power, was to 'patronize the metropolitan capitalist entrepreneurs which would be mutually sustaining and yielding economies of scale and profits from both vertical and horizontal combination of enterprise'.[47] Rather, this process weaned away the savings of the native people. Many tea companies and private planters had bid for opium licenses for the purposes of supplying their 'coolies' with opium with the result that ordinary traders found it difficult to compete at auction with the large companies.

The *farming system* began to face criticism as it had induced a spirit of unhealthy competition with the licensees making up for the high purchase price of the *mehals* by charging exorbitant price from the consumers. It was also suspected that such a system would seriously affect the labour market and hence it was proposed that no person should be allowed to purchase more than one *mehal*.[48] The result was that the quantity of opium consumed in 1881-2 was less by 103 maunds or about 6 per cent, than the quantity in 1880-1 and was less than it had been in any year since the auction system was first introduced in 1877.

Moreover, the heightened intervention of the *mahaldars* who had formed 'coalition of interests' was neither favourable nor desirable to the interests of the Government. The Marwari traders were accused of biding at 'abnormally high prices' for the shops. The influential Marwari merchant Harbilas Agarwala who owned two shops in the Dibrugarh subdivision was accused by other vendors of selling opium at 6½ *annas* per *tola* against a selling price of 8 *annas* per *tola* 'to ruin other lesses'.[49] The Assamese and Bengali merchants formed a syndicate to counteract the influence of the Marwari traders, including inducements offered to the Deputy Commissioner of large license fees.[50] Fierce competition amongst the two syndicates often caused violent fluctuations, which was unfavourable to the Government interests who tried to prevent the formation of monopolies.[51]The Board of Revenue, proposed the need to do away with the *mahaldars* 'who now stand between the

Government and the retail shopkeeper' and confer the 'right of selling opium direct to the keeper of the shop'.

Through the shop system, which was reintroduced from 1883 onwards, an attempt was made to refurbish the administration of excise opium in Assam. The basic principle of issuing licenses as was proposed was to ensure that a sufficient number of shops were licensed to supply the legitimate demands of the different localities. It involved first the substitution of licensed individual shops for the opium *mehals* from 1 April 1883. This followed an enhancement in the retail price of opium by 23 per cent. As an experiment, Malwa opium was introduced in place of Behar opium, following complaints of the poor quality Behar excise opium. By substituting the Malwa drug for Bengal opium for excise purposes, the outturn of opium manufactured for export to China was sought to be increased.[52] The experiment proved ineffective and excess stocks of Malwa opium that could not be disposed off were proposed to be routed to Burma, Chittagong or Orissa.[53]

The Royal Commission on Opium and Assam

The Royal Commission on Opium 1893 (hereafter RCO 1893) affirmed the efficacy of the existing Government policy as the most appropriate under existing conditions in India of lack of unanimity on the question of prohibition. The Commission was against any authoritative interference like recommending of restrictive legislation. Many of its recommendations on regulation and control were absorbed into the provincial laws. However, many among the Indian elite were found to be apathetic to the question of opium suppression and regarded it as 'interference in the internal affairs', which could invite discontent. Ever since 1857, the colonial Government had as its keynote policy – 'the promotion of the welfare of the country as a whole'. The States had passed reciprocal agreements with reference to the mutual extradition of criminals and the assimilations of systems of regulating the production and distribution of salt, drugs and intoxicating liquor.[54] The incident leading to the *Phulaguri* uprising (1860) was noted by J.D. Anderson, the Deputy Commissioner of Darrang, who stressed on exercising caution and called for a gradual reduction in the treasury price of opium.

> It was a remarkable fact that this crowd was composed entirely of the opium eating Assamese. The liquor consuming classes were conspicuously absent. It is cruel and tyrannical to expect a sudden withdrawal from opium by the people. Every man's hand would be against us and smuggling would be practised on an enormous scale. When two years ago, the retail price of opium rose to 12 *annas* a *tola,* my *cutchery* was thronged with petitions who begged that I would take steps to make the drug cheaper. Only a few days ago, I received a petition asking for the opening of a new opium shop on the ground that the *ryots* had to go over 5½ miles to get their supply.[55]

Infact, many among the Assamese elite, including litterateurs and those in prominent social positions, remained divided in their opinion on the issue of total suppression of opium. While a section of the educated Assamese intelligentsia including Gunabhiram Barooah, Trinayan Kakati, Harbilas Agarwala, were in favour of opium prohibition as a general policy excepting on medical grounds, Hemchandra Barooah and Jagannath Barooah were against opium prohibition as interference in the socio-cultural practices of the people. Around three hundred members of the Jorhat Sarvajanik Sabha, which claimed to be representing 'the wishes and aspirations of the people to the Government, explaining to the people the objects and policy of the Government and generally ameliorating the condition of the people', signed a memorandum to the Commission stating that,

> [...] the people of Assam, in common with those of other provinces of India, have been in the habit of using opium and other narcotics from the remotest times. Opium is an invaluable medicine in many disorders of the stomach, it alleviates pain and possesses a sedative power of restoring health. It is useful after 40 years of age in prolonging life and is an undoubted preventive against malaria. The hard working classes in the malarious plains of Assam require some stimulant to keep up their powers. Overall, opium is positively necessary for a large number of the people earning their livelihood by manual labour in the swampy rice fields and in the tea gardens of Assam and of boatmen and others....[56]

In their statements made before the RCO 1893, Hem Chandra

Barua and Benudhar Barua, were unanimous that, 'The people of Assam are naturally disposed to use opium for non-medicinal purposes and are not, I believe, willing to bear any part of the cost of prohibitive measures, nor can they afford to do so. Sale of opium by the Government should not, be prohibited for non-medicinal purposes. Such prohibition is not, practicable.'[57]

That the Assamese 'Western educated' intelligentsia at large, remained uncritical supporters in this colonial enterprise provides an angle of thought to understanding as to why though proclaimed an 'evil' requiring 'eradication', the colonial policy always stopped short of prohibition. Viewed in this context, Rajen Saikia's statement is enlightening, 'As a class, it [the middle class] is torn between two value systems and therefore, unable to develop a compact personality; courage and creativity coexisted with masochistic instincts and blurred vision.'[58]

The Commission was convinced that the great mass of Indian opinion was opposed to the proposal of prohibition as unnecessary restrictions on individual and an interference with the established customs and habits.

In 1895, acting on the recommendations in the report of the Royal Commission on Opium, certain amendments were made in the Opium Act I of 1878, which was in force in the province along with the Bengal Excise Act VII of 1878 as amended by Act IV of 1881 and Act I of 1883. Under the amended Act, all Local Governments and administrations were forbidden to issue licenses to shops for the sale of preparations of opium used for smoking while not attempting to prevent the manufacture of such preparations by individuals for the purposes of private consumption.[59] The limit of legal possession of opium by private individuals was reduced to 1 *tola* down from 5 *tolas* along with strict prohibition of the manufacturing of smoking preparations of opium.

With the exception of the Government of Bengal, which proposed legislation for the suppression of opium smoking saloons on the lines of the law enacted for the suppression of gambling, the majority of the Local Governments and Administration, including Assam, were against the measures suggested by the Royal Commission. They opposed it mainly on the ground that, (i) it would become a means of extortion and oppression on the part of subordinates in the Police and the Preventive Departments and (ii) that it might result in making the practice of opium smoking in private more general than it had hitherto been.[60]

International Surveillance and Colonial Assam

The crusade in the Chinese Empire against the growth of poppy and the production and use of opium, prohibitionist voices at home, and American appreciation of the magnitude of the opium problem following the Philippine Opium Committee marked the internationalizing of the anti-opium movement. From the middle of the nineteenth century some measures for narcotics control were taken in a number of countries, example, in 1845, a French law facilitating the control of poisons (including narcotics) was passed, while between 1895 and 1906 various states and territories of the United States of America enacted special regulations for the control of opium and other narcotics. The Philippines Opium Commission of 1903 was the first federal government enquiry into the use and effects of intoxicating substances. Bishop Brent[61] headed it and its findings contradicted those of the earlier RCO 1893. The latter had found opium related problems in India 'comparatively rare and novel', thereby legitimizing continued British participation in the trade. The Philippines Commission found that the unregulated sale of opium had a grave effect on the health and moral capacity of users. It recommended that the import, sale and use of opium should be based on medical need only, thereby ending centuries of 'long tradition of unregulated and promiscuous use in South-East Asia'. The influence of the Christian Missionaries did not end with this measure. Brent and Crafts lobbied the Roosevelt administration to convene an international opium conference. This was a significant step and it marked the beginnings of US 'narco-diplomacy'.

The influential missionary groups had therefore set out two important principles. First, the use of intoxicating substances was morally wrong and injurious and that national governments had the responsibility to step in to prevent people from doing harm to themselves. Second, this could only be achieved by reducing the supply of narcotic substances from cultivator and producer countries. This prohibitionist-supply side focus shaped the structure and orientation of the international regime that was to emerge. The British, Dutch and other significant stakeholder countries were prepared to concede the need for regulation of the opium trade but they emphasized regulation over prohibition. The British had already moved towards a ten-year supply reduction agreement with China. The Shanghai Opium Commission of 1909 urged upon governments the (i) the desirability of the gradual suppression of opium smoking (ii) the restriction of the use of morphine for medical purposes only and (iii) the national control of morphine and other derivatives of opium. The efforts of the Shanghai delegates were largely responsible for the conclusion three years later at The Hague (in Netherlands) of the first International Opium Convention that established 'narcotics control' as an institution of international law on a multilateral basis.

The Shanghai Commission (1909) did lead to the realization of enforcing stringent preventive and fiscal arrangements for regulation of opium use, particularly opium smoking. Accordingly, the administration in Assam was asked to impose necessary restrictions on opium smoking.[62] A general enquiry was conducted into the possibility of legislative action against opium smoking and the feasibility of raising the issue prices of opium as the 'only direction in which we can safely proceed in attempting to reduce opium consumption'.[63]

Nonetheless, since 1901, consumption registered an increase owing to the recovery of the country from the effects of earthquake, disappearance of unhealthiness and better seasons.[64] Demand rose from Rs. 17,23,238 to 17,79,917. The consumption of treasury opium increased from 1,205 to 1,274 maunds. There was an increase of 52 maunds in the consumption of opium in the Assam Valley districts. The habit was increasing among the cultivating classes, especially in Kamrup and Darrang and among the people of the hills, especially the Mikir Hills. It was suspected that the migrant tea garden labourers had been substituting opium for the country spirit. Hence it was proposed to remove some 19 shops from the vicinity of the tea gardens. Most of the licenses were held by the tea garden managers, many of whom were the *keyas* (local term applied for Marwari traders) – 'one of whom is to be found on almost every tea garden'.[65] The following are the remarks from the Board's review of the Report for 1907-8 in explanation of the increase,

> The causes which have led to increased consumption of opium are the same as those which have led to the expansion of ordinary cultivation among the Assamese *ryots.* Satisfactory natural growth of Assamese population, their recovery from the effects of malarial unhealthiness, kala-azar, earthquake and floods, a succession of years of agricultural prosperity and good public health, and the influx and circulation of cash, particularly among the laboring classes and hill and forest tribes in consequence of railway construction and activity in the lac trade were all causes contributing to the increased consumption of opium.[66]

The rate of consumption was high among the Kacharis (who inhabit the submontane tracts of the Brahmaputra valley and the low hills) and the Mikir population. Serious apprehension was expressed on the efficacy of the restrictive measures as the enquiry revealed a considerable diminution of opium consumption with corresponding increase in use of *ganja.*[67] Explicitly stating that, 'Experience has shown that as the Assamese give up opium; they are liable to take to other intoxicants, the younger educated classes in towns to spirituous liquor, the villagers as a rule to *ganja*, but among certain tribes to spirit.'[68]

Prohibition and Policing People

With the formation of the legislative councils, the anti-opium discourse entered a new phase. Among the leading Assamese members in the council, only Padmanath Gohain Barua continued to give vent to his indignation. His friend, Ghanshyam Barua, exposed the hollowness of the Government policy on opium and called for some drastic steps, but the government refused to concede anything. Members of the Assam Association, including Ghanshyam Barua and Rai Bahadur Nilambar Datta, suggested a course of action, wherein organization of temperance societies was at the top of their agenda. Amidst growing concerns over the continuous upward trend of consumption of both *ganja* and opium and in view of the resolutions at The Hague Convention of 1912,[69] where India formally committed to suppressing opium in all its provinces, the Government of Assam, conceded to the native demand for an enquiry into the opium situation.

In December 1912, was appointed the Commiitee to Enquire into Certain Aspects of Opium and Ganja Consumption in Assam (also called the Botham Committee), with A.W. Botham as the Chairman and Kaliprasad Chaliha, Kutubuddin Ahmad, Radhanath Phukan as members. Altogether 482 witnesses were examined across the province.[70] It submitted its report in 1913, though it was made in public only in June 1925. Interestingly, a major revelation of the Botham Committee was the widespread prevalence of smoking *madak* and reported on the increase in the habit since the prohibition of poppy cultivation in 1860. Presenting a detailed description of the nature of the opium smoking habit and its proliferation, it hinted at the possible spread of the opium habit through propagation of the semi-religious use of the drug at the *Kania Seba* (opium assemblies) held at some of the *Namgoas* (religious assemblies). Hence, it proposed that the smoking of opium in company should be forbidden by law and declared a penal offence.[71]

Meanwhile, the Botham Committee authenticated the Government contention that further restrictions on the sale of opium would involve the danger of diverting consumption to more deleterious stimulants, as *ganja*, cocaine and morphia.[72] It reported that the consumption of *ganja* in the Kamrup district had increased from 68 maunds in 1904-5 to 125 maunds in 1909-10 and its use had reportedly found to have been popular among the Assamese populace. The Committee reported an increase of 88 per cent for *ganja* consumed in the five upper districts of the Brahmaputra valley between 1901 and 1911, largely to a marked spread of the *ganja* habit amongst Assamese Hindus of all castes and classes. With a view to check the growth of the habit, an enhancement of the retail price to 8 *annas* a *tola* was proposed. The Committee did not overlook the danger of diverting consumption from excise *ganja* to wild bhang, which 'grows freely throughout the Assam valley and is largely consumed by those who cannot afford the excise article'.[73]

It advocated caution on the smuggling of cocaine and morphia from Burma into Assam, and was against prohibition or stringent restriction. Instead, it stressed on greater public awareness by mobilizing village councils headed by a *gaonburah* (village headmen) or a *mauzadar* (revenue official) to oversee the ban on smoking opium in company.

The report was revealing but it failed to have any impact on the official policy. It remained buried in official labyrinth till 1925 when the uproar in legislature to make its results public could not be ignored by the government. It concluded that a severe restriction on opium, without similar restriction on *ganja*, would divert consumption from one drug to the other. It refused to recommend a system of personal registration of opium-eaters. It merely prescribed 'prohibition of smoking in company' as a deterrent.

Most of the witnesses to the 1913 committee were in favour of a restrictive registration though the Committee's final verdict was against prohibition. Whilst agreeing that any system of restrictive registration is not necessary or practicable in Assam, the 'native' members of the Botham Committee, Rai Bahadur Kali Prasad Chaliha, Khan Bahadur Kutubuddin Ahmad and Radhanath Phukan were in favour of simple registration without any restriction (except one of age) on the registration of new consumers or on the quantity of opium to be allowed to each consumer. They proposed that only persons who had attained the age of 20 years should be registered. The object of their proposal was to prevent the consumption of opium by minors.

There was also some disagreement among the members of the Committee as regards the extent and nature of the problem. While Kali Prasad Chaliha argued for 'special measures of prevention', to the other members of the Committee, including Khan Bahadur Kutubuddin Ahmad and Radhanath Phukan did not regard the 'evil as at present widespread'.[74] The Committee recommendations against prohibition echoes the concurrence of view against prohibition as upheld by the Secretary of State by Lord Hardinge's Government in 1911,

> The prohibition of opium eating in India we regard as impossible, and any attempt at it is fraught with the most serious consequences to the people

and the Government. We take our stand unhesitatingly on the conclusion of the Royal Commission which reported in 1895, viz., that the opium habit as a vice scarcely exists in India, that opium is extensively used for medical and quasi-medical purposes, in some cases with benefit, and for the most part without injurious consequences; that the non-medical uses are so interwoven with the medical uses that it would not be practicable to draw a distinction between them in the distribution and sale of the drug; and that it is not necessary that the growth of the poppy and the manufacture and sale of opium in British India should be prohibited except for medical purposes. Whatever may be the case in other countries, centuries of inherited experience have taught the people of India discretion in the use of the drug, and its misuse is a negligible feature in Indian life. Even if it were possible to suppress the cultivation of opium in India, geographical and political limitations would place it beyond our power to prevent illicit import and consumption on a serious scale.[75]

Following the Government's recognition of 'prohibition as impossibility', any increase of restrictions was considered – 'unnecessary and unadvisable'.[76] To satisfy the demand of reformers, it approved minor amendments in the Assam Opium Rules in 1916. This included measures to prohibit the transmission by inland post of opium and morphia drugs, excepting certain medical preparations.[77] The Committee insisted on strengthening temperance associations, with permanent committees in each town and subdivision of the Valley. The anti-opium reformist discourse in the early years of the twentieth century was focused on advocacy of temperance. In Assam, an anti-opium conference was convened in 1907 at Dibrugarh. It urged upon the Government to check the opium menace and call out for a formation of the Assam Temperance Association. Two measures were resolved on with the object of combating the evils attendant on the use of opium, (i) To consider submitting a memorial to the Government asking for the habit to be checked and (ii) to form an *Assam Temperance Association* with permanent committees in each town and subdivision of the valley. In 1912, an anti-opium conference was organized at Dibrugarh, with the *Satradhikar* of Dinjay *Sattra* as the president, where a temperance society was formed. It recommended the opening of a public register of opium-eaters, as has been successfully done in Burma, with a view to check the further progress of the habit.[78]

Excise Violations as Subversion, 1883-1919

Since 1883, the authorities had been perplexed by a pattern of a steady though gradual decline in opium consumption. This was more marked in the Upper Assam districts.[79] Opium being the great mainstay of excise revenue in Assam, particularly in Upper Assam, where the residents were regarded as avid consumers of opium,[80] the wide fluctuations and local variations were a 'serious irritant' to the Government. Official statistics placed the excise revenue of the district of Sibsagar to nearly three-fourths of the land revenue while in Lakhimpur it was put up at twice the land revenue. The authorities suspected smuggling and the explicit involvement of the *keyas*,[81] particularly following the introduction of Malwa opium. Although there was another set of opinion that held the view that, 'the present generation of the Assamese does not indulge in the drug so much as their predecessors probably partly owing to the spread of education'. However, this found favour only amongst a minority. Smuggling of opium, had according to a majority of official opinion, emerged as a potent factor than education aiding in the decrease of the consumption of excise opium. Licensed opium in Assam was expensive as compared to most other British provinces. The Assam opium market remained a seductive field for the black marketers. Clandestine opium was reported pouring in from Nepal and Malwa.[82]Aside from imported opium, there was considerable 'illegal' traffic in opium. Excise Department records reveal that on an average more than two-thirds of the opium violations involved 'illicit' trade in 'illicit' opium. The price fluctuated dramatically from district to district which encouraged speculation and opium moved regularly from low-priced regions to high priced regions.

Opium was smuggled into Assam from Manipur while the Marwari traders were suspected of bringing in illicit Malwa opium. Smuggling was reported not only into Assam but also from Assam to the Hills district.[83] In 1899-1900, the consumption was reported to have touched the lowest figure on record (1,301 maunds) with only 750 shops settled against 1,397 shops settled in 1880-1 (and consumption of treasury opium being 1,686 maunds – a difference of 385 maunds). This entailed enormous loss of revenue to the Government to the tune of Rs. 5,69,800. With opium selling at

Rs. 37 a seer in Assam, opium smuggling proved a lucrative affair for the traders from the native states of Rajputana and the immigrants from Nepal. Government anxiety over 'illicit' importation is well reflected in a passage from the Excise Report for the same year, 'Smuggling must be enormous otherwise licensees could not afford to pay practically the same price for shops when the consumption of opium is 1,300 maunds as they did when the consumption was nearly 1,700 maunds. The fact that a license was a valuable asset to the smuggler of opium as it enabled him to dispose off the contraband article with comparative safety.'[84]

The formation of monopolies or syndicates of Marwari opium licensees against the Assamese and the Bengali licensees is well documented in official reports. An official statement mentions an 'important and influential Marwari' merchant, Harbilas Agarwala, who held licenses for two opium shops in the Dibrugarh subdivision and sold opium at 6½ *annas* per *tola*, in order to ruin other lessees, forcing them to lower their price. Instances were reported of inducements offered to the Deputy Commissioner of large license fees with a view to creating monopolies.

There was also a suspicion that the license was used as a cover under which foreign opium was smuggled into the province by the licensees themselves. The introduction of Malwa opium, which bore much resemblance to that used by the Marwaris in their native country, had apparently offered increased opportunities for defrauding the revenue. Names of a few Marwari merchants of Upper Assam, chiefly from Dibrugarh, Sibsagar and Lakhimpur – Chunia Agarwala, and Brahma Datta Agarwala of Dibrugarh, Pannalal and Chunnilal of Lakhimpur and Ramjas Agarwala of Sibsagar found mention in the official reports as accused of smuggling opium from Rajputana (area of Rajasthan) into Assam. Apart from the Marwaris, traders hailing from Afghanistan (they were called as *Kabuli* – as they hailed from Kabul province in Afghanistan) were actively promoting the opium trade. The 'Pathan coolies' – also from Kabul were believed to be their allies in the 'illicit' trade – particularly those employed on the Assam-Bengal Railway. The Gurkhas of Nepal were also suspected of bringing in Nepal opium for sale in Assam.[85] The Manipuris were also suspected of smuggling opium into Assam and

Burma. The opium manufactured locally in Manipur was popular due to its excellent quality and bore great similarity to the excise opium.[86] To stop the illicit traffic in opium and *ganja* between Manipur, Cachar and Burma, the prohibition of the cultivation of poppy and hemp was suggested along with arrangements for the sale within the state, of excise opium obtained from the Manipur treasury.[87] The Tibetan traders were also suspected of large illegal importation of Chinese opium.[88] Official enquiry mentioned the hill tribes, particularly the Rangpang Nagas near Margherita and the Miju and Digaru Mishimis on the Upper Lohit-Brahmaputra as chief consumers of Chinese opium brought by the Tibetan traders.[89] Excise officials also reported on smuggling of contraband and excise opium from the cheaper districts of Bengal and Behar. The illegal cultivation of opium in the districts of Nowgong, Sibsagar and Lakhimpur and the frontier tract of Sadiya by the hill tribes bordering the province, the use of short weights by retail vendors in the province, as well as instrumental in exposing the manufacture of opium had seriously affected the sales of treasury opium. Short weight sales as a system of fraud affected not only the treasury sales but also the poorer classes who were in the habit of spending a certain sum on their weekly supply of opium.

As early as 1895, the Bombay Government suggested the organization of a small detective department working under the authority of the agents to the Governor-General in communication with the various provincial police departments with a view to the suppression of the trade in opium smuggling.[90] Upon consultation, the heads of the local administration appeared divided in their opinion citing financial involvements as an important pre-condition for setting up an adequate establishment.[91]

Acknowledging the necessity to prevent the 'illicit trade' of opium in Assam, in 1899, P.G. Mellitus, proposed an enquiry to consider the feasibility of a special establishment to prevent smuggling. It was expected that the establishment would direct its attention to illicit sales, possession or retail sale in excess of limit, vendors not keeping accounts, etc. He proposed raising a 'frontier blockade'. Nevertheless, a section of official opinion was of the view that such a department would mean interference and cause harassment to the people owing to the difficulties of time and space, insufficient superior establishment and inexperience of district officers. They were in favour of the 'self-acting detective system' – the licensed vendors – who would in their own interest report any irregularity interfering with their profits.

In March 1907, with the sanction of the Government, a conference in Burma in order to discuss the question of opium smuggling and to devise means for its prevention was organized. A detailed report on the subject was submitted to the Government.[92] Detailed measures were proposed to ensure better cooperation between Burma, Bengal and Assam to halt illicit practices of retail vendors.[93] In 1912, in light of the questions dealt with in view of the recommendations of the Shanghai Opium Commission and the proposal for setting up of an 'Opium Smuggling Prevention Bureau', M.B. Comber and R.A. Stephen, in a report, held in official circles as 'most serious indictment of our excise opium system in India',[94] advocated uniformity of laws and increased vigilance over licensed opium vendors and sales. It stressed on greater inter-provincial co-operation and collaboration. It was also proposed to introduce a system of official vend of opium to add a harmless reagent to Excise opium in order to distinguish it from non-government opium.[95]

Conclusion

The twentieth century introduced a new phase of active propaganda against opium. Led by the medical men and the missionaries, the anti-opium lobby now led a virulent global campaign against the use of opium. The colonial power in India was forced to review its official stance in the wake of the emerging international narcotics control regime. A vital component of which was the curtailment of use and trade of opium and opiate based preparations, except under medical supervision. The reverberations were felt in Assam as well. The traditional use of opium was challenged and opium eating and smoking became signs of physical and mental decadence. The repercussions, however, created a crisis. It led to a rising use of *ganja*. *Ganja* had replaced opium as the 'drug of choice' by the mid-twentieth century. Cocaine made its way into the province. The stringent controls moreover drove the opium market underground and an illegal market now flourished. Huge seizures of cheap Nepalese, Malwa, China and even Afghan opium revealed how the official policy of restriction on opium use had boomeranged.

Notes

1. Amalendu Guha, *Medieval and Early Colonial Assam: Society, Polity, Economy*, Calcutta: K.P. Bagchi and Company, 1991, pp. 280–96.
2. Shrutidev Goswami, *Aspects of Revenue Administration in Assam, 1826-1874*, Delhi: Mittal Publications, 1987, p. 54.
3. A soil analysis by Piddington revealed certain peculiarities in the soils of Assam. It was found that the soil exhibited poor yellow loamy characteristics of soil quality. It contained no carbonate of lime and only traces of phosphate and sulphate. Iron was almost wholly absent in the state of carbonate of iron. Such soil was considered unsuitable for growing of cotton, tobacco, opium or sugar cane but was utterly conducive to the growth of the tea plant. H. Piddington, 'On the Soil Suitable for Cotton, Tobacco, Sugar and the Tea Plant', *Transactions of the Agricultural and Horticultural Society of India*, vol. 3, Calcutta: Baptist Mission Press, 1839, pp. 31-6.
4. In 1853, A.J. Moffat Mills, Judge of the Sudder Court on deputation to Assam, visited Goalpara, Gauhati, Lakhimpur, Nowgong, Sibsagar and Darrang. His administrative report is an invaluable historical document on all aspects of the conditions prevailing in the province in the early days of the British rule. A.J.M. Moffat Mills, *Report on the Province of Assam*, Guwahati: Publication Board, Assam, 1984 (rpt.), 20.
5. 'Treaty between the East India Company and Poorunder Singh, Raja of Assam, 1833.' Nagendra N. Acharya, *Historical Documents of Assam and Neighbouring States*, New Delhi: Omsons Publications, 1983, pp. 58-65.
6. Goswami, *Aspects of Revenue Administration in Assam*, pp. 54–60.
7. Jenkins believed that taxing the *bari* lands would provide a stimulus to the *ryots* to cultivate commercial crops as sugar cane, mustard, mulberry, lac and tobacco. It is interesting to note that tobacco production was sought to be encouraged as a substitute for opium as tobacco was believed to be 'less hurtful'. See, Goswami, *Aspects of Revenue Administration in Assam,* pp. 56–7.
8. Lands in Assam proper were divided into three classes, *basti* and *bari* (homestead land), *rupit* (low land fit for late rice) and *faringati* (high land fit for early rice and cold weather crops). See, Barpujari, *The Comprehensive History of Assam,* p. 23.

9. Appendix J, 'Observations on the Administration of the Province of Assam by Baboo Anandaram Dakeal Phookan', in the Mills, *Report on the Province of Assam*, pp. 110-11.
10. Mills, *Report on the Province of Assam,* 19.
11. On an 'experimental' and 'preparatory' basis, in 1844-5, *abkaree* (excise) opium was first introduced in the district of Goalpara, yielding a revenue of Rs. 59,450 in the year 1849-50. The Board of Customs, salt and opium intended to introduce the sale of Behar opium to undersell the native product. Although the tax was yet not general throughout the province, there was an excise duty on the sale of spirits and drugs at Sudder stations of Kamrup, Nowgong and Darrang. Goswami, *Report on the Revenue Administration of the Province of Assam*, pp. 42-4.
12. Mills, *Report on the Province of Assam,* pp. 19-22.
13. Malwa opium was opium grown in territories of the princely states, which were not under the direct control of the British administration. Opium grown in Malwa had posed a serious challenge to the monopoly trade of the East India Company. It is as much a story of challenge to the British capitalist enterprise as it led to the emergence of the Indian capitalist class. For details refer, Amar Farooqui, *Smuggling as Subversion: Colonialism, Indian Merchants and the Politics of Opium*, New Delhi: New Age International, 1998, pp. 6-7.
14. 'Correspondence from Deputy Commissioner's Office. Rangoon, 26th December 1852', *Friend of India* 4(1846).
15. Opium was already a contraband commodity in China and the British were themselves exploring avenues of routes for their commercial missions in China. *The Asiatic Journal and Monthly Miscellany* 23(1837).
16. Townshed identifies four possible motives that may influence a Government in considering the imposition of a particular tax. As (a) To exact from a certain class of citizens an equitable contribution as economically as possible (b) To minimize disadvantages due to inequalities of wealth (c) To divert consumption from noxious to wholesome commodities and (d) To divert production from one set of commodities to another for the sake of anticipated military, social, political or purely economic advantages. Refer, Meredith Townshed, *The Annals of Indian Administration*, vol. 4, Serampore: J.C. Murray, 1859, p. 240.
17. In a memorandum presented on 1 May 1857, the Assam Company urged upon the Governor-General to prohibit the cultivation of opium altogether. H.A. Antrobus, *A History of the Assam Company, 1839-1953*, London: T. and A. Constable, 1957.
18. Jenkins had expressed strong disapproval at any policy leading to immediate suppression and instead proposed to impose a tax. On fiscal grounds, C.W. Smith, Member of the Sadar Board of Revenue expressed his unwilling-

ness at Government's proposed interference in the cultivation of poppy, claiming that it would generate evils of oppression and bribery. Even Frederick Halliday, Lieutenant Governor of Bengal, believed that the prohibition would fail as a financial measure. Refer, Goswami, *Aspects of Revenue Administration in Assam, 1826-1874.*

19. Goswami, *Aspects of Revenue Administration in Assam, 1826-1874*, p. 58.
20. Guha, *Medieval and Early Colonial Assam*, pp. 280-96.
21. Measures included the prohibition of unlicensed sale, imposition of duty raised by gradual enhancements from Rs. 14 a seer; in 1860 to Rs. 37 a seer in 1890-1 and Rs. 40 in 1909-10, the imposition and enhancement of license fees and reduction in the number of retail shops. Annual Excise Administration Reports, ASA.
22. The quantity of crude opium that was lawful to sell retail to one person at one time was fixed at 5 *tolas* in Assam, Bengal and Berar. In Bombay and Central Provinces it was 2 *tolas*; in Madras it was 3 *tolas* [1 *tola* = 180 grains]. T.L. Seccombe, *Statement Exhibiting the Moral and Material Progress and Condition of India during the Year 1860-1*, London: John Edward Eyre and William Spottiswoode, 1862, p. 30.
23. Guha, *Medieval and Early Colonial Assam*, p. 284.
24. Henry T. Prinsep, *History of the Political and Military Transaction in India*, vol. 2, London: Kingsbury, Parley and Allen, 1825, p. 58.
25. John F. Richards, 'Opium and the British Indian Empire: The Royal Commission of 1895', *Modern Asian Studies* 36(2002): 375-420.
26. In his Memorandum to Moffat Mills, Anandaram Phukan advocated for the gradual suppression of the opium habit as he recognized it as a remedy against dysentery and warned against its sudden abolition, which would cause great difficulty to the people. A.J. Moffat Mills, 'Observations on the Administration of the Province of Assam by Baboo Anandaram Dakeal Phookun', pp. 110-11.
27. Around 106 km east of Guwahati and 17 km west of present day Nagaon district, the *ryots* of the small village of Phulaguri in Assam organized as is claimed, the first peasant revolt in Assam. It was less of an 'opium eater's revolt' and more of an outburst against the interference in their traditional ways of life. The introduction of exorbitant taxes had frayed the limits of their endurance and they rose in protest. The death of Lt. Singer was construed by the British as an unacceptable Act of crime committed by a savage nation and they unleashed terror among the people of the village. Mahendra N. Karna, *Agrarian Structures and Land Reform in Assam*, Shillong: North East Hill University, 2004, pp. 18-56.
28. Barpujari, *The Comprehensive History of Assam*, pp. 204-9.
29. Nearly one person in every village held a government license. In 1873-4, there were as many as 5,137 opium shops in Assam. The number of villages

in the Assam Valley according to the census of 1881 was 6,776. Thus, there was nearly the same number of shops as there were villages. *ACOECR*, 1925, p. 22.

30. Government of Bengal, *Annual Report on the Administration of the Bengal Presidency*, Calcutta: Bengal Secretariat Press, 1868, p. 177.
31. Ibid.
32. In his memorandum, Major Lees stated that between the years 1859-60 and 1864-5 the opium revenue had risen from Rs. 21,044 to 1,435,426 (the returns exhibiting an increase in consumption in the face of an increase in the price of the drug). He also points out that a large portion of the silver expended by the planters which was returned to the treasuries in payment for opium. *The Calcutta Review* 45(1867), pp. 172-3.
33. The rates of fees for licenses granted were Rs. 4 for 3 months, Rs. 7 for 6 months, Rs. 10 for 9 months and Rs. 12 for one year. *Annual Assam Administration Report 1876-7*, Shillong: Assam Secretariat Press, 1878, ASA.
34. The terms for the sale of opium *mehal* included (a) the purchaser of the *mehal* shall have the monopoly of sale within the plains part of the district (b) no more than fifty retail shops were to be allowed (c) the opium was to be purchased from the Treasury at Rs. 24 per seer (d) No new retail shop could be opened nor an existing shop be transferred without permission from the Deputy Commissioner (e) the licences for the retail shop were mentioned in the forms and no violation was permitted (f) 1/4th of the price was to be paid on the day of auction and the remaining 3/4th in installments (g) the Deputy Commissioner was invested with the power to annul the agreement for breach of its conditions and (h) in the event of the agreement being annulled for breach of its conditions, the security as well as the portions of the price paid in advance was liable to forfeiture.' Letter from H. Luttman-Johnson Officiating Deputy Commissioner of Cachar to The Secretary to the Chief Commissioner of Assam', Revenue Department, No. 15 R, 8 January 1877, ASA.
35. In the Assam valley, the area of a license was the *mauza* (revenue divisions) there being from three to five retail shops in each *mauza*. The settlements of opium shops were made in February and March every year. In December, the Deputy Commissioner prepared lists of shops of each class for the ensuing year. This was forwarded to the Commissioner of Excise for approval. When that was obtained, notices showing the dates of sale, sites of the proposed shops and the sanctioned upset prices were circulated throughout the district as also in the adjoining districts. The dates of sale were fixed in consultation with the Deputy Commissioner of the neighbouring districts so that the sales may not clash with each other and opportunity was hereby given to intending bidders in the other districts to be present at the sales. The rates on being completed were submitted to the Commissioner of Excise for confirmation and no settlement was

regarded as final unless confirmed by him. Government of Assam, *Annual Excise Administration Report for the Province of Assam 1874-75*, Shillong: Assam Secretariat Press, 1875, ASA.

36. The largest concentration of shops were reported in places which were trading centres of lac, cotton and mustard seeds, the market places (hats) in the vicinity of tea gardens and close to the Mikir hills.
37. *ACOECR*, 1925, p. 22.
38. In 1860, the price charged was Rs. 14 a seer, in 1862 it was Rs. 20, in 1863 it was Rs. 22, in 1873 Rs. 23, in 1875 Rs. 24, in 1879 Rs. 26, in 1883 it was Rs. 32 and in 1890 it was Rs. 37. Government of Bengal. *Annual Report on the Administration of Bengal Presidency of Calcutta*, Calcutta: Bengal Secretariat Press, 1865.
39. It refers to a house where opium was sold and consumed in a gathering. Benudhar Kalita, *Opium Production in Assam in Phulagurir Dhewa (The Uprising at Phulaguri)*, Deurigaon: Nowgong, 1861, pp. 48-53.
40. The SSOT in a memorandum submitted to the imperial government in Britain, alleged 'houses licensed by the Government in many towns of India for smoking opium and its products on the premises were causes of great demoralisation'. 'A Memorial Submitted to the Right Honourable Viscount Cross, Her Majesty's Principal Secretary of State for India,' no. 68 (Revenue), 30 July 1890, NAI.
41. 'Letter from F.C. Daukes, Secretary to the Chief Commissioner of Assam to The Secretary to the Government of India.' Finance and Commerce Department, no. 466 Revenue, 31 January 1891, NAI.
42. 'Letter from Colonel William Agnes, Officiating Commissioner of Assam to the Officiating Secretary of the Board of Revenue Lower Provinces', no. 117, 1870, NAI.
43. Official narratives mention of a great decrease in the number of petty thefts, following the introduction of Government opium. 'Correspondence from A.J. Moffat Mills to Cecil Beadon, Secretary to the Government of Bengal', 24 July 1853. Mills, *Report on the Province of Assam,* pp. 56-280.
44. Baulmer, *The Chinese and Opium under the Republic*, p. 69.
45. Timothy Brook and Bob Tadashi Wakabayashi, *Opium Regimes: China, Britain and Japan 1839-1952*, Oakland, California: University of California Press, 2000, p. 100.
46. Refer to Appendix III – List of opium *mehals* in the Sudder subdivision of Kamrup for the year 1877-8 sold in public auction as on 29 March 1877. 'Letter from S.O.B. Risdale, Secretary to the Chief Commissioner of Assam to the Deputy Commissioner of Assam Proper', 13 March 1877, ASA.
47. Ganguly, *An Economic History of North East India,* pp. 8-12.
48. By an order from the Chief Commissioner, separate opium licenses for the tea gardens were not permissible. Planters were required to purchase

mehals or arrange with purchasers for the establishment of shops. 'Letter from Secretary to the Chief Commissioner to Nowgong Deputy Commissioner. Assam Chief Commissionership 1877', no. 875, ASA.

49. *Report on Administration of the Excise Department in Assam*, 1882, 11.
50. Ibid.
51. The Government, however, had its own reasons. By settling shops individually with different persons, it attempted at playing one lessee against the other. Moreover, in the absence of any preventive establishment, it would afford greater facilities for smuggling and would be difficult to restrain. A monopoly in one year also increased the difficulties of settlements in the next. The Government was also anxious of losing revenue as a monopoly could induce 'smuggling and Secret Use of Drugs'. 'Letter from A.W. Davis, Commissioner of Excise Assam to the Secretary to the Chief Commissioner of Assam', no. 1015, *Report on the Administration of the Excise Department for the Year 1899-1900*, Shillong: Assam Secretariat Press, 1901, ASA.
52. It was expected that the number of chests for export to China would increase by around 3,000 chests up from 1,374 chests of opium that were exported to China in 1882. The Malwa Excise scheme had been suggested by Mr. Carnac and was sanctioned by the Government in 1882 to set free a larger quantity of Bengal opium for export. 'Letter from Government of Bengal,' *Finance and Commerce*, no. 89024, September 1883, NAI.
53. It was suggested that the opium be made into *abkaree* (excise) at Ghazeepore, getting rid of as much of the oil as possible and then to have it sent down to Calcutta to be disposed of to the best advantage. It was decided to limit the purchase of the Malwa drug to 2,000 maunds until greater success had been obtained in the experiment and in case the yield of Bengal opium turn out to be unsatisfactory. 'Note by Mr. Reynolds on Malwa Abkari Opium. Proceedings of the Finance and Commerce Department.' July 1883, Pros. no. 953, *Finance and Commerce*, 15 March 1883, NAI.
54. *Statement Exhibiting the Moral and Material Progress and Condition of India*, 11.
55. Evidence of J.D. Anderson, Deputy Commissioner Darrang before the Royal Commission on Opium. July 1894. *Finance and Commerce*, nos. 12-126, ASA.
56. 'The Humble Memorial of the Jorhat Sorvajonik Sabha, From The President and Secretary, Jorhat Sorvajonik Sabha To William Erskine Ward, Chief Commissioner of Assam.' RCO, 1893, Appendix XXXVI.
57. See RCO, 1893.
58. Saikia, *Social and Economic History of Assam, 1853-1921*, pp. 213-21.
59. 'Letter from the Officiating Secretary to the Chief Commissioner of Assam

to The Secretary to the Government of India', *Finance and Commerce*, 16 April 1896, ASA

60. It was also cited by the Local Governments that prohibition had been imposed in 1891 in respect to smoking opium in shops, which was calculated to gradually extinguish the practice. *Report on the Administration of the Excise Department in Assam for the Year 1892*, ASA.
61. Charles Henry Brent (April 1862 to 27 March 1929) was an American Episcopal bishop who served in the Philippines and western New York. He served on several international commissions to stop narcotic traffic.
62. On the report of the Opium Commission, the Government of India requested all Local Governments to cease to license shops for the sale of preparations of opium used for smoking commonly known as *madak* and *chandu*, while not attempting to prevent the manufacture of such preparations by individuals for the purposes of private consumption and legislate against the use of premises for opium smoking either by the public generally or by so-called clubs. 'Letter from W.M. Hailey, Deputy Secretary to the Government of India to the Secretary to the Government of Eastern Bengal and Assam,' *Separate Revenue*, no. 5396, 25 October 1909, ASA.
63. 'Letter from Secretary to the Board of Revenue, Eastern Bengal and Assam to the Secretary to the Government of India', *Finance Department*, no. 1713EX-T, 20 October 1910, ASA.
64. The year 1901-2 was the year in which opium consumption in the Assam valley reached its lowest ebb. *Report on the Administration of the Excise Department in Assam for the Year 1901-02,* ASA.
65. 'Letter from Major W.M. Kennedy, Commissioner of Excise and Salt, Eastern Bengal and Assam to the Secretary to the Board of Revenue, Eastern Bengal and Assam', no. 4885E, 27 September 1910, ASA.
66. Excise Commissioner's Letter No. 2314 E of 17 July 1908 to the Secretary to the Board of Revenue submitted to Government with the Board's letter of 9 January 1909, ASA.
67. Jim Mills in his exposition of the cannabis use in India refers to an 88 per cent increase in the consumption of cannabis preparations between 1901 and 1911, a 34 per cent increase in consumption, which he asserts, was far in excess of any increase in population. For further details, refer to, Jim H. Mills, *Cannabis Britannica: Empire, Trade and Prohibition, 1800-1928*, Oxford: Oxford University Press, 2003.
68. 'Letter from J.T. Rankin, Secretary to the Board of Revenue, East Bengal and Assam to the Secretary to the Government of Eastern Bengal and Assam', Municipal Department, no. 244 Ex/T, 27 May 1910, ASA.
69. In The Hague Convention of January of 1912, the gradual suppression of opium smoking was agreed upon; the use of manufactured narcotic drugs

(morphine, cocaine, etc.) was limited to medical and legitimate purposes and their manufacture, trade and use were made subject to a system of permits and recording. This Convention changed the obligation on its participants to cooperate in the international campaign against the drug evil from a moral obligation to a duty under international law. Hamilton Wright. 'The International Opium Conference', *The American Journal of International Law*, 6(1912): 865-89.

70. Centres at Gauhati, Nalbari, Barpeta, Kalaigaon, Mangaldoi, Tezpur, Dibrugarh, Dumduma, Dakshipur, Sonas, Nazira, Sibsagar, Jorhat, Golaghat, Dinajpur, Kamrup and Nowgong. Commissioners, Deputy Commissioners, tea garden managers and the Adhikar Gossains of the leading *sattras* were consulted by the Committee, *Botham Committee Report*, 1913, p. 1.
71. The proposed prohibition was to extend even to two persons smoking together, an exception being made only in the case of husband and wife. *Botham Committee Report*, pp. 2-3.
72. *Botham Committee Report*, p. 7.
73. 'Letter from A.W. Botham, Second Secretary to the Chief Commissioner of Assam to The Secretary to the Government of India', Department of Commerce and Industry, no. 7939 M, 29 November 1913, NAI.
74. *Botham Committee Report*, 1913, p. 7.
75. For details, refer, 'The Abolition of Opium Smoking in India', *Bulletin on Narcotics*, Issue 3: 1-7, Geneva: United Nations Office on Drugs and Crime, 1957.
76. Telegram to the Secretary of State for India, no. 1226-G.D, 12 March 1917, NAI.
77. Excise-A February 1916, nos. 10-11. Proceedings of the Department of Commerce and Industry, 1916, NAI.
78. Saikia, *Social and Economic History of Assam,* p. 296.
79. The Excise Reports ascribed the high figures to the increase in the issues of opium taken out by dealers in anticipation of the rise, which was enforced.
80. The plains population was broadly divided into the tea 'coolies' the 'Sylhetias' and the Assamese. The use of country spirits was presumed to be confined to the 'coolies', *ganja* to the Muslim population of Sylhet and Cachar and use of opium, to the Assamese. Extract from the Proceedings of the Chief Commissioner of Assam, *Revenue Department*, no. 1876, 6 November 1882, ASA.
81. The Marwaris handled most of the opium trade in Upper Assam districts in the nineteenth and twentieth centuries.
82. The findings of *ACOECR*, 1925, had asserted that the real danger to the country districts of Assam was not so much from the internal cultivation of poppy as from the smuggling of opium into the country from outside,

especially the Malwa opium which was brought in by the traders and the merchants. *ACOECR*, 1925, p. 44.

83. Opium was suspected to have been smuggled from Sibsagar to the Naga Hills. *ACOECR*, 1925, p. 36.
84. 'Mr. Mellitus's Note dated 12 October 1899, regarding the entertainment of a preventive establishment to check opium smuggling and other illicit practices.' Deposit-R, no. 40, November 1899, ASA.
85. C.J. Lyall, *Extract from the Proceedings of the Chief Commissioner of Assam in the Revenue Department*, no. 3226, 17 September 1887, ASA.
86. 'Letter from L-Colonel P. Maxwell, Political Agent Manipur to the Secretary to the Chief Commissioner of Assam', no. 92 X, 21 May 1904, NAI. However, the Superintendent of Manipur in his report on the cultivation of opium in Manipur regarded that the outturn of the opium crop cultivated in Manipur, chiefly by the Mahomedan population, was not sufficient enough to affect the consumption of the drug in the British territory. About 3½ seers of opium were obtained from 1 *bigha* of poppy cultivation. Locally grown opium was sold in Manipur at the rate of 3 *tolas* a rupee, nearly Rs. 27 a seer. Enquiries tend to show that in ordinary years about 15 maunds of opium were obtained in Manipur from a cultivation of 192 bighas of land. The cost of producing a seer of opium could not be more than Rs. 7, so the drug could very easily be sold for much less than Rs. 27 were the price not regulated by some competition outside the small local demand. The annual local demand was estimated at about 7½ maunds with an additional stock of 7½ maunds which was meant to be disposed either in Assam or Burma. It was held that there being no restriction to the growth of poppy and the manufacture of opium there from Manipur, the quantity grown for export would be greater than 7½ maunds. 'Letter from F.J. Monahan, Secretary to the Chief Commissioner of Assam to the Secretary to the Government of India', *Finance and Commerce Department*, no. 684-2880, 11 August 1904, NAI.
87. 'Letter from J. Campbell, Under-Secretary to the Government of India, Finance and Commerce Department to The Honourable Chief Commissioner of Assam', no. 6782 Ex., 26 October 1904, NAI.
88. 'Letter from J.T. Rankin, Secretary to the Board of Revenue, Eastern Bengal and Assam to The Secretary to the Government of Eastern Bengal and Assam', *Financial Department*, no. 1427 Ex.-T, 18 August 1908.
89. 'Note by Mr. Williamson, Assistant Political Officer, Sadiya in the Annual Administration Report of the Excise Department in the Province of Eastern Bengal and Assam', 1908-9, ASA, p. 15.
90. 'Letter from The Lieutenant Colonel D.W.K. Barr Officiating Agent to the Governor General in Central India to the Secretary to the Government of India', Foreign Department, no. 2127, March 1895, NAI.

91. 'Letter From The Agent to the Governor-General in Central India.' Diary no. 85-I (a) no. 2127-G, 15 March 1895, ASA.
92. 'Letter from F.P. Dixon, Officiating Secretary to the Board of Revenue, Eastern Bengal and Assam to The Secretary to the Government of Eastern Bengal and Assam.' Financial Department, no. 433, T. Excise, 26 August 1907, ASA.
93. 'Letter from Captain W.M. Kennedy, Commissioner of Excise and Salt, Eastern Bengal and Assam to The Secretary to the Board of Revenue.' *Eastern Bengal and Assam*, no. 1918E, 10 July 1907, ASA.
94. 'Report by Messrs. M.B. Comber and R.A. Stephen on the Subject of Opium Smuggling from India to Burma', *Separate Revenue* 'A', nos. 40-2, February 1912, NAI.
95. 'Letter from the Government of Burma', no. 2396 M-SE 7, 18 November 1910, NAI.

CHAPTER 6

Opium Reduction Campaign: 1921-1938

By 1920, THE anti-opium crusade in Assam had acquired national recognition, a new crusader, a new temper and a new dimension. The non-cooperation resolution for Assam, passed at the instance of M.K. Gandhi, had as it's goal the promotion of temperance among the people of Assam, through voluntary effort and public propaganda. This was a marked departure from one of much interpreted and questioned silence of the Indian National Congress on the opium question during the tour of the Royal Commission on Opium in 1893.[1] The changing political contours resulted in a reorientation in the social life of the Assamese middle class. Already a credible force on the social landscape, the Assamese intelligentsia was now besotted with a new fervour.[2] This 'trend of radicalisation within the Assamese middle class', as Guha remarks, was marked by the ascension of a new breed of Assamese nationalists who believed in action oriented political agitation.[3] Most of them were members of the Assam Association. With its inception in 1903, the Assam Association had significantly articulated the political aspirations of 'Western-educated Assamese elite'. Highly oriented in their initial stages to the moderate line of political thinking, the early leaders of the Assam Association – Gangagovinda Phukan, Ghanshyam Barua, Kamakhyaram Barua, Chandradhar Barua and Taraprasad Chaliha – stood opposed to the idea of a mass movement. They were votaries of Assamese 'sub-nationalist sentiment' and held that any such move would dilute that ideal. Such a stand received further momentum with the formation of the Axom Chhatra Sanmilan (Assam Students Conference) in 1916 and the Axom Sahitya Sabha in 1917. Uncertainty and disillusionment, however, prevailed and exacerbated differences amongst two factions within the Assam Association until members of the Assam Association headed by Nabin Chandra Bordoloi (1875-1936)[4] met M.K. Gandhi at the Nagpur session of the Indian National Congress (INC). After his second meeting with Gandhi at Calcutta, he turned from a *cooperator* to a *non-cooperator.* The Association declared that the movement in Assam would aim at the restriction and limitation of excise articles and promotion of *khadi* and *swadeshi* goods. At the insistence of the Assamese Congressmen, at the Nagpur session of the INC in December 1920, Assam was recognized as a separate Congress Province.[5] In the very same year, in accordance with the provisions of the Government of India Act of 1919, Assam was given the status of a Governor's province.

The prominent votaries of the new spirit of action oriented political campaign as Chandranath Sharma (1889-1922), Ambikagiri Raychaudhari (1885-1967), poet and litterateur, Tarun Ram Phookan, Nabin Chandra Bordoloi, Trigunacharan Barua, Kanak Chandra Sharma, Padmanath Jain, K. Chaliha and many others led meetings at various districts as Sibsagar, Jorhat, Dibrugarh and Nowgong, explaining and convincing the masses that 'Assam must remain in the mainstream of nationalist politics, she could not remain aloof'.[6]

The Bardoli decision (1922) of Gandhi, following the Chauri-Chaura violence disillusioned nationalist workers. As the fervour of mass upsurge was 'killed' and this 'failure' resulted in a reorientation of strategies. Following the withdrawal of the Non-Cooperation movement in 1922, the legislature was employed as a powerful platform for propaganda and influence Council politics in Assam was instilled with fresh vigour.[7] Both the non-cooperators in the Congress and the Swarajists bound in a symbiotic relationship were more determined than ever to 'defeat the government' and push for reforms. Under the surcharged political atmosphere, opium took the centre stage as international activism emboldened. Council sessions witnessed vehement protest against the downplaying of the large extent of opium smoking and came down heavily on the Government of Assam for it's complacency as regards a plausible solution of the opium menace in the province. Legislative activism was directed against the discrepancies that could be discerned in the colonial opium policy of *Maximum Revenue and Minimum Consumption.* The Legislative Council where opium policies were discussed and resolutions were debated, give a good indication of how legislative intervention had added momentum to the anti-opium campaign. Opium was enmeshed in the changing contours of nationalist politics and its eradication a matter of recouping provincial pride. A great impetus to the movement came from international activism that was initiated by the League of Nations. This arose out of concern of a global proliferation of opium abuse further strengthened domestic enforcement efforts.

Drive Out Opium and get me *Swaraj*

With Gandhi's clarion call to shun all intoxicants – opium, *ganja*, liquor, etc., the anti-opium agitation in Assam was enthused with a new spirit of an awakening. Being an avid reader as he was, Gandhi was aware of the devastation that opium had caused in China and had been tremendously influenced by the work of Ellen LaMotte (1873-1961).[8]Abhorrence of drinks and drugs was included as an agenda of the constructive programme of the Non-Cooperation movement. It was on his personal insistence following his meeting with the leaders from Assam that temperance promotion became the anchor of the Satyagraha movement in the province. This gave a boost to the anti-opium agitation in the province. Gandhi's action *packed* programme appealed to the young minds, who participated with fervour in picketing shops selling liquor, opium and *ganja.*

Promotion of temperance while adhering to the principle of non-violence was a unique achievement and received tremendous appreciation. The ceaseless campaign by the local Congress volunteers had enabled the buildup of a massive public opinion against the use of intoxicants. Student participation under the aegis of Asom Chhatra Sanmilan enthusiastically supported the resolution for boycott and temperance adopted by the All India Students Conference at Nagpur in December 1920.[9] This further served to validate and strengthen elite activism in Assam which had specifically aimed at political consciousness of the masses. Students under the vibrant leadership of Congress leaders – Chandranath Sharma, Ambikagiri Raychaudhary, Trigunacharan Barua and Muhibuddin Ahmad toured villages, persuading the people to give up intoxicants that were responsible for the ruin of Assam and its people. A *Kani Nibarikaran Andolan* (Give up Opium Campaign) was launched at their behest. *Kani Nibarani Samitis* (Opium Prohibition Societies) and Anti-Intoxication League[10] were organized, which had as its aim the education of people into temperance voluntarily and not by coercion. Managers of tea gardens and in some cases even the European owners of the tea gardens set up or facilitated the formation of temperance units,[11] which is also a unique facet of the movement. Youth participation ensured that each village in the districts had their temperance units. In their lectures to the masses, the leaders appealed for boycott of excise opium, *ganja*, liquor and cigarettes, which were 'tools of imperialism' that had brought Assam on the brink of poverty and effeminacy. The functionality of the message of 'charkha and temperance' can be gauged from the emergence of a wave of antipathy among the public for all excise articles and foreign cloth. The need for suppression of all intoxicants became a commonplace of nationalist rhetoric in Assam. The Act of renouncing and denunciation of *ganja* pipes and opium hookahs began to be perceived as a sign of freedom from colonial bondage. Purged of the noxious habit, the suffering masses were to prepare for self-rule, as N.C. Bordoloi claimed how the temperance movement had 'practically concentrated in them the progressive realisation of the highest ideals of freedom, morality and sacrifice for the country'.[12] Gandhi's visit to Assam and the strenuous agitation of the temperance workers had resulted in a drop in the opium consumption by nearly 26 per cent.[13] Gandhi's close comrade, C.F. Andrews asserted, 'Assam is no longer the "black spot of India" as it was in the previous years.' Official reports though, had a different story to tell. The fall in the consumption of opium claimed to have resulted due to measures taken by the Government.[14]

The Non-Cooperation movement was in a sense, only the beginning of a long yet phased struggle, against driving out the 'opium evil' which was later to be fought on the floor of the

Legislature in Assam. However, with the Non-Cooperation agitation, the Congress was elevated into a mass political platform. The demand to revamp the official excise policies was high on the agenda of the Council. Legislative Council members including Congress leaders, Kuladhar Chaliha, Rohini Kanta Hatibarua, Taraprasad Chaliha, Maulvi Faiznur Ali and Sarbeswar Barua took up the mantle of reform in the legislatures and the administration of the Excise department was attacked, with some success, during the Non-Cooperation movement. Unmoved by government indifference, in 1920-1, Nichols Roy (1884-1959)[15] in response to the Council deliberation on excise matters, moved a resolution in the Council in March 1921. The resolution sought, (i) a total prohibition of the sale of opium except to present *bonafide* opium-consumers on medical prescription, (ii) introduction of a system of personal registration only for a limited time fixed according to circumstances for such registration after which no new names will be registered, and (iii) shop rations and personal registration were to be decreased every year such that in 10 years time the whole opium trade in Assam was to be 'abolished together'.

A census of opium eaters was conducted in 1921.[16] The Government introduced rationing of all opium shops from 1 April 1921.[17] The commissioners were empowered to authorize deputy commissioners to vary from time to time the ration of any individual shop. Although the Government had clearly laid down that under no circumstances the rations fixed for each district was to be superseded,[18] there were instances when the government allowed relaxations citing inconvenience of the consumers due to insufficient rations.[19] The government, perplexed at the vigorous anti-opium agitation introduced certain administrative changes in the excise regulations. In supersession of the practice of realizing two months fees in advance at the time of settlement, the system of depositing a certain sum, not less than one month's fee, as security by the vendors of excise and opium shops settled under the vend fee system was introduced. The system of *restricted auction* of excise and opium shops was abolished. In order to restrain malpractices, license holders of *ganja* and opium shops were ordered to keep scales of approved pattern and to weigh the drug in the presence of the purchasers.[20] As an experimental measure, a system of settling shops by tenders in the district of Sibsagar was also introduced.

Becoming an Agenda of the Congress Agitation

Following the withdrawal of the Non-Cooperation movement in 1922, the legislative politics became a powerful platform for propaganda and influence of the Assamese nationalists. More so, with the formation of the Swaraj party, a new element of activism was introduced in the campaign for *Swaraj*. Although it needs to be mentioned that most of the European and Assamese members had vested economic interests and stake in the administration, the party clearly lacked a 'populist base.' Ambiguity in the functioning of the ministers was reflected well enough with a number of members unwilling to obstruct the working of the Council. They were desirous of participation in discussions on important policy matters. Opium appeared as a convenient 'political' issue. Already, the constructive programme of the Non-Cooperation movement had amply displayed the mass fervour and cooperation that it aroused. Though criticized for its 'lackluster performance' and 'poor legislative output', it did succeed in ensuring that the Government agree to open a annual register for opium eaters. In opium, the nationalists had found 'imperialism's weakest link' and they were not to let go of this opportunity. The consolidation of the international narcotics control regime had further emboldened them to pursue a course of confrontation with the colonial rulers. The Government could not choose to play truant, which could result in potential damage to legitimacy in the international arena. To the Councillors, their opinion against opium was an expression of the public opinion against its use, yet on many occasions it was not able to influence the government. Whatever reforms were carried out can be safely adjudged as 'by-product' of the agitation of the Non-Cooperation movement. The Government agreed to open a register of opium eaters although it refused to implement a time-bound programme of eradication. The Council decried 'foul play' by the Government's move at opening of the registers with reports of large-scale malpractices threatening to erode the credibility of the system. Nilmoni Phukan, the Assamese nationalist and fiery orator, apprised the Council of the efficacy of the *Sadiya System*, 'No Pass Book, No Opium.'[21] He suggested the introduction of the *Sadiya System* for rationing the opium eaters of the Assam. He also called for the appointment of a committee of official and non-official members for investigating and introducing effective legislations against smoking of opium on the evidence collected for the purpose.

The Government, however, ignored these suggestions. Nevertheless, the Council carried on its relentless struggle against the official opium policies and members continued to assert the various issues in curtailing opium consumption in the valley. Nilmoni Phukan brought to notice, the issue of short-weight opium, particularly in the Dibrugrah subdivision, carried on with the connivance of the *mahaldar* and sales clerk under the contract system. He asked for the matter to be investigated by appointing a joint committee of the Local Advisory Committee and the Excise Department.[22] Towards the end of March 1924, 'Excise' had been classified as a 'Provincial' subject in the major provinces of India, though in Assam, it continued to remain a 'Transferred' subject until 1928. Although the Government of India held the view that provinces should solve their own excise problems, it was in mood to forego its official control and stressed on continued cooperation between the Local and the Central Government. This question first received attention in 1921 when as a sequel to the examination of India's position in relation to the 1912 Hague Opium Convention; the Department of Commerce in a correspondence of 6 April 1921, called to consider the desirability of controlling the practice of opium smoking by provincial legislation. It declared that, 'To ensure that the independent action of this kind would not prejudice the harmonious working of the Excise Administration as a whole, it appears to the Government of India to be desirable that every province should keep in close and constant touch with fresh developments in the other provinces so that each may know where it stands.'[23]

Urging strong action to contain the menace of drug addiction, a petition signed by about 400 persons representing the societies over which they presided, on behalf of 206 members, was sent from

India. Among the signatories were M.K. Gandhi, C.F. Andrews, Rabindranath Tagore, Ramanada Chatterji, Ferrain Benolt, H.C. Morris, Balvir Singh and Kana Karayan Paul, which read,

[...] the undersigned, viewing in the growing addiction to narcotic drugs a deadly menace to individuals and nations, an insidious rapidly-spreading poisoning of the human race, which can be overcome only by cooperation among all nations, respectfully petition the International Opium Conferences ... to adopt measures adequate for the total extirpation of the plants from which they originate, except as found necessary for medicine and science in the judgment of the best medical opinion of the world.[24]

This was a 'sufficient answer' to the representative of the Government of India to the Geneva Conference in 1923, who remarked on the total indifference of the Indian leaders including M.K. Gandhi towards the entire opium question. In the Imperial Assembly at Delhi, in March 1925, during the debate on the opium question, Basil Blackett, the Finance Minister held out the hope that if the local governments agreed, the Government might be willing to hold an enquiry by a representative to see if any changes might be necessary, 'What is the new opium policy to which the leaders of the Indian thought are looking forward?' They objected to the fact that opium had been declared a 'transferred subject' in which people's choice should prevail. The delegate to Geneva had been appointed by the Executive power and not by the Legislative Assembly. They also strongly objected to the delegate chosen to represent India.

In Assam, dominated as it was by the Congress *Swarajists*, the Second Reformed Council (1924-6) failed to play any constructive role as it merely wavered between 'effective obstruction' and 'responsive cooperation'.[25] Meanwhile, over increasing voices of dissent on the opium policy pursued by the Government, on 3 March 1924, the Council accepted the resolution of Congress representative, Kuladhar Chaliha who recommended immediate legislation to prohibit the consumption and sale of opium in Assam, except for medical and scientific purposes. His demand was further strengthened by the resolution of the 1925 Geneva Narcotics Conference.[26]

The Indian representatives to the 1925 Opium conference at Hague led by Surendra Kumar Datta[27] (1878-1948) of the Imperial Legislative Assembly were appalled by the conduct of the official Indian representative at the World Conference on Opium, John Campbell's 'policy of obstruction'.[28] Dr. S.K. Datta, Pandit M.M. Malviya and Pandit Motilal Nehru openly expressed their displeasure with the official explanations for the mess at Geneva. They argued that they would willingly forfeit the opium revenue that is obtained out of this disreputable traffic.

Echoing the view of S.K. Datta, in the Assam Legislative Council, Congress member Rohini Kanta Hatibarua, sought an appraisal to be addressed to the Government of India over the incongruity of views expressed by Campbell.[29] In Assam, opium smoking was prevalent to a considerable extent.[30] The tension engendered by the misquote had hardly subsided when Assam was declared 'Black Spot' with consumption in excess of the League of Nations standard at 30 seers per ten thousand of population (for India)[31] which led to a demand by the Congress for an appraisal of the scenario of opium consumption in the province.

In 1925, the Report of the Botham Committee was made public at the insistence of the members of the Congress leaders of Assam. The report revealed much novel information on the patterns of opium and *ganja* consumption in Assam. Apart from this, there were many private and semi-official investigations, which included those made by the National Christian Council of India, Burma and Ceylon and this resulted in fresh evidence regarding opium consumption in many of the provincial districts of India. The figures based on the official government statistics for 1922-3 presented by S.K. Datta in the Imperial Legislative Assembly in March 1925, put an entirely new complexion to the overall problem of the internal consumption of opium in India. Meanwhile, the Joint Health and Opium Committee in the League of Nations laid down an index figure for medical consumption of opium. This index figure generally accepted as a standard sets it at 30 seers per ten thousand of population for India. In Assam, the figures were much higher than the standard set by the League.[32]

The Assam Congress Opium Enquiry Committee 1925

Confounded at having the 'blackest records in India', the Assam Provincial Congress Committee recommended a 'non-official' enquiry into the opium habits of the people of Assam and the effect upon them of the opium policy of the Government. The All India Congress Committee (AICC) appointed C.F. Andrews to conduct an enquiry in collaboration with the Assam Provincial Congress Committee.

The Assam Congress appointed a leading Assamese Congressman Kuladhar Chaliha as the President and Rohini Kanta Hatibaruah as Secretary. The other members of the committee were, C.F. Andrews, Tarun Ram Phookan, Nabinchandra Bordoloi, Krishnanath Sarmah, Ambikagiri Raychaudhary and Omeo Kumar Das. The report discussed in detail each facet of the opium problem in Assam. To the Congress in Assam, the report was a great legislative victory. They were able to influence both national and local opinion of their commitment to deal with the 'scourge of humanity' in consonance with the International Opium Conventions. Opium became a celebrated legislative issue and the Congress declaration of the 'desire to set our country entirely free from the opium habit', earned it wide acknowledgement and political acceptance among the people of the province. The Report endorsed the restriction of consumption to medical and scientific needs and the need of 'education of public opinion' and 'a great anti-opium campaign to be carried on by entire peaceful means'.[33] The Report also advocated the promotion of anti-opium associations and temperance societies to carry on the temperance propaganda. In consonance with the prevailing international opinion and in conformity with the evolving notion of addiction as a disease, the Report recommended all opium addicts to be treated as medical patients.[34] It affirmed that, 'the Indian non-official members of the Legislative Council are practically unanimous in condemning the opium excise policy and look forward to a time-limit for non-medical consumption and to an immediate registration of confirmed addicts'.[35] The Report had succeeded in creating an 'identifiable social awareness' and envisaged the remedy of the opium evil to lie in total prohibition. It reported on the consensus prevalent in Assam as regards prohibition. 'All are for prohibition', it declared, 'only questions with regard to the time limit for final prohibition vary slightly'. The futility of the Government opium policy had been amply portrayed in its failure to contain the consumption, which 'merely wavered, now going up and now going down'.[36]

In 1925, the Assam Opium Smoking Bill was introduced. Drastic measures were implemented to enforce registration of consumers and strict rationing of opium and subjecting it to stringent administrative regulations.[37] Strict surveillance over the system was to be ensured by the officials of the excise and revenue department. Rohini Kanta Hatibaruah and Maulvi Faiznur Ali apprised the Council of the harassment of the opium eaters due to the malpractices resorted to by the Excise staff. They demanded an enquiry into the system of leasing of the opium shops.[38] These revelations invited a flurry of dissent in the Council as regards the Excise administration. To Sadananda Dowerah, the method of settling opium shops was, 'a scandal . . . an open secret', to which the Government owed both responsibility and explanation.[39] Supporting the motion to distribute opium rations by Government agency, which would stem the illicit contraband opium sales and remedy the rot in the Excise department, he suggested the issue of opium to the agents in sealed packets as a remedy to the issue of short-weight of opium. The Planters constituency representative, W.K. Karren opined in favour of the *ticket system* introduced by the Government and called for a year's trial of the scheme before being finally implemented. The Government was not prepared to accept the resolution and it was voted out.

Gauhati hosted the forty-first Congress session from 26 to 28 December 1926. In his inaugural address, Tarun Ram Phookan as Chairman of the Reception Committee of the Session, referred to 'willful slow poisoning of the people of Assam' by the unjustifiable excise policies of the colonial government.[40] Opium policies, however, did not figure as an agenda during the session. Nevertheless, with the Gauhati session of the INC, the Assam Pradesh Congress Committee (APCC) acquired a popular mass base. Meanwhile, the controversy over the Assam Opium Smoking Bill was carried on also in the columns of the Press. The *Times of Assam* in two successive issues in 1926 vigorously opposed the principle of the Government Bill on opium smoking in Assam.[41] The *Asamiya* carried reports on the congregation of villagers in Kolongpar (Nagaon), under the aegis of the 'Kolongpar Ryot Sabha' and of the opium eaters, the 'Kania Samajai Mel' in Chapaguri where the contents of the Bill were discussed and debated. It reported on 18 opium eaters surrendering their pass with a pledge never to touch opium ever in their lives. The *ryot* sabha also expressed its satisfaction at the Bill aimed at doing away with opium that had wrought destruction upon Assam.[42] Concerns about the efficacy of the regulative efforts were voiced also by the *Asamiya*, which reported the swelling in number of the opium consumers and the perversion of the use of passes for securing increased issues of opium from the treasury and selling it to *gupptokaniyas*.[43] It stressed on the need of consulting local opinion.[44] It appealed to the Council to relook into the pass-system and concluded with a dismal appraisal of the increase in the number of consumers,

> Those who had given up opium during the non-cooperation days have again reverted to the habit. Besides, the *mahaldars* are indulging in illicit practices, which has boosted the sales of opium and swelled the number of opium consumers. It is pathetic. If such illicit practices are allowed to continue unabated, how would Assam be ever free from the scourge of opium? We appeal to the Council to give a serious thought to the issue. (Translation mine.)[45]

An important precondition to ensuring the effectiveness of the laws aimed at curbing the spread of the habit was inter-provincial collaboration. The high price of excise opium in Assam had resulted in smuggling[46] of cheap and also adulterated opium from the Central Provinces. At the inter-provincial conference held in 1926, representatives from Assam and Bihar at the Inter-Provincial Conference on Excise Policy[47] complained of rampant smuggling from Nepal. It was brought to the notice of the Conference that the restrictive policy had served to replace 'licit' opium with 'illicit' supplies from the states of Rajputana and Central India. However, Punjab, Ajmer and Central Indian representatives were unanimous that the uniformity of retail prices was a pre-requisite to curb smuggling – while in other states the retail price of opium was in the range of Rs. 23 to 50 a seer, in Assam, opium was being retailed at Rs. 140 a seer, while there were buyers for smuggled opium at Rs. 280 a seer.[48] Most of the provinces, however, regarded registration to be an unpopular measure.[49]

The unease over absence of uniformity in laws pertaining to excise became a dominant feature of provincial and centre relations. A clash of interests was destined to ensue over the issue of implementing a system of prohibition, which raked up a violent storm, which was ascribed to the divergences of policy. In a memorandum, the Central Board of Revenue enquired, 'Should a Local Government have the constitutional right to introduce and enforce (supposing that it could do so) a system of prohibition?' The Central Board of Revenue opined that adoption of a system of prohibition was 'unthinkable',

> As to Prohibition, that is obviously a question, which cannot be looked at merely from the point of view of Revenue, nor can it be regarded merely as a question of Excise administration. Its importance far transcends such narrow limits. The adoption and particularly the hasty adoption would certainly have consequences whose gravity and far-reaching nature cannot be exaggerated. It might well lead to widespread demoralization among large classes of the population . . . it might arouse discontent and a spirit of resistance to established authority, the political results of which would be extremely serious and might strain the forces of law and order to the utmost . . . if adjacent provinces should adopt varying policies the situation on their frontier could hardly fail to resemble a state of war. [50]

The suggestion put forward by the Board as a solution revealed the underlying discrepancies in the official position. The Board asserted that the Government of India should retain the right to 'interfere decisively should any Local Government go to dangerous lengths in this matter'. Further, it called for clearly defining the powers of control to be exercised by the Government of India over the legislations, policy and actions of the provincial governments.[51] The issue raised fundamental questions of the future relations between the Central and Provincial governments and was certainly more political in nature than constitutional. In October 1924, the Government of India put on the agenda for the Conference of Finance members for that year, the suggestion that any province embarking on any new policy in Excise matters should furnish full information to the Central Government, which would in turn pass the information to other provinces. In 1925, the Government of India decided to convene a Conference of representatives of Provincial Governments and certain local administrations to discuss certain matters of all-India importance, relating to Excise.[52]

This inter-provincial conference was meant to discuss issues relating to securing uniformity in the matters of penalties by legislation and in particular, demand a revision of the conclusions of the RCO 1893. Another important issue that was taken up was the suggestion of the Taxation Enquiry Committee that the revenue from excise on opium should be made a Central subject.[53] In keeping with the first Resolution of the Conference held at Geneva on 19 February 1926, important steps were proposed to be taken with respect to internal and external control of raw and manufactured opium and of hemp drugs.

The provincial governments of Punjab, Central India, Ajmer, Burma, United Provinces, Assam, Bihar and Orissa, favoured the setting up of a bureau with a detective staff. It was also decided that the Provincial legislatures should legislate concerning the internal control of drugs.[54] Meanwhile the reassertion of the traditional policy regarding internal consumption of opium by the Government of India Resolution of 17 June 1926, invited virulent verbal duels in the Indian Legislative Assembly from member S.K. Datta. He called for a reassessment of the findings of the RCO 1893, particularly in light of the recent advances in medical science related to medicinal use of opium and the findings of the 1913 Botham Committee Report in Assam along with the report of the 1925 Assam Congress Opium Enquiry Committee.[55] He also cited the conclusions of the Taxation Enquiry Committee, which recommended uniformity of retail rates of excise opium. The Report was also apprehensive of the auctioning system and suggested the extension of the registration system to Assam and the need to introduce modifications in the official vend system.

Opium in the Politics of the Council

India being a signatory of the Hague Convention, the Assam Opium Smoking Act was passed in 1927. It was aimed at prohibiting

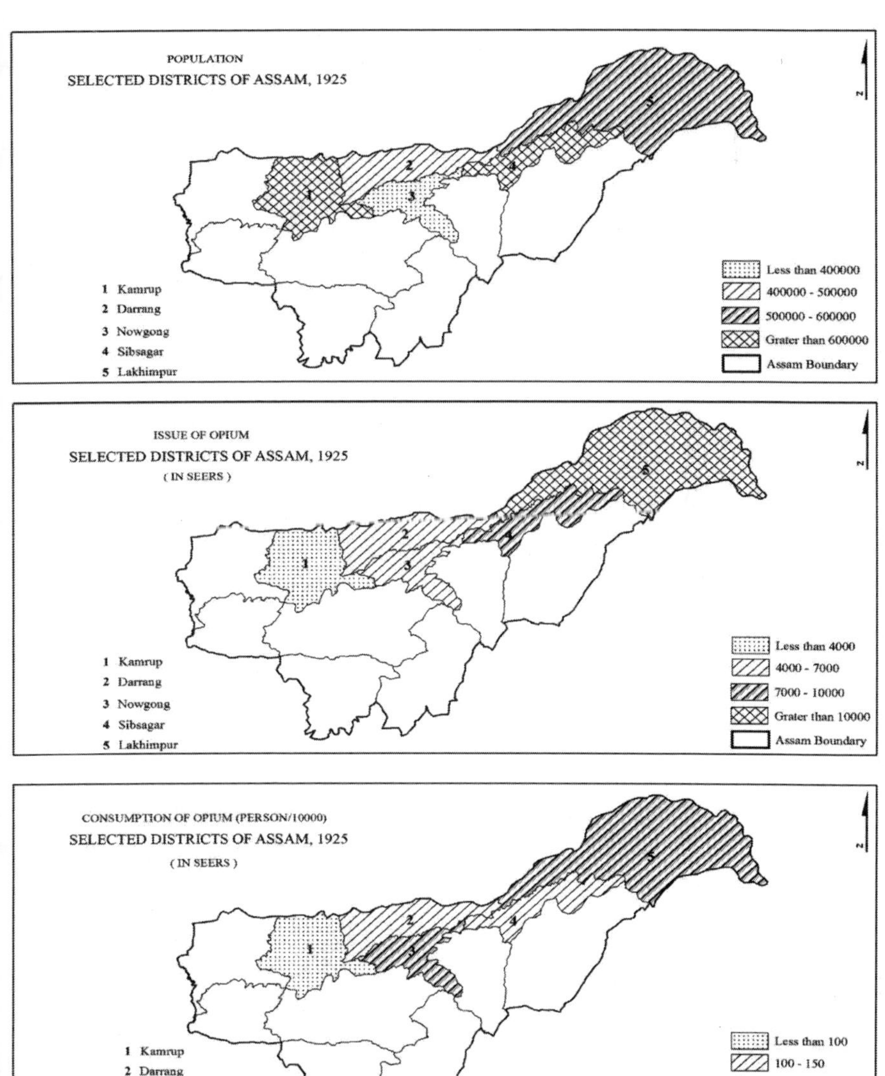

Source: Based on the Findings and Data as mentioned in the Assam Congress Opium Enquiry Committee Report 1925, ASA.

MAP 6.1: MAP SHOWING POPULATION, ISSUE OF OPIUM AND AMOUNT OF CONSUMPTION PER TEN THOUSAND OF POPULATION IN SELECTED DISTRICTS OF KAMRUP, DARRANG, NOWGONG, LAKHIMPUR AND SIBSAGAR.

opium smoking. Under the provisions of the Act, smoking opium in company or in an opium smoking assembly, the possession of opium making and smoking apparatus, was declared a penal offence attended with imposition of fines, or imprisonment or both. The Government was apprehensive of increased 'subversion' following the 10 per cent reduction in rations and the Council voted for setting up a separate preventive department to prevent smuggling. Perturbed over the growing trend of substitution of opium with *ganja* and liquor, Jatindra Mohan Deb's censure motion pointed to a serious flaw in the official policy regarding intoxicants.[56] Lending his support to the censure motion, Rohini Kanta Hatibarua complained of the double standards of the Government including the Excise Department.[57]

The Council members' continuous tussle against the abuses of the Excise Department reflects not only the legislative interventions to tackle a crisis in the society but also the political imperatives and the social and economic dimensions of the opium question in Assam. The Legislative activism at what it conceived as the failure of the Government to introduce effective measures was nonetheless an effective instrument in negotiating necessary changes in the Excise system.[58] The proceedings in the Council evoked great interest in the Assamese press and the *Asamiya* featured a column called *Axom Councilor Adhivekhon* (Proceedings of the Assam Council). *Asamiya* in its feature on Council proceedings lamented on the lack of unanimity that had seriously impeded effective implementation of laws and provisions to do away with the opium menace. It severely criticized the eccentricity 'of native members many of whom had actively participated in 1921 opium restriction campaign of the Non-Cooperation movement and in 1927, many of them have been following a position of compromise with the Government for the sake of power and money'.[59]

The Government faced increasing criticism on the floor of the Legislative Council for going too slow with implementation of the recommendations of the Council. The complicity of the officers and staff of the Excise Department in opium smuggling had resulted in total disorder.[60] Legislator Nabin Chandra Bordoloi likened the conduct of the Excise establishment to a 'Football Game', where the excise officers are 'players' and the *mahaldars* the 'football', with the Advisory Committee as the 'linesmen' and the Deputy Commissioner as the 'goal-keeper'.[61] Interestingly, with no 'referee' – with the result, that there prevailed a complete chaos. Anybody could kick the ball (*mahaldar)* as he likes and ultimately if it pleased the goal-keeper (Deputy Commissioner) who allowed the ball (*mahaldars*) to pass through the goal. It is a 'Standing Scandal', he remarked and accused the Government of facilitating and being a party to the trade. To him, the entire excise system had become 'rotten' to the core, which was hindering the formulation of any definitive policy. He called upon the Council members to prevail upon the Government for an urgent redressal of the opium excise system and ensure that 'economic welfare' of the 'poverty-stricken opium consumers' is given priority.[62]

Following such active propaganda, the Government was inclined to accept the Council resolution moved by Rohini Kanta Hatibaruah, recommending that the ration of opium eaters below 50 years of age be reduced by 10 per cent. The Government contention was that any attempt at prohibition would only push the addicts to other noxious drugs.[63] *Ganja* consumption was gradually registering an upward trend.[64] However, the Council activity but public apathy often resulted in official indifference to the issue.[65] Although the Government agreed as an experiment to an annual, 10 per cent reduction provided the Council voted the provision for preventive staff required to deal with smuggling. The enforcement of the scheme of 10 per cent reduction of rations had resulted in a decrease of the total rations of persons fewer than 50 by approximately 13 per cent. However, the Council expressed concern at the widespread complaints received regarding the hardships caused by excessive reduction of rations. Cases of riot and looting of the opium shops were reported at various places. After long and anxious consideration, it was decided to supplement the preventive action of the staff and the increased supervision over the licensed vendors by taking up the registration of hitherto unregistered consumers.

Opium in the Whirlpool of National Politics

By the 1920s the phase of mass politics had assumed a different hue. The 'regionalization of politics'[66] was to radically alter the dynamics of nationalist agitation. It witnessed the emergence of 'separate ethnic and religious movements, rivaling each other enviously'.[67] As subsequent developments were to prove, the communal politics would take priority over all other issues. As Bipan Chandra rightly remarks of the ubiquity of communalism as the dominant ideology beginning the second decade of the twentieth century.[68] In Assam, picketing of opium and liquor shops was one of the main plank of action.[69] There were forcible seizure of opium passes, heavy fines were imposed on those using opium, tobacco and *ganja* followed by social boycott of opium addicts at many places in Assam.[70] The decline in excise revenue was estimated at Rs. 5,692,313 from 6,621,535[71] amounting to a loss of more than 1 per cent of the total provincial revenues in a single year. While the Government declared that it 'had no intention of a shift from the position adopted in accordance with the expressed wishes of the Council', it sought, '[...] all possible assistance rather than mere adverse criticism from those who claim to champion the discouragement of opium consumption ... wish that there were more tangible evidence by the advocates of opium reduction of practical cooperation and clearer recognition of the practical difficulties recurring day by day.'[72]

It stressed on creating greater public awareness against what it believed to be 'social evils' rather than 'sources of revenue to a Government which is endeavouring to suppress them'.[73] A Directorate of Public Instruction publication on general knowledge including hygiene, temperance and sanitation was circulated in all the schools. The Directorate of Public Health complemented this initiative by circulating notices in Assamese, explaining the evil effects of the opium habit.[74]

Meanwhile, the central government suggested to the provincial governments to appoint committees of enquiry to investigate separately the causes of excessive rates of consumption in each isolated locality where it is more than five times the rate of 30 seers to 10,000 inhabitants. Each committee was to contain members acquainted with the local conditions of each district along with a degree of uniformity in the conditions affecting different localities.[75] Consumption in excess (267 seers per annum per 10,000 population) of the standard set by the League of 30 seers per 10,000 of the population per annum, ensured Assam was summoned at the 'Black Spot' Conference of May 1930, convened at Simla.[76] There were representatives from Madras, Bombay, Bengal, Punjab, United Provinces, Bihar and Orissa, Assam, Baluchistan and Ajmer. In Assam, the five upper districts of the Assam valley, Lakhimpur, Sibsagar, Darrang, Nowgong and the Sadiya Frontier Tract, were identified as 'Black Spots'.[77] However, Assam had already committed itself to a policy of total suppression at the initiative taken by the Legislative Council with a stringent system of registration and rationing with a progressive annual reduction of 10 per cent of the ration. This, as a general policy was, however, not acceptable to most local governments. There were increasing apprehensions that the severe restrictions had given a boost to short weight sales and malpractices in the shops. It was proposed that caution be exercised, as any further restriction would result in jeopardizing the policy of the Government.

Clearly, the British Government in India was keen only on observance of commitment as signatory to the League of Nations as is apparent from the inaugural speech of the Viceroy, yet resonating the theory of relative harmlessness of opium upon Indians, upheld by the 1895 Royal Commission on Opium,

> [...] for the greater part of the country, no opium evil exists. The average consumption in India as a whole is less than twice the 'League of Nations standard' of 6 seers per 10,000 of population. But this standard is not applicable in India. It was framed for purely medical needs of countries with highly organised medical services, where the uses of opium as an indulgence, so common in India, is entirely unknown. In India, apart from this 'euphoric' use there is and for many years to come must continue a large quasi-medical use, especially in malarial tracts, which whatever its real value or the reverse (apart from merely palliative effects) could not be interfered with without causing grave and widespread discontent or indeed without positive inhumanity.[78]

Council Dissatisfaction and Government Apathy

Increasing sale of *ganja*, opium and liquor coupled with increasing revenues had exposed the hollowness of the Government stand of decrease in consumption. The ambivalent official policy had all along been a bone of discontent between the Assamese councilors and the Government. Though there was lack of unanimity among themselves as regards the best possible course of action against opium use. Moving a censure motion, Sarvesvar Barua informed the Council as to how in utter disregard to the opinion of the Local Boards and in contravention of their professed policy of reduction, the Government had sanctioned the settling of new opium and liquor shops at Dibrugarh and Lakhimpur. The province was passing through a serious deficit, but the Government was 'replenishing its coffers by this immoral drink and drug traffic at the expense of the moral and physical well being of our people.'[79] Nilambar Datta questioned the Government motives, which were to suit the convenience of licensed opium consumers. He informed the Council that the Excise Superintendent was pulled up for his failure to curb the practice of opium use. Challenging the substance of the censure motion, representative of European community, W. Douglas, remarked that contrary to revenue gains, the Government is losing out to the smugglers. He cited the poorly paid subordinate staff as one of the important reasons of this.[80] The censure motion was defeated.

The Government maintained that huge seizures of contraband articles were proof that of the dynamism of the Excise establishment. Abdul Hamid of the Muslim League informed the Council that the existence of the Excise Department was essential to effective implementation of the policy of 10 per cent reduction of opium rations. He also informed the Council of the need of preventive staff to step up vigilance as smuggling from China into Assam was proving a deterrent to the successful implementation of the reduction policy.[81] Though the Congress members protested and deplored the Government's lackadaisical attitude in the manufacture of opium tablets to prevent the shortweight sale and other malpractices resorted to by the opium vendors.[82] The Council was informed of the hiring of services of a private chemist in Calcutta to test the feasibility of the manufacturing of opium tablets by means of ordinary pill making machinery. This saw much protest in the Council where this was regarded as insincerity on the part of the Government to tackle trafficking.

The Council members enquired if the Government was aware that following the reduction of rations, the opium eaters have resorted to supplementing their rations by purchasing contraband opium, at an abnormal price of Rs. 4 to 10 per *tola*. This, as they argued, had wreaked havoc and ruined many families of opium eaters. Jogendranath Gohain enquired if the Government proposed to give any medical aid to the opium eaters whose rations are reduced so that they can do without the reduced quantity of opium without any detriment to their health. The Government claimed it could and would not. 'We cannot arrange for the 82,000 opium eaters in this province whose rations have been curtailed', remarked Abdul Hamid.[83]

Irked at such apathetic attitude of the Government, member Pyari Mohan Das moved a resolution calling for withdrawal of the policy of 10 per cent reduction of opium rations. 'That this Council recommends to the Government of Assam that the Government opium policy of an annual 10 per cent reduction of rations and restriction of opium eaters be withdrawn with a view to eradicating the evils of smuggling of opium into, and the cultivation of poppy in the province of Assam.'[84]

The Assam Opium Enquiry Committee Report 1933

As the members of the council clamoured for sincere efforts on the part of the Government, on 6 March 1933, the Assam Legislative Council voted, to institute a seven member non-official committee with a mandate of reviewing the Government's opium policy. The Council voted for the following as members of the Committee, James Joy Mohan Nichols Roy as Chairman, Brindaban Chandra Goswami, Nilambar Dutta, Mahendra Nath Gohain, Abdur Rahim Chaudhari, E.S. Roffey and Rohini Kumar Chaudhary. The Commissioner of Excise was appointed by the Government as a member and secretary of the Committee. One hundred and thirty-four witnesses were examined, including some thirty-five opium eaters, six Civil Surgeons, five European Medical Officers of tea gardens, a retired Civil Surgeon who had served in Burma and one private practitioner.

The Committee focused on a review of the opium policy, to identify the extent of threat posed by the existence of contraband opium, including the prevalence of short weight including investigation into the case for total prohibition, which was yet to receive acceptance as a government policy. It also attempted to explore effective instruments of opium eradication, including registration of addicts and massive public education campaigns and called for strengthening control and regulatory mechanisms.

For a comprehensive understanding of the various aspects of opium problem and the policies adopted, it had included the Botham Committee (1913) recommendations, the conclusions of the Assam Congress Opium Enquiry Committee (1925) and the findings of the Ekstrand Commission (1931). Although medical opinion did play an important role in the deliberations, the report was highly reflective of the major international interventions. The Shanghai Conference of 1909, The Hague Convention held in 1912, The International Opium Convention of 1925, The League Convention for Limiting the Manufacture and Regulating the Distribution of Narcotic Drug in 1931 which expressed concern and stressed on action to regulate the demand and supply of psychoactives. In Assam, The Assam Congress Opium Enquiry Committee, 1925, the promulgation of the Assam Opium Smoking (Prohibition) Act, 1927, The 'Black Spots' Conference, 1930, and the appointment of the Assam Opium Enquiry Committee, 1933, are but visible manifestations of the multilateral efforts, at international, national and local level.

The 1933 Report is rich and multifarious. It proceeds to outline in the broadest terms, yet with many detailed recommendations, a major reorientation of policy and attitudes, along with major change in laws and public policies. Being of a non-official character, it was acknowledged as being reflective of public opinion. Both native and official opinion poured forth into the hearings with great spontaneity. The Committee noted with great satisfaction at the social response it had aroused. It had for the first time, attempted a comprehensive understanding of the causation, extent, effects of the opium problem to outlining the government policy, the consumption pattern, the international treaty obligations on reduction and suppression. In comprehending the issues of demand-supply, reduction including the legal framework to control offences related to opium trade and revenue, it recommended an effective 'opium eradication policy'.

The Assam Opium Enquiry Committee accepted addiction to be a medical problem. Although it lamented on the lack of necessary infrastructure for the treatment of addicts, yet it suggested that Dr. Modino's cure[85] could be given a trial in the jails of Assam. Reiterating the 'nationalist stand' adopted by C.F. Andrews, in the *Assam Congress Opium Enquiry Committee,* the report argued that opium's classification as a poison in Britain shows that the drug demands the greatest care and discrimination. Here, it is worthy of mention that in 1926, the Bengal Government published in the *Calcutta Gazette*, draft rules which they had made under the Indian Poisons Act, for the control of particular poisons. Opium and its derivatives had been placed in Schedule A as being 'dangerous poisons'. These rules did not apply to 'excise opium'.[86]

Based on the recommendations in the *Report of the Assam Opium Enquiry Committee 1933*, in 1934, detailed instructions for the future working of the policy of the annual 10 per cent reduction of opium ration of persons 'under 50 years of age' were issued by the Government. According to this resolution, no new pass for consumption of opium could be granted merely on the ground of addiction without the production of medical certificate from recognized medical practitioners. No monthly allowance exceeding 2½ *tolas* was permissible in any case without the sanction of the Government. The first attempts at 'legal prohibition' of opium in Assam were initiated in 1937, following the provisions laid down in the Government of India Act of 1935. Though the Act of 1935 made no explicit reference to 'Prohibition', it certainly empowered the Provincial Governments to 'legislate' with respect of 'narcotic drugs and intoxicating liquors'.

Radical Politics against 'Opium Government'

Throughout the period under survey, opium suppression had been high on the agenda of the councilors who were in no mood to disengage from the policy of stamping out the opium vice.

One of the most prominent legislators to get involved in the crusade against opium was Krishna Nath Sharma, a militant nationalist who along with Rohini Kumar Chaudhary led the front in the Council for harsh regulations against smugglers, though there were differences over the course of policy, which was to be pursued as regards the addicts. While Krishna Nath Sharma favoured medicalization, Rohini Kumar Chaudhari advocated penalties for addicts including capital sentence for the smugglers, 'If we want to tighten the grip to punish the smugglers, then we have no compunction of heart if they are hanged. I should be satisfied if they are actually hanged. The opium addicts must be dealt with first and then pursue the smugglers.'[87]

This intolerant attitude became rather a feature of the debates in the second decade of the twentieth century. The council members considered death penalty as a deterrent to the crime. 'If two lakhs of people can die in this province from cholera and malaria and other diseases, let another two lakhs die from want of opium. That does not matter much.'[88]

What did matter was that Assam had a problem with opium and 'to purify the people and defend the state', no sacrifice was big enough. Opium had earned Assam the infamy as 'black spot' and this had struck the Assamese nationalists as an assault on the identity of what was once termed as *Sonar Asom* (golden land of Assam). It intensified its agitation against the 'imperialism of opium'. Their anger was directed also at those Assamese lessees who had collaborated with the British to secure opium leases.[89]

Denouncing the attitude of the Government, Krishna Nath Sharma disparaged the insensitivity of the medical community and the callousness of the Government towards the seriousness of opium poisoning in Assam.

When opium is considered as a dangerous poison to the Chinese, the Europeans and the other Eastern nations, why it is considered as a saviour of life to the people of Assam. While the Government of India could sacrifice annually rupees 9.96 crores of opium revenue to save the Chinese and the Eastern nations, why they cannot forego 1,45,000 rupees to save people under their own charge. Our people have fought crusades after crusades and have filled the Assam jails. Yet the Government has not cared to stop this habit.[90]

He accused the Government of India for being unable to resist revenue accruing from opium consumption and of 'fleecing' Assam of its resources, which would have otherwise been utilized to develop the province and empower its human resources.[91] Opium eradication was an considered an integral part of the 'nation building activities' and the intelligentsia in Assam denounced the apathetic attitude of the Government of India.

> The Government of India get from petrol and kerosene alone 157 lakhs and 30 lakhs from income tax . . . in addition to jute export duty, the Government of India annually get more than two crores of rupees and as an act of gratefulness for this, they are forcing upon us this inhuman and immoral traffic to poison our people? The Government of India is robbing the infant province of Assam of it's mother's milk and supplying poison in its place.[92]

'Better die than survive on the moral and physical ruin of the people. We must be content to let this vicious revenue go', declared Kashinath Saikia.[93] Echoing a similar sentiment, Krishna Nath Sharma, declared the present Government as an 'Opium Government' – contended as it was in thriving on the proceeds of the opium revenue, which had wrought misery and degradation upon the people of Assam.[94] The Government's intention was challenged. Despite championing the cause of temperance and prohibition, it had reopened the registers to ensure passes on medical grounds. The members also prevailed upon the Government to ensure that no opium lessees were henceforth to be awarded to 'foreigners'. This was reflective of the growing intolerance against the traders, most of who came from Rajputana and the Central Provinces as also those from Bengal.[95]

Conclusion

The virulent attacks in the Council on the opium policies build up a new political awakening, which was rejuvenation of the people to ensure the regeneration of Assam. Opium had by the mid-twentieth century become 'that vulnerable heel of the British Achilles'.[96] The institutionalization of global narcotics surveillance regime had catalysed domestic activism against opium. The deluge of mass participation and the huge impact that the *Kani Nibarani Andolan* revealed the great deal of public enthusiasm for opium eradication. Thus was opium made a celebrated legislative issue. When the fight against opium was carried on the floor of the legislatures, the opium issue was both a 'tricky' and a 'sticky' affair.[97] It revealed certainly how ambiguity towards the use of opium marked middle class sensibilities about the drug while it pushed hard for anti-opium legislation. The Council politics made certain that the issue of opium use and its eradication was regarded as a matter of policy in ensuring the health and welfare of the people. The nationalists ensured that the fight for 'purging the nation of this noxious habit' would entwine with the larger vision of freedom from alien rule and nation-building.

Notes

1. An anti-opium lobby was in existence in India as early as 1870s with Keshab Chandra Sen and Dadabhai Naoroji actively challenging the ethics of the opium trade. The Indian National Congress was not until the 'self-purification campaign' by M.K. Gandhi, sensitive to the issue. Divergent views on its avowed policy of non-interference was seen to emerge from a variety of factors as unanimity of views among representatives of various interests which prevailed in the party (it was even held that INC was protecting the interests of the private parties who had vested interests in the liquor and opium trade); religious and social sanction to the use of opium in the country, etc. Julia Buxton, *The Political Economy of Narcotics: Production, Consumption and Global Markets*, Canada: Fernwood Publishing, 2006, p. 29. It is the latter use of opium in India that inspired J.F. Richards to interpret the INC assuming an identical stand on the issue with the Government as they viewed the anti-opium agitation in India as a form of 'cultural imperialism'. See, John F. Richards, 'Opium and the British Indian Empire: The Royal Commission of 1895', *Modern Asian Studies* 36(2002): 375-420. It was at the Belgaum session of the INC in 1924 that it passed a resolution against 'Drink and Opium Traffic', and declared in clear terms its avowed apprehension of the colonial policy and called for abolition of the drink and drug habit which 'as a source of revenue is detrimental to the moral welfare of the people of India', *Report of the Thirty-Ninth Indian National Congress, 1924*, vol. 30, pp. 115-18.
2. In the wake of Montague Chelmsford reforms, the political atmosphere in Assam as in the rest of the country was charged up. While the Assam

Association geared up its demand for 'major province status' for Assam, a Surma valley delegation of both Hindus and Muslims placed their demand for transfer of Sylhet to Bengal.Feelings of'uncertainty and jealousy' surfaced following such developments. Guha, *Planter-Raj to Swaraj,* pp. 112-13. H.K. Barpujari contends that the emergence of the Assamese middle class as a byproduct of the Western education played on their psyche atleast for a long time. He writes of how the newly emerging intelligentsia, which included Anandaram Dhekiyal Phukan, Gunabhiram Barua, Jagannath Baruah, Ganga Govinda Phukan, etc., chose to deal diplomatically with issues of social reform and favoured a policy of conciliation instead of revolution. It was with the formation of the Assam Association in the early part of the twentieth century and the struggle against partition in the Swadeshi campaign which infused the first sparks of nationalistic fervour. Refer, Barpujari, *The Comprehensive History of Assam.* This view is echoed in Rajen Saikia's nuanced analysis of middle class sensibilities.The widespread addiction of the populace to opium was one such significant issue that brought to fore the complexities in its tacit approach to the anti-opium movement. He puts up an interesting picture of the adherents and dissenters for the colonial opium policy among the emerging Assamese intelligentsia. He mentions of how litterateurs, citing the instance of Hemchandra Barua, writer of the *Kaniyar Kirtan* (a satirical composition highlighting the evil of opium) and Lakshminath Bezbarua, chose to use soft satire in place of criticism for venting their views against the various social evils including use of opium. For details see, Saikia, *Social and Economic History of Assam,* pp. 193-225.

3. Guha, *Planter-Raj to Swaraj*, p. 118.
4. A lawyer and an entrepreneur, Nabin Chandra Bordoloi was the son of a high-ranking Government official, Madhav Chandra Bordoloi and son-in-law of a pioneer Assamese tea planter, Malbhog Barua. He presided over the annual conference of the Assam association in 1915. He was chosen to lead a delegation of the Assam Association to London to plead for the granting of major province status to Assam in November 1918. Guha, *Planter-raj to Swaraj,* p. 119.
5. Assam was being represented through the Bengal Congress Provincial Committee until December 1920. Girin Phukon, *Assam: Attitude towards Federalism*, New Delhi: Sterling, 1984.
6. At the initiative of leaders like Nabin Chandra Bordoloi, Krishna Kanta Bhattacharya and Chobilal Upadhyay, the Assam Association merged itself into the Assam Provincial Congress Committee (APCC) in 1921. Subsequently, an ad hoc committee of APCC was formed in June 1921, with it's headquarter at Guwahati and Kuladhar Chaliha as its president. Later Tarun Ram Phookan became the president and the reconstituted the APCC

elected Phookan, Gopinath Bordoloi, Bimala Prasad Chaliha, Chandranath Sarmah, Krishna Nath Sarmah and Kanak Chandra Sarmah as members of the AICC. Under the initiative of the new committee, Gandhi's visit to Assam materialized in 1921 to propagate the message of non-cooperation amongst the masses. His visit gave tremendous impetus to the Congress workers to carry out the Non-Cooperation movement and implement the principles of Swadeshi. For details, refer Guha, *Planter-Raj to Swaraj*, pp. 123-6.

7. A group of Congressmen led by C.R. Das, Motilal Nehru, Hakim Ajmal Khan and V.J. Patel launched upon a strategy to carry the battle inside the legislatures. The issue of Council-entry aroused much controversy within the ranks of the Congressmen. In January 1923, the formation of the Swaraj party was officially complete. Tarun Ram Phookan was entrusted with the setting up of the Assam wing in July 1923 with Rohini Kumar Choudhary, Gopinath Bordoloi, Bishnuram Medhi, Kamakhyaram Baruah, Dhaniram Talukdar and Jadovchandra Das as the office bearers. Nabinchandra Bordoloi and Kuladhar Chaliha remained 'orthodox non-cooperators of Assam'. They forced T.R. Phookan to resign his presidentship of the Assam Pradesh Congress Committee. A new committee was formed which was headed by Kuladhar Chaliha as the President, Nabinchandra Bordoloi as the general secretary and Hemchandra Baruah as the assistant secretary. A 'compromise resolution' resulted in cooperation to achieve a 'common objective'. Guha, *Planter-Raj to Swaraj,* pp. 154-68.
8. Ellen Newbold LaMotte was an American nurse. She recounted her travel to Asia and described herself as a witness to the 'horrors of opium addiction' in *Opium Monopoly* (1920), *Ethics of Opium* (1922) and *Opium in Geneva: or How the Opium Problem is Handled by the League of Nations* (1929).
9. The Congress volunteers stood outside the excise opium shops and implored the village people not to buy the drug. Jadav Prasad Chaliha, a tea planter and proprietor of several tea gardens remarked, 'The effects of the Non-Cooperation movement, so far as the temperance side was concerned, was marvelous on the people-in matters of all sorts of drugs and spirituous liquors. However, the Government imprisoned the workers and did everything to suppress the movement.' *ACOECR*, 1925: 29.
10. During their visit to Assam, Madan Mohan Malviya and Rajendra Prasad had asked the Congress workers to actively enlist the support of women in the temperance agitation by forming an Anti-Intoxication League and form *Nari Mandali* (Women's Association) to pursue the programme. Arun C. Bhuyan (ed.), *Political History of Assam,* vol. II, Guwahati: Publication Board Assam, 1999, pp. 80-1.
11. We come across a reference to the organization of an opium prohibition committee of the Dipling Tea Estate. The committee included the Manager

of the estate, W.G. Braff (who later joined as Superintendent of the Jorhat Tea Company), the supervisor, Tirtheswar Borkotoki. The committee also found support in the supervisor of Timon Tea Estate, Lila Prasad Chaliha (later the Manager), and Harkumar Barua who was employed as a staff at Dikom Tea Estate. Other members included Dr. Suresh Chandra Sen, Kulsi Phukan, and Khagendranath Gogoi, Jagat Chandra Bora, Benudhar Hazarika (later Leader of the Tea Labour Union), Surendranath Mishra (later Secretary of Sonari branch of Indian National Trade Union Congress [INTUS]). An abandoned shop used for retailing opium served as a makeshift office which was also used for treating of the opium addicts. Padmanath Borthakur, *Swadhinata Ranar Sangsparksat* (Freedom Movement in Context), Dibrugarh: Kasturba Prakashan, pp. 171-80.

12. *ACOER*, 1925, p. 56.
13. Ibid., p. 28.
14. The treasury price of opium was increased from Rs. 68 to 75 a seer and the maximum retail price was raised from Rs. 1-8-0 to 1-12-0 a *tola* in all districts. The consumption of opium fell from 39,717 to 36,421 seers respectively. The total receipts rose from Rs. 56,81,294 to 62,24,778. *Extract from the Proceedings of the Governor in Council in the Judicial and General Department*, no. 4386 G.J., dated 18 September 1924, ASA.
15. James Joy Mohan Nichols Roy had been elected from Shillong urban constituency.
16. In a resolution dated 23 March 1921, 'all vendors of opium shall now be required to record the name, caste, age, occupation and village of each purchaser of opium and also the amount and date of every purchase made. The *mauzadars* in the Assam valley and the *sarpanches* in the plains district of the Surma valley, while in the hill districts, the work was to be done by the agency at the disposal of the Deputy Commissioner.' The total number of opium eaters was reported at 13,214; in Darrang, 10,630; in Nowgong, 25,754; in Sibsagar 25,016 and in Lakhimpur 43,282. ALC Proceedings, 1923, ASA.
17. Ibid. The rations for the individual shops were fixed by the Deputy Commissioners, subject to the control of the Commissioner. The ration was fixed in consideration of the requirements of the consumers served by the shop. Deputy Commissioners, when authorized by the Commissioner had the power to vary from time to time the ration of an individual shop in their districts, provided the total ration sanctioned by the Government for the district is not exceeded.
18. The rations fixed for the district were Kamrup 91 maunds; Darrang 126 maunds; Nowgong 185 maunds; Sibsagar 250 maunds; Lakhimpur 273 maunds; Sadiya Frontier Tract 26 maunds 28 seers and Balipara Frontier Tract 1 maund 20 seers. ALC Proceedings, 26 September 1924, ASA.
19. Ibid.

20. *Report on the Administration of the Excise Department in Assam for the Year 1922-23*, ASA, 5.
21. Under the Pass Book system, a license would be issued to every opium eater in the form of a Pass Book that would be renewed every year. ALC Proceedings, 1922, ASA.
22. ALC Proceedings, 27 September 1922, ASA, pp. 805-6.
23. *Memorandum Regarding Interchange of Information between Local Governments on Legislation and Policy*. Finance Department (Central Revenues), 21 October 1924, NAI.
24. British Bulletin of the Society for the Suppression of the Opium Trade. January 1925, NAI.
25. Only 13 members of the previous Council could retain their seats out of a total of 39 elective seats of the Assam Council. Although Nilmoni Phukan (Dibrugarh-rural) and Sivaprasad Baruah (Jorhat non-Muslim) had to face defeat, they were later nominated to the Council. Rohini Kanta Hatibarua (Jorhat), Kamakhyaram Baruah (Gauhati), Jogeshchandra Gohain (Dibrugarh) Sarvesvar Baruah (North Lakhimpur), Jonaram Borah (Nowgong) and Faiznur Ali (Dibrugarh) of the Swaraj party were elected to the Council. Muhammad Sadullah, elected as an Independent candidate, joined the Government as a minister to work under the dyarchy. Padmanath Sarma, Bishnuchandra Borah, Sadananda Dowerah and Md. Sadullah expressed their inability to act up to the obstructive programme of the Swaraj party. However, the former three supported the Council in all-important matters, pp. 98-9. The Assam Valley Responsive Cooperation Party held a meeting at Gauhati in September 1926, in wake of the Responsivist Party formed at Bombay by M.R. Jayakar, Kelkar and Moonje, after their withdrawal from the Swaraj party following dissatisfaction with the obstructionist policy. It believed that such a policy was proving detrimental also to the interests of the people. In Assam, it was led by Radhikananda Choudhary, Kaliram Barman, Hemchandra Goswami, Jyotish Chandra Das and Sivaprasad Baruah as members. See, Barpujari, *Political History of Assam*, p. 107.
26. It endorsed an 'opium suppression campaign', which obliged all members to cause a 10 per cent reduction annually and limit production to medical and scientific necessities as ascertained by the consensus of world medical opinion and to enforce an equitable rationing system.
27. Surendra Kumar Datta was an Indian Christian who had been nominated member of the Imperial Legislative Assembly (1924-31) to represent the Indian Christian community. He had earlier served as the national secretary of Young Men Christian Association's (YMCA) of India, Burma and Ceylon (now Sri Lanka) from 1919-27. He had also attended the Second Round

Table Conference in December 1931. G.H. Anderson, *Biographical Dictionary of Christian Missions*, London: William B. Eerdmans, 1999, p. 169.

28. Mr. John Campbell was regarded as reactionary in his approach to the American proposals. The Indian leaders believed in these American proposals throughout. They wished to join hands with America in carrying through a world reform and they were entirely opposed to Mr. Campbell's policy of obstruction.
29. John Campbell had opined that opium smoking was almost non-existent in the country; also that opium was a transferred subject in every province of India. *The Contemporary Review*, London, 1925, pp. 163-9.
30. In February 1924, the Central Legislative Assembly voted the formation of a Reforms Enquiry Committee (also known as the Muddiman Committee). Among the recommendations of the Committee, it suggested that 'Excise' in Assam be placed under Transferred subjects. Excise became 'Transferred' in Assam in 1926.
31. Considering that India had a long tradition of opium consumption which in many parts of the country enjoyed socio-religious sanction, the League of Nations for India had set the maximum standard of consumption as 30 seers per ten thousand of population.
32. Refer Table in Appendix F.
33. *ACOECR*, 1925, pp. 51-2.
34. Ibid., pp. 51-2.
35. Ibid., pp. 71-2.
36. The *ACOER* revealed sharp discrepancies as consumption of opium (1,748 maunds) was reported to be 17 per cent in excess of the consumption for 1885-6 (1,446 maunds) although the indigenous population had increased only by 10 per cent, followed by a steady rise of revenue up from Rs. 12 lakhs in 1875 to Rs. 44 lakhs in 1920. *ACOER*, 1925, p. 24.
37. By this, the purchase of opium was permitted only to the holders of a pass to be granted by the Deputy Commissioners and subject to the conditions stated in the pass. Public notice of the introduction of the new system was given and opium eaters had to apply at once for the names to be entered by the *mauzadar* on the list of persons recommended for passes, which the *mauzadar* would prepare. The Deputy Commissioner would fix the amount to be allowed to each applicant for a pass. He could reduce the amount of monthly ration fixed for individuals from time to time according to his discretion. Each pass holder should be registered for the shop at which he would make his purchases and he would not be bound to purchase opium at any particular shop. The pass was to be issued on plain paper with the form enclosed and should bear the signature and seal of the Deputy Commissioner. A register of passes was to be maintained

either *mayawari* or *thanawari* and the quantity mentioned in the paper was to be entered on the register. The passes of those who die was to be collected by the excise officials. 'Letter from G.T. Llyod, Second Secretary to the Government of Assam to the Secretary to the Government of India.' Finance Department (Central Revenue), 1926, NAI.

38. *ALC Proceedings*, The Assam Gazette, March 1926, ASA, pp. 330-1.
39. Ibid., May 1926, ASA, p. 360.
40. Speech by Tarun Ram Phookan at the Forty-First Session of the INC. For details, refer K. Suresh Sharma, *Documents on North-East India: An Exhaustive Survey*, vol. 3: *Assam, 1664-1938*, New Delhi: Mittal Publications, 2006, pp. 227-98.
41. While the Bill introduced by Nichols Roy made opium smoking itself an offence, the Government Bill makes opium smoking in company an offence. *The Assam Gazette*, 21 July 1926, ASA, p. 692.
42. *Asamiya,* 22 May 1927, Department of Historical and Antiquarian Studies, Assam (hereafter DHAS), 3.
43. This term was used to denote those *kanias* (opium eaters) who were invisible/secretive (*guppto*), denoting those newly addicted to the habit, chiefly the younger generation and without pass to purchase legitimate opium. *Asamiya,* 21 August 1927, DHAS, 4.
44. *Asamiya*, 21 August 1927, DHAS, 2.
45. Ibid., 28 August 1927, DHAS, 4.
46. The Kabulis, Pathans, Nepalese, Marwari and Bengali traders were found to be engaged in the sale of contraband opium. The Marwari traders were known to carry on a very systematic trade in smuggling opium and selling it without license in Lakhimpur, Sibsagar and other districts of upper Assam.
47. The Government of Assam had suggested certain important issues to be taken up for discussion at the Conference. Among them was: (a) the system of settling opium and excise shops (b) a reappraisal of the Taxation Enquiry Committee (c) the exercise of more efficient control over the sale of excise opium in Indian states within the jurisdiction of the local governments. It was reported that because of lax control and lower retail price in other provinces, opium was being smuggled into Assam (d) the difficulties experienced in introducing a measure of consulting local opinion in settling excise shops and (e) Measures to prevent smuggling. 'Letter from G.T. Lloyd. Second Secretary to the Government of Assam to the Secretary to the Government of India).' Finance Department (Central Revenues), 11 August 1926, NAI.
48. 'Notes on the Proceedings of the Inter-Provincial Conference, 23 September 1926,' no. 2780, Local Self-Government, 1926, NAI.
49. Ibid.

50. Central Board of Revenue (CBR), no. 522 EO 27, dated 17 October 1927, NAI.
51. The Government of India was empowered to interfere not only in circumstances in which the previous sanction of the Governor-General is required under Section 80(A)(3) of the Government of India Act, to legislation by a Provincial Legislative Council or in which under Rule 49 of the Devolution Rules, the Governor-General in Council is authorized to exercise his powers of superintendence, direction and control over a Local Government, but also whenever it was of the opinion that the policy or actions of a Local Government or Legislature can produce serious and undesirable repercussions. Central Board of Revenue (CBR), no. 522 EO 27, dated 17 October 1927, NAI.
52. The important measures related to (a) penalties for offences relating to drugs and the legislation relating thereto (b) Internal control of raw opium and Hemp Drugs should remain with the Local Government (c) effective preventive measures against the smuggling of opium and *charas* and (d) the setting up of a bureau with a detective staff. 'Excise Conference, Shimla, 21-3 September 1926.' Excise and Opium (E&O), no. 2780, LSG, NAI.
53. E&O., no. 2780 LSG, 20 March 1926, NAI.
54. This included consumption for purpose other than medicinal use.
55. 'An Indian Critique of the Opium Policy of the Government of India', Speech by S.K. Datta in the Indian Legislative Assembly on 10 March 1926, in Gerald N. Grob, *Narcotic Addiction and American Foreign Policy: Seven Studies, 1924-1938,* New York: Arno Press, 1981.
56. *ALC Proceedings. The Assam Gazette*, 17 August 1927, ASA, p. 993.
57. Ibid., p. 995.
58. Various suggestions were forwarded to the Government by the members including J.J.M. Nichols Roy and Rohini Kanta Hatibarua including the appointment of permanent vendors on salary to sell specially opium, substitution by opium pill forms of standard weights so that there could not be selling of short weights. ALC Proceedings, *ALC Proceedings, The Assam Gazette*, 10 August 1927, ASA, pp. 760-1.
59. *Asamiya*, 11 June 1927, DHAS, 5.
60. *ALC Proceedings, The Assam Gazette*, 10 August, ASA, pp. 1126-7.
61. Ibid., 25 April 1928, ASA, pp. 348-9.
62. Ibid.
63. *Report on the Administration of the Province of Assam for the year 1926-27* had recorded increase in the consumption of *ganja* among tea garden labourers while the habit of smoking cigarettes was on the increase among influential families.
64. There was an increase in consumption from 569 maunds 2 seers to 580 maunds 32 seers. Detection of hill *ganja* cases, opening of new shops,

growth of immigrant *ganja* smoking population. Substitution of small quantities of *ganja* for opium consumers whose rations had been reduced was also reported in two districts. The no. of shops increased from 231 to 235. *Report on the Administration of the Province of Assam for the Year 1929-30*, ASA, p. 32.

65. Ibid. It was maintained in official reports that although the local bodies were consulted in regard, they expressed no suggestions in connection with the methods of trading, hours of sale, excise, etc., but confined themselves to the questions of shop sites only.
66. Dietrich Reetz, 'Ethnic and Religious Identities in Colonial India (1920s-1930s): A Conceptual Debate', *Contemporary South Asia*, 2(1993): 109-22.
67. Ibid.
68. Bipan Chandra, *Communalism in Modern India*, New Delhi: Vani Educational Books, 1984.
69. Since Assam had no suitable salt mine, no salt law was in force, which could be violated. Even the *chaudhari* tax was realized only in Goalpara and its violation was possible only in the district.
70. There was a decrease of around 24.1 per cent. In Kamrup, the temperance movement had a marked effect but in other districts, the decrease was due to the continuance of the pass system, the further reduction of rations of consumers below 50 years of age and the fall in the price of lac, jute and other products. *Report on the Excise Administration of the Province of Assam for the Year 1930-31*, ASA, p. 8.
71. Picketing, Temperance propaganda along with the 10 per cent reduction of the rations of consumers below the age of fifty years, along with introduction of the pass system and the civil disobedience movement was ascertained as the causes of the fall in revenue.
72. To the Government, the Civil Disobedience movement was 'wholly bad in its conception and execution'. It was not aimed at temperance but the embarrassment of Government and its result the diversion of consumers from controlled to uncontrolled sources of supply. 'Extract from the Proceedings of the Government of Assam in the Medical Department', no. 1575, dated 17 December 1929, ASA.
73. *Report on the Administration of Excise of the Province of Assam for the Year 1930-31*, ASA, p. 3.
74. Ibid.
75. The Central Government was even considering appointing that incase the Provincial Governments do not approve of the idea of conducting local enquiries, the Government would even consider setting up of a general enquiry unless effective steps are taken by the Provincial Governments to enquire into and remedy the abuse of opium in the areas of admittedly

excessive consumption. Central Board of Revenue. R. Dis No. 491, E&O 1926, NAI.

76. Ibid. The Conference composed of representatives of Local Governments was convened for considering issues relating to the use of opium and other narcotics including the Reports of the Local Committees appointed in certain provinces to investigate the apparently high average consumption of opium in those areas. The issues discussed were: (1) Smuggling from Indian states as an obstacle to temperance measures in certain parts of British India. The policy of raising sale prices was stated to be limited in its effectiveness by this illicit traffic and from the point of view of expediency by the danger of driving consumers to substitutes other more pernicious indulgences such as cocaine or *ganja* or cocaine, (2) An attempt on the part of the local governments to equalize sale-prices on their respective borders by mutual consultations, (3) The supply of opium in the form of wrapped tablets and (4) The Conference was in favour of a Central Intelligence Bureau under the Government of India to collect, collate and disseminate information regarding the illicit drug traffic, especially in its international and interprovincial aspects.
77. The consumption per 10,000 inhabitants in 1926-7 for those areas was Sadiya Frontier Tract, 175 seers, 153 seers for Lakhimpur; Sibsagar, including Mikir Hills, 91 seers; Darrang, 72 seers and Nowgong, including Mikir Hills, 119 seers. *ACOER*, 1933.
78. 'Press Communiqué, Simla.' Finance Department (Central Revenues), 21 August 1930, NAI.
79. *ALA Proceedings*, *The Assam Gazette,* 27 April 1932, ASA, p. 547.
80. Ibid., pt. VI, 27 April 1932, ASA, pp. 548-9.
81. Reports of smuggled opium reaching Assam from Cooch Behar, Orissa, Nepal, Tripura and China were major hurdles in proper implementation of the restrictive measures. *ALC Proceedings*, 20 May 1931, ASA, pp. 642-3.
82. The experiment in the sale of opium tablets to the tea garden labourers of Kanjikhowa Tea Estate in Lakhimpur district had been a success. The pills were very popular with the coolies. However, the experiment had to be abandoned as the Ghazipur factory found manufacturing of opium in tablet form a costly affair. *Report on the Excise Administration of the Province of Assam for the Year 1930-31*, ASA, p. 9.
83. To the members of the Assam Muslim League, opium was certainly not a worthy issue of consideration. While in principle, they pledged their support to development measures, it is noteworthy that a serious initiative was lacking.
84. *ALC Proceedings*, *The Assam Gazette*, 9 November 1932, ASA, pp. 1048-9.
85. In 1932, the League of Nations communicated the positive results of treatment of drug addicts by the 'Modinos treatment' (it was treatment by

injecting serum obtained from blisters artificial that were developed on the patients' skin to enhance the immune system of the addicts) in the Netherlands Indies. The Inspector-General of Prisons in Burma introduced it in the prisons of Burma and the news of experiments with Modinos caught the fancy of the 1933 Opium Enquiry Committee who suggested a similar trial in Assam. Gerard M Kelly, 'Opium Addiction and its Treatment', *Irish Journal of Medical Science*, 10(1938): 627-36.

86. 'An Indian Critique of the Opium Policy of the Government of India', Speech by S.K. Datta in the Indian Legislative Assembly on 10 March 1926. Grob, *Narcotic Addiction and American Foreign Policy.*
87. *ALA Proceedings, The Assam Gazette*, 13 May 1936, ASA, pp. 666-7.
88. Ibid., Statement made by Nagendra Nath Chaudhary, 9 November 1933, ASA, p. 1063.
89. In 1932, a number of opium shops were settled with the non-Assamese, those hailing from United Provinces, Bombay Presidency, Bihar, Bengal and even from the Surma valley were deemed 'outsiders' and this had incurred a lot of displeasure among the Assamese intelligentsia. As a matter of policy, non-Assamese were not being awarded any opium lessees as they were suspected of malpractices and of spreading the opium habit amongst the people. *ALC Proceedings, The Assam Gazette*, 11 May 1932, ASA, pp. 745-7.
90. *ALC Proceedings*, 27 October 1937, ASA, pp. 1116-17.
91. Ibid.
92. Ibid.
93. *ALC Proceedings, The Assam Gazette*, April 1935, ASA, p. 916.
94. Ibid., 22 September 1937, ASA, p. 489.
95. Ibid., 5 December 1938, ASA, p. 853.
96. Adaptation from Original quote-'Ireland, that vulnerable heel of the British Achilles', Samuel T. Coleridge, *The Friend: A Series of Essays*, London: Gale and Curtis, 1812, p. 431.
97. Saikia, *Social and Economic History of Assam,* p. 213.

CHAPTER 7

Towards Total Prohibition: Opium Eradication Campaign in Assam, 1935-1959

> Such a radical policy as prohibition would not meet with success but would be very difficult to check. It seems better to allow the policy to run its normal course in the hope that, by that time, the people in Assam will have realised that the opium habit is an evil, which must be eradicated (*Assam Opium Enquiry Committee Report, 1933*).

DISMISSING THE IDEA of 'Prohibition', the 1933 Assam Opium Enquiry Committee Report, had upheld the efficacy of the policy of gradual eradication of the opium habit by reduction and rationing. Moreover, it had endorsed the recommendations of the 1925 Assam Congress Opium Enquiry Report in propaganda work and organization of temperance societies begun at the initiative of M.K. Gandhi. The research findings of the Calcutta Tropical School of Medicine, had greatly facilitated a scientific understanding of the progression of the opium habit and the various forms of medical treatments available for prevention and treatment of opiate abuse.[1] The Opium Enquiry Committee Report 1933 clearly outlined the inefficacy of incarceration of the opium users. Instead, it stressed on undertaking the treatment of opium addicts in hospitals where addicts could be entitled to proper medical care and supervision.

The victory of the Congress-led coalition government in 1939 with Gopinath Bordoloi as leader of the government marked the beginning of a new phase in the history of opium regulation in Assam. In February 1939, the coalition Congress ministry announced an 'opium eradication campaign' to be launched on 15 April 1939.

It was decided to launch a mass treatment programme which was to be conducted by doctors from the School of Tropical Medicine in Calcutta. Addressing a gathering at Sibsagar on 24 February 1939, Gopinath Bordoloi, in an emotive speech appealed to all sections of people to extend their full cooperation towards ensuring success of the *Kanee Barjan Andolan* (Give up Opium Campaign).[2] Elucidating the various facets of the campaign, he called upon the opium addicts to come forward for treatment and cooperate with the Government. He also apprised the people of the financial losses, which the Government would undertake, remarking, 'if we deem it a responsibility to make sacrifices for the cause of public good, no sacrifice would seem so big and success is guaranteed. But what is essential is public support'.[3] Emotions ran high as newspapers reported on how in the charged atmosphere many opium addicts immediately vowed in the presence of Gopinath Bordoloi, to give up opium altogether and pledged to report at the treatment centres for necessary medical intervention.[4]

The move towards opium eradication represented the culmination of the schedule for elimination of the 'opium evil' from Assam. Perhaps the most rousing facet of the prohibition drive was the tremendous outpouring of public enthusiasm, which reminded of the days of the Non-Cooperation movement of 1921-2, when under M.K. Gandhi the 'opium restriction campaign' witnessed a deluge of active cooperation from the people of the province.

The Addict as a 'Patient:' Medicalisation of the Problem of Opium

There were important addiction-related studies in the 1920s. In January 1923, a joint sub-committee of the League of Nations Health Committee and the Advisory Committee on Traffic in Opium, consisting of Dr H. Carriere (Vice-President, Director of the Swiss Federal Public Health Department, Berne), Dr W. Chodzko (delegate of the Polish Government to the Office International d'Hygiene), Dr. O. Anselimo (German Minister of Health) and J. Campbell (representative of the Government of India on the Opium Advisory Committee) presented a report which stated, '[...] the medical use should be considered the only legitimate use, all non-medical use should be recognised as an abuse; and that in the opinion of the doctors, opium as a stimulant could not be considered legitimate even in the tropical countries.'[5]

In 1925, John Palmer Gavit,[6] an American journalist, in a letter to the weekly *Westminster*[7] referred to Professor Elie Metchnikoff's[8] work, remarking on the relation of narcotic drugs to infectious diseases such as malaria and cholera. According to Metchnikoff, 'in every case those (animals) treated with the narcotic died, because the leucocytes, on account of the narcotic action of opium, were tardy in coming up'.[9] Thus, his results confirmed that the presence of opium in blood makes it impossible for a patient to resist the onset of disease. Following this revelation, Gavit's claim of a direct relation between the 'almost universal saturation of opium in India and the cholera mortality of 50 per cent aroused much international interest'.[10]

Researches carried out by Arthur B. Light and Edward G. Torrance of the Philadelphia General Hospital and members of the Philadelphia Committee for the Clinical Study of Opium Addiction Research on opiate addicts showed that the 'withdrawal from opiates is not life threatening and usually not dangerous'.[11] In 1928, Charles Terry and Mildred Pellen (of the Bureau of Social Hygiene's Committee on Drug Addictions), in collaboration with the US Public Health Service produced a classic study of the epidemiology of drug addiction and published an important paper, titled, 'The Opium Problem'.[12] In this paper, they argued that addiction maintenance is the most appropriate treatment for addicts who are not able to sustain abstinence. Their views were viciously attacked and only years later 'The Opium Problem' would be recognized as among the best treatise on opiate addiction ever written.

In Britain, the report of the 1926 Rolleston Committee chaired by Humphrey Rolleston, the then President of the Royal College of Physicians in Britain outlined a system of adopting a medico-legal and health approach to the enunciation of drug policies in Britain. This served as the foundation for the British system of treating addiction. It affirmed that addiction is the 'manifestation of a disease and not a mere form of vicious indulgence'.[13] In the first three decades of the twentieth century, medical treatments for narcotic addiction continued to focus on managing the mechanics of withdrawal from narcotics.

In India, Lieutenant Colonel Ram Nath Chopra[14] and his team at the School of Tropical Medicine, Calcutta (now Kolkata) carried out pioneering studies on the opium habit in the country.[15] They divided the drug addicts into three main groups: (i) moderate users, who used the drug for its medicinal properties rather than for its euphoria inducing effects, (ii) those who indulged deliberately for the sake of euphoria-inducing and aphrodisiac effects, and (iii) those accustomed to using the drug following fatigue and hard work. A series of papers by Colonel Chopra[16] and Colonel R. Knowles[17] contained an analytical study of the opium habit. Their findings had great relevance to our understanding of the progression of opium habit in Assam. Colonel Chopra's major contribution to the field of addiction studies in India was acknowledged in the 1933 Assam Opium Enquiry Committee Report. The observations made by Colonel Chopra in the studies mentioned earlier were a harbinger of the emerging politico-medical discourse, which emphasized on state participation and medical collaboration in tackling a public health menace effectively. Scientific investigations and studies had confirmed that opium addiction could be treated effectively with the help of medical involvement.[18] It was expected that the involvement of the medical community would combine the twin objectives of scientific expertize and rational administration designed to promote social welfare by safeguarding public health. Colonel Chopra lamenting on the lack of specialized institutions catering to the medical requirements of drug addicts in India, suggested the establishment of 'abstinence sanatoria' so that addicts could be treated along scientific lines in areas where the incidence of drug addiction was high. Addicts were classified according to the suitable mode of treatment, i.e. sudden or gradual withdrawal.[19]

The Indian Drug Addict

On the basis of his findings on opium addicts and the etiology of addiction in India, Colonel Chopra was convinced that the 'non-institutional method of treatment', was best suited for conditions prevalent in India where the medical fraternity was ignorant of advances in the field of addiction and its treatment. The country's apathetic attitude was evident in the lack of specially equipped institutions, such as the 'abstinence sanatoria' in the West, which precluded the possibility of institutional treatment of addicts along scientific lines. In addition, Colonel Chopra felt that the gradual withdrawal method[20] was the most suitable mode for detoxification of Indian patients.

> The shock of sudden withdrawal would be too much for many of the addicts and even those with strong will power, determined to get rid of the habit. It would make the most willing and determined of them to lose confidence and they would end by refusing to go through the treatment. We have often heard inveterate opium eaters remark that they would rather endure hell than the abstinence syndrome.[21]

Colonel Chopra cited minimal discomfort as the major advantage of the gradual withdrawal method. Another advantage was that post-withdrawal insomnia, an extremely distressing condition, was much less frequent. It was believed that this would encourage other addicts to seek treatment and help prevent relapse. Moreover, with slow withdrawal, it generally took about 3-6 weeks to effect a cure in most Indian addicts. In a paper published in 1931,[22] Colonel Chopra had emphasised the role of a certain 'psychic element' which facilitated addiction to opium. It also played a role, he stated, in the production of withdrawal symptoms.

He reached this conclusion because he had come across persons addicted to large doses of opium (20 to 100 grains a day) and then had been sent to jail. The supply of opium had inevitably been stopped. However, they had not suffered from the marked abstinence symptoms that some others did. Thus, he stressed that proper attention was to be given to the psychological rejuvenation of the patient. Building a congenial doctor-patient relationship was imperative for the recovery of the patient. Colonel Chopra also pointed out that while trying to get rid of their opium habit, bio-chemic preparations such as gentian and nux vomica, in pill form, could largely or totally replace the drug without the patients realizing it.

The findings of Colonel Chopra were included in the 1933 Assam Opium Enquiry Committee Report, which had upheld the efficacy of the policy of gradual eradication of the opium habit by reduction and rationing. Highlighting the inefficacy of incarceration of opium users, it stressed the need to cure opium addiction in hospitals where addicts could be properly 'policed'. Complete rehabilitation was ruled out. Considering the paucity of proper institutional set-up in India, Col. Chopra and his team of doctors decided to confine the scheme to the treatment of withdrawal symptoms.

Addicts were obliged to personally attend the treatment centres and no addicts were to be treated at home. In addition to government and local board staff already working in dispensaries in the sub-division, additional doctors were engaged temporarily, including in the tea garden hospitals. There were altogether 149 doctors working in the prohibition area. Every centre had a doctor on the spot to treat the addicts reporting for treatment.[23] There was considerable demand for treatment in all parts of the prohibition area as was apparent from the preliminary phase of treatment scheme. The Public Health Department surveyed the area under total prohibition with the cooperation of the Excise Department and Voluntary Local Prohibition Committees. In the Dibrugarh sub-division, a total of 31 treatment centres and 3 outreach centres while in Sibsagar subdivision, 23 treatment centres and 32 outreach centres were opened. These included all public health, local board and medical dispensaries and hospitals in the area, 8 each in Dibrugarh and Sibsagar. Treatment centres were also opened by medical officers of the tea gardens in their tea estates – 72 of these in Dibrugarh and 28 in Sibsagar. A total of 189 places were set up where treatment was made available to addicts. During this preliminary period, temporary doctors who were recruited for the prohibition treatment scheme were given a short course of training. All doctors who were in regular charge of dispensaries were also included in this training. The tea gardens were also invited to send their doctors. The training was done at Dibrugarh and Sibsagar where Colonel Chopra conducted the training sessions. The course lasted for two or three days and consisted of clinical demonstrations of withdrawal symptoms and of the treatment, which was to be followed. However, civil surgeons could exercise their discretion to modify the procedure as per local exigencies.

During the preliminary phase of the scheme, there was considerable demand for treatment in all parts of the prohibition area. The Public Health Department, with the help of the Excise Department and voluntary local prohibition committees, surveyed the area under total prohibition.

Provincial Politics and the Beginning of 'Opium Prohibition Campaign'

The Congress Coalition ministry led by Gopinath Bordoloi was to encounter not only the 'meshes of the imperialist Government of Assam and their stooges' but also the 'resourceful and strong League Ministry'.[24] Apart, certain European members represented in the Council, particularly the tea garden lobby was keen to veto any move towards total prohibition of opium. Proposals for total prohibition were defeated or had to be withdrawn in the Council.[25] Nevertheless, the Coalition Government of Assam[26] laid out an ambitious plan and a detailed agenda for a phased suppression of opium, which had elements of both revenue-oriented approach and strict suppression. In his budget speech on 9 March 1939, Bordoloi, announced the intention of the coalition government which he headed, to launch, 'A comprehensive measure to enable all consumption of intoxicants to be prohibited when the time is ripe in each case and meanwhile to make the experiment of stopping all consumption of opium . . . with the object of stamping out the habit completely within two years.'[27]

Dibrugarh and Sibsagar subdivisions, considered as having a large populace of opium consumers were selected for the first phase of the programme. [28] It was to initially run for a period of one month with effect from 15 April 1939.

Committed to 'uplift and betterment of the masses' as part of its agenda, the introduction of the motion on the *Prohibition of Opium* in March 1939 was as much a political as a social welfare initiative. The opium suppression campaign had been in operation before the assumption of power by the Congress Coalition Ministry, Bordoloi was keen on scripting the tale of its final demise from Assam. 'It is a heart rending story to give a picture of our downfall. I would ask all of you to see the condition of the people', he exclaimed, lamenting on the statement made by Syed Muhammad Sadulla of the Muslim League, and leader of opposition in favour of expansion of primary education instead of launching a costly prohibition scheme.[29] Allaying opposition fears at the prohibition scheme being 'launched in haste and may end in failure', Bordoloi justified his Government's attempt to muster all forces to 'save our nation from a ruinous habit'.[30] While F.W. Hockenhull, representing the planter constituency, expressed his support for the scheme, yet, he apprised the Government of 'attempting too much at one time which may endanger the success of the experiment', which would involve huge investments. Nevertheless, he called for an unanimous resolve to make a success of this effort, 'for the good name of Assam'.

Moving the government motion on the prohibition of opium, Akshay Kumar Das, called for unanimous acceptance of the scheme and sanction of funds within the limit of Rs. 1,25,000 for prohibition expenses. However, despite the strong anti-opium sentiment, the motion for prohibition faced stiff opposition citing other important issues requiring urgent attention. Allaying apprehensions of the opposition members, Bordoloi informed the Assembly that it is the proceeds from the opium revenue, which will be spent for the good of the public. Out of a receipt of Rs. 10,40,000 as opium revenue, the government had placed a proposal of incurring an expenditure of around Rs. 6 lakhs leaving a balance of more than Rs. 3 lakhs, which could be utilized under other heads of social expenditure. The government's policy of about 10 per cent reduction in the state supply of opium and *ganja* placed under scanner in the premises of the house. An important issue, which rocked the house, was a cut motion on the subject of non-settlement of excise shops with the Assamese people, the Government proposes to make an enquiry into the matter of policy.

10,150 opium passes with an aggregate monthly ration of 5 maunds 3 seers in these areas were cancelled and 61 opium passes were closed down from this date. The area of the Sibsagar subdivision under prohibition was 1,012 sq. miles and population estimated at 3,31,052 while Dibrugarh subdivision area under prohibition at 2,040 sq. miles with an estimated population at 5,30,178. There were 6,426 registered addicts in the portion of Dibrugarh subdivision under prohibition and 3,724 in the Sibsagar subdivision.[31] The implementation and effectiveness of the prohibition programme, however, varied from place to place. The Opium Prohibition Scheme which had been introduced in the 'Included Areas' of the province was extended to the partially excluded areas of Sibsagar and Nowgong districts from 1 December 1941 and to the partially excluded areas of Khasi and Jaintia Hills district from 1 March 1942. The introduction of total prohibition of opium throughout the included areas of the province, partially excluded areas of Garo Hills and Mikir Hills tracts in the districts of Nowgong and Sibsagar with effect from 1 March 1941 necessitated the amendment of rule 6(1), 7, 9, 32 and 35 of the Assam Opium Rules, 1926 and necessary amendments were made.[32]

'Registration, Licensing and Cures'

During the first phase of the reforms, the Prohibition Committee threw itself with fervour into a mission to wipe out 'opium evil from Assam'.[33] The first step was identifying the addict. Ordinary residents of the Dibrugarh and Sibsagar subdivisons of Assam found themselves subjected to increasingly intrusive measures. Residents were subjected to a census designed not only to identify opium smokers and record their age and occupation but to ascertain the severity and length of their habit. The system of registration, licensing and cures established under the plan allowed the government to arrange users into different categories so that they could be dealt with appropriately. This information was used to set deadlines for opium smokers to give up their habit. In many cases, it was used to determine precisely the amount of their opium ration as they gradually weaned themselves from the drug. Those identified as addicts and registered for the rationing programme were issued licenses. Prohibition volunteers carried out much of the monitoring/ documentation and enforcement of the campaigns. Mass meetings were organized, leaflets were distributed, lantern lectures were organized by the Kani Nibarani Sabhas (Opium Eradication Societies) to disseminate information about the evils of opium. The *Sattradhikars* (chiefs of the Vaishnavaite monasteries, *Sattra*) played a pivotal role in convening meetings, educating the people of the health risks associated with opium consumption. Newspapers reported on meetings and action committees formed by the anti-opium societies to disseminate information on the scheme of medical treatment to galvanize the public in action. The Gormur Sattra Kani Nibarani Samiti may be cited as an instance.[34] Anti-opium societies sprang up also in many *mauzas*, viz., the Panidihing Mauza Kani Nibarani, Kalugaon Kani Barjan Samiti, the Congress committees at North Lakhimpur, Lahowal, Doomdooma and many places in Lakhimpur. The Excise Department was also reported to have sprung into action as local newspapers reported on seizures of contraband opium followed by arrests of smugglers in many parts of the Province. Appeals were made through the newspapers to the lawyers to desist from taking up cases of excise law breaches and opium smugglers. In addition, the Congress legislators were requested to refrain from providing any sort of 'clandestine support' to those indulging in illicit opium trade.[35] Articles and press releases, eloquent speeches formed part of the propaganda to enlist both popular sympathy and support for the movement, which was crucial to the success of the campaign. This propaganda informed people that this campaign unlike many before was to be taken seriously. It emphasized on the health aspects of the opium policy encouraging people to renounce opium and purge their body of noxious substance and leading productive lives by voluntarily reporting at the treatment centres. The local newspapers, *Asamiya* and *Tini Diniya Asamiya*, played a significant role in attempts to encourage mass enthusiasm propagating the movement of prohibition of opium, applauding the efforts of the Government, exhorting people to join the movement while also criticizing loopholes in the eradication movement. It did succeed in sustaining the popular support towards anti-opium campaign. Applauding the public welfare policies of the Congress government, particularly the movement to root out the opium evil, the *Asamiya*, called for severe punishment for any person suspected of attempting to sabotage the movement of eradication by indulging in smuggling or selling opium.

> Such persons are traitors. The police complicity in smuggling and selling opium to raise profit is endangering the success of the eradication movement. It is disheartening that many among our own people are indulging in such treacherous activities. The Congress Government should not spare such enemies of the Assamese nation.[36] [Translation mine]

Interestingly, with the announcement of the Opium Prohibition Campaign, medicines claiming to cure opium addiction began to be advertized in local newspapers.[37] The Government launched a massive propaganda highlighting the benefits from the treatment. Assistant Surgeons on tour to the villages gave magic 'lantern demonstrations', 'gramophone entertainments' and lectures. Officials claimed more than 700 such demonstrations attended by around 70,000 people. Public health propaganda in school was carried out by means of Assamese and Bengali pamphlets illustrating the 'Evils of Opium Eating'. Grants and prizes to the pupils and teachers were allotted to local boards and municipal boards. Instruction in the principles and practice of hygiene and sanitation was stressed in the Public Health Department attempted to 'bring about a steady uplift amongst the people in matters pertaining to the enjoyment of good health. . . '.[38]

The Beginning of the Mass Treatment

The experiment with a three-phased intervention of detoxification, withdrawal management and recovery made Assam a pioneer of sorts in prevention and cessation of opiate addiction – a model later emulated by other provincial governments, as Orissa, which also had reported a sizeable number addicted to opium. The addicts reporting at the detoxification clinics were to undergo a process of registration, which was organized under two heads: (i) total number of addicts with opium passes and (ii) total number of addicts without passes. They were required to fill in forms mandatorily with personal details including details of their affliction and association with use of intoxicants. These copies were to be deposited with the Primary Prohibition Committees and District Prohibition Committees. It was designed as a six-week programme which began with registration which enabled classification according to the intensity of addiction, which was based on factors as daily dosage, age, duration of addiction, etc.

TABLE 7.1: CLASSIFICATION OF ADDICTS

Number treated in each group	Percentage	Daily Dosage (in grains)	Maximum Age (in yrs)
Group I 4,800	60	15 and <15	40
Group II 2,400	30	16-30	50
Group III 800	10	31 and <31	70

Source: Reproduced from R.N. Chopra and I.C. Chopra, 'Treatment of Drug Addiction: Experience in India', *Bulletin on Narcotics* 4(1957): 21-33.

Group I: consisted of 4,800 (60 per cent) of whom all were below 40 years of age and were taking the drug in doses of less than 15 grains a day. The average duration of addiction in this group was shorter than in groups II and III.

Group II: 2,400 or 30 per cent who consumed between 16 and 30 grains a day, the highest age in this group was 50 years.

Group III: 800 or 10 per cent of persons who took the drug in doses of over 30 grains a day and the average duration.

The initial phase was an experimental phase. It was to operate under severe limiting factors such as logistic and financial bottlenecks, which could render results 'meagre and inconclusive'. The propaganda and relief component of the prohibition programme was headed by Omeo Kumar Das, member of the Assam Legislative Assembly. Das was appointed as the Honorary Prohibition Commissioner to hold charge of the non-official organizations formed for carrying out the prohibition scheme. The Excise Commissioner with the general responsibility of carrying out the entire operations was left with the main concern of controlling of the Excise staff and their work. The Honorary Prohibition Commissioner organized the work under three heads, viz., propaganda, relief and vigilance through the non-official agency. Two central prohibition committees were formed – one at Dibrugarh and the other at Sibsagar with branch committees in the interior localities. In many places within the prohibited area, public meetings were held. In these meetings, the aim of the prohibition scheme was explained to the public and appeals were made to them to cooperate in every respect. Local committees also recruited volunteers. The committees instructed the opium eaters to take medicine for their cure and helped them in being treated at the centres of medical treatment. *Musti Bhikshyas* (donations), were collected from the public by the volunteers to provide rations of food free to the addicts and their relatives during the period of medical treatment. There were free offers of services by the members of the tea garden authorities and the Local Boards in various ways like collection of statistics, disseminating information and investigating the mechanisms of addiction. After release from the medical centres, the ex-addicts were to be kept under vigilance with a view to protect them from being supplied with illicit opium and to see that their friends and relatives might not come with opium from unprohibited areas and that the addicts might not migrate to these places.

With a view to effect the necessary legislation for introduction of prohibition, a Prohibition Bill was introduced in the Assembly. However, pending the passage of the Bill, the rules under the existing Opium Act were amended for the purpose. It was also decided by the Government to enforce accelerated reduction of rations in the remaining parts of the province (non-excluded areas) with a view to effect quarterly reduction of rations on all passes at the rate of one-eighth per *tola* according to a prescribed scale from 1 June 1939.

The Directorate of Public Health, Assam was in charge of the medical treatment of the addicts in close collaboration with the Excise Department, the Voluntary Local Prohibition Committees, Local Boards, Medical Dispensaries and Hospitals in Dibrugarh and Sibsagar and a two-day training programme for the doctors was organized at Dibrugarh and Sibsagar by G.S. Chopra of the School of Tropical Medicine of Bengal. Instruction manuals were prepared and issued to the doctors and the medical staff involved. It was expected that around 1,000 addicts would voluntarily apply for treatment. It was decided to embark on a three-month trial period and accordingly arrangements were made. However, the number of addicts who presented themselves for treatment at the centres far exceeded the initial figure of 1,000 and the entire scheme had to be recast to cater to the addicts reporting for treatment. There were around 10 per cent more addicts who were not registered. A formal announcement from the government was made that those unregistered addicts who voluntarily reported for treatment would not be penalized. The ratio of registered addicts to the general populace was estimated around 5 per cent.

Considering the financial constraints and the nature and extent of the scheme, the mode of treatment was confined to the treatment of withdrawal symptoms[39] – relief from withdrawal symptoms and counteracting the effects of opium on the system. All substitution treatments were rejected as being a costly venture involving hospitalization of the addict, liable to abuse and the formation of a new addiction habit. The Modinos system of treatment was rejected as totally unacceptable following painful procedure and increased risks of infection.[40] All substitution treatment procedures were rejected as being costly, involving hospitalization of the addict, liable to abuse and the formation of a new addiction habit. Under such limiting conditions, the treatment involving the use of lecithin and glucose, the 'Vitamin Cure' was deemed to be best suited.[41]

Glucose Lecithin Therapy for Withdrawal Management

The treatment that was adopted in Assam was arrived at by a process of exclusion. Due consideration was given to the number of persons who would have to be treated, the duration of treatment that would be practicable and the local conditions under which the work would have to be done. All substitution treatment therapy was rejected as being costly involving hospitalization of the addict, liable to abuse and the formation of a new addiction habit. Two methods of treatment were experimented with in Assam: (i) Vesicatory serum therapy of Modinos, and (ii) the glucose-lecithin therapy.[42]

The civil surgeons who experimented with the treatment of drug addicts by Modinos detoxification method were convinced of the efficacy of the treatment in jails and hospitals of Assam. Extensive trials of Modinos treatment were already underway on drug addicts in Burma following its approval by the health section of the League of Nations in 1932. The trials, covering 353 opium addicts confined to prison in Burma, were conducted under the supervision of Jail Superintendents. The treatment was hailed as a valuable method of withdrawal and 'denarcotisation'. However, contrary to claims of cure, it appeared to provide only temporary relief. Further, the injection of autogenous serum was not considered suitable and came to be regarded as a difficult and painful treatment.

In the Modinos detoxification method, the patient was to receive injection for about five weeks under strict observation in a hospital. His consent was required for an incision to be made and an injection of serum to be produced from his blood. The process was painful and patients resisted the treatment. Moreover, whereas the estimated addicts in Assam was around 40,000, only a few of the 193-odd dispensaries had provision for indoor patients. In addition, owing to the risks of septic infections and other complications, which could discredit the scheme and raise opposition to its continuance, the Modinos treatment was discontinued after a few trials. The only treatment that appeared to suit the conditions prevalent in Assam was the use of lecithin and glucose, both to counteract the effects of opium on the system and the treatment of other symptoms. Colonel Chopra had studied this system in detail in connection with his study on the treatment of drug addiction in India.

The treatment consisted of a three-phased intervention: (i) detoxification, (ii) withdrawal management, and (iii) recovery. The dosages of lecithin and glucose depended on the severity of the symptoms. Lechitin could be administered at a dosage of 10 grams twice or thrice daily while glucose was to be administered orally in solution or by intravenous injection (25 per cent solution). Throughout the period of treatment, addicts were encouraged to report voluntarily to treatment centres. On admission, they were subjected to a complete medical examination which included recording their detailed medical history as well as their name, age, sex, religion, occupation, social status, income, amount of opium consumed, duration of habit, reason for the habit, general health, state of heart, lungs, bowel, kidneys, urine and also details of their mental condition. Depending on the above, the patient was subjected to specific and symptomatic treatment under constant observation and control. Patients with signs of 'toxaemia' (weak pulse, yellow eyes, furred tongue and dry skin) were immediately put on isotonic saline intravenously along with a dose of diffusable cardiac tonic mixture. For 'elimination of opium through the intestinal tract', the patient was administered a full dose of calomel, ranging from 1 to 3 grams and some sodium bicarbonate at night. This was followed by a dose of magnesium sulphate to help restore the functioning of liver. However, this was discontinued if the patient had diarrhoea and then milk or curd was fed to the patient. Lecithin was administered in the form of pills from the second day, for a period of five to seven days. One pill thrice a day, along with approximately, 30 to 50 gms of glucose, was believed to ameliorate the withdrawal symptoms.

Symptomatic treatment was followed for withdrawal symptoms that usually appeared within 36 hours. Nausea and vomiting were managed by sodium bicarbonate. In severe cases, ten drops of adrenaline hydrochloride solution (1 in 1,000) were given under the tongue every two or four hours for relief. The most common complaint following the withdrawal was diarrhoea, which was treated with minimal doses of opium, in the form of Dover's powder, spread over a period of three to four days. Chronic diarrhoea was treated with bismuth salicylate, pulvis createa aromaticus – the dose varying from 10 to 15 grams. Restoratives such as brandy, spirituous ammonia aromaticus and digifortis strycnine were used to relieve low blood pressure, a feeble pulse and sinking sensation. To relieve insomnia, paraldehyde, sulphonal or chloral hydras were administered, while general weakness was sought to be alleviated by using tonics such as iron, strychnine or small doses of quinine.[43] Other 'intercurrent diseases' such as asthma, abdominal discomfort, dyspepsia, etc., were treated symptomatically.

Special attention was given to diet. During the detoxification phase, when the appetite was almost nil, the patient was fed well cooked rice with milk along with large doses of glucose (about 30 gms per day), two or three times daily. This was believed to act effectively on patients suffering from jaundice and in overcoming symptoms of shock and collapse. The use of intravenous injections of glucose was restricted to chronic cases. Once the withdrawal symptoms had eased, the patient was fed on a balanced diet consisting of eggs, milk, fish, mutton, chicken, beans, vegetables, fruit, vegetables, butter, and *ghee*, in addition to the regular meal of rice, pulses and curd.

The most important of the changes in the method of treatment was the general adoption of intravenous injections of glucose, in addition to oral glucose. The normal dose of injectable glucose was reduced from 25 to 10 ml. Stock mixtures were used for the treatment of symptoms. It was at first thought that intravenous injections, or for that matter any kind of injections, would be unpopular and end up being an obstacle to the success of treatment. The first supplies of glucose were from a German pharma company, Merck; these were later replaced by a solution of glucose, which was prepared and tubed locally at the Pasteur Institute in Shillong. Meanwhile, Messrs Smith, Stanistreet and Company Limited of Calcutta was also approached at the initiative of Colonel Chopra for the local manufacture of lecithin. This not only ensured a steady supply but also stimulated local enterprise and generated great interest in various parts of the country.

The administration of intravenous injections were, therefore, restricted to the hospitals and the regular dispensaries, where addicts could be kept under observation and control. It was found that during the preliminary period of treatment, when intravenous injections were given, the relief of the symptoms was so immediate that the addicts clamoured for these injections. Once it was found that it was possible and feasible to use the method safely under the prevailing conditions in the prohibition area, permission was given for its use in most of the centres. The duration of treatment was generally around 10 days. Though the normal practice was to examine the urine samples to determine the level of morphine, this could not be done in Assam, as the necessary reagents could not be obtained. Had it been possible to conduct such a test, it would have facilitated a comparison between the condition of those who had undergone specific treatment and those who had got over their withdrawal symptoms without any specific treatment. The official records reported on the positive results of treatment and their efficacy in the management of withdrawal symptoms and associated reactions. '[...] the patient develops a distate for the drug . . . the craving for the drug disappears and the patient's whole outlook improves. His appetite improves; he gains weight, with a great improvement in general health. The patient becomes more active and begins to take greater interest in himself and his surroundings.'[44]

However, the treatment scheme received its share of bouquets and brickbats. It came under heavy criticism with reported death of fifteen addicts. They were presumed to have died as a result of treatment or on account of the withdrawal of opium and of addicts having committed suicide by hanging or drowning and even of addicts having committed murder. *Tinidiniya Asamiya*'s report on the death of an addict at Kaluagaon de-addiction centre[45] was challenged by Bhabanath Bhattacharya of Kalugaon Kani Barjan *Samiti*. Bhattacharya claimed that in this case the addict was suffering from pneumonia and died a natural death. Such attempts at 'sabotaging' the prohibition scheme by creating fear and confusion in the minds of the public did not go unnoticed in the Assembly. Satyendra Nath Lahiri considered the desirability of appointing a special tribunal to enquire into the deaths of persons undergoing treatment. Denying such allegations, Gopinath Bordoloi informed the Assembly on weekly assessments of the prohibition scheme and denied the stoppage of opium as anything to do with the deaths and termed the reports about murder and suicide as 'unfounded' and 'untrue'.[46] The *Tinidiniya Asamiya*, carried a public plea made by Omeo Kumar Das against the sale of an anti-opium medicine, 'Amal Saraban' an ayurvedic preparation manufactured by one Ghanashyam Medicines of Ajmer, by Marwari merchants. On examination, it was revealed to have been a decoction of opium. Arrests were made and severe penalties imposed for selling the preparation.[47] *Tinidiniya Asamiya* carried advertisements of medicines claiming to cure opium addiction.[48]

Col. Ramnath Chopra recalled it in his article, as 'a unique campaign unparalleled in the history of drug addiction anywhere in the world'.[49] Apart from etiological factors, the intensity of drug addiction, principal withdrawal symptoms, relationship between age of addict, dosage, duration of addiction and the success of treatment all enabled the collection of a massive database which focused on important aspects of drug habits. Out of a total of 8,000 addicts who had reported for treatment (on the basis of data collected and available), 35 per cent reported developed the habit in association with friends and relatives, 25 per cent had started using it as a medicine, 20 per cent used it to overcome fatigue, for a 15 per cent it was for pleasure giving effects, while a 5 per cent reported using it as a substitute for alcohol.

On the question of success or otherwise of the prohibition scheme inaugurated by the Congress coalition ministry, the remarks of Durgeswar Sarma, the officer selected by the Congress coalition ministry to carry on the work would be apt. In a note dated 10 February 1940, Sarma admitted, 'the success is more or less a guess work. But continuous work for some years will certainly bring the situation to a steady and satisfactory position. The habit of a nation formed through centuries cannot be set right overnight. The present success in Sibsagar is near about 70 per cent and in Dibrugarh is between 40 and 50 per cent.'

Sarma had indeed struck a right chord. Continuous and persistent effort was required and the government in proposing an expenditure of around Rs. 8 lakhs during the budget session argued on the same logic. This was not to the taste of the opposition which decried the sum as 'sheer wastage' when Assam was reeling under a deficit of Rs. 17 lakhs.[50] The option as J.J.M. Nichols suggested was that 'the money was to be found elsewhere'. He informed the Government of demands for more dispensaries, demand for education which he believed neccessitated immediate and urgent attention. Echoing a similar view, Syed Muhammad Sadulla questioned the logic of the introduction of the opium prohibition campaign when a phased programme of restriction and reduction had already been in operation from 1929 onwards.

While the planter's constituency in general applauded the government for its initiative and courage to go ahead with such a bold experiment, voices of dissent were also heard amongst them. They expressed their apprehension at the efficacy of the treatment procedure. D.B. Moore, representing the planters' constituency remarked on how the lop sided attempts had only exacerbated the risk environment as more than 80 per cent of the tea garden addicts had access to illicit supplies. Moreover, he stated the dissatisfaction of the majority of opium addicts with the treatment who were unwilling to submit to any future treatment procedure. Nonetheless, the combination of educative propaganda and therapeutic intervention was a novel initiative as it had certainly aroused public empathy for the opium users. It marked a paradigm shift in the outlook of the general public towards the opium users who were no longer looked down as offenders but as patients who needed medical care and attention.

Sadulla Ministry and Prohibition Politics

In November 1939, the Congress coalition in Assam, following the decision of the All India Congress Committee (AICC) resigned from the ministries. After the resignation of the Congress coalition ministry, the Sadulla government claimed to have speeded up the momentum of opium prohibition in Assam. 'Undoubtedly the success achieved was a substantial degree and there is no reason to doubt. We believe that public experiment lies in a courageous extension of the experiment and in harnessing and utilizing the imagination, sympathy and effort of all well-wishers of the addicts and their dependents.' The Sadulla ministry was actively considering on introducing total prohibition in the partially excluded areas,

> It is in the confident hope and expectation of receiving wide public cooperation that this Government have embarked on this momentous measure, in spite of the great loss of revenue and increase of expenditure involved therein. There is no doubt that smuggling is rampant and big cases have been successfully detected. With the suppression of this habit of opium eating it is essential to check the addicts from diverting to the habit of taking excisable articles like liquor and ganja. If diversion is needed, it should be to the least injurious habits like tea drinking.[51]

The Sadulla ministry endeavoured to highlight its priority to public health. In 1941, a sum of Rs. 90,000 was passed for the Opium Prohibition campaign. Apart, various other social welfare initiatives as the Mass Literacy Campaign, Compulsory Primary Education in the urban areas and the establishment of a Tuberculosis Hospital at Shillong, were launched. It was claimed that these measures would 'to effect an all round improvement of the people of the country and in the best interests of the province'.[52] In the same year, the Sadulla government also modified rules 5 and 7 of the revised instructions regulating the settlement of opium and excise shops. The settlement of excise shops was to be made with due regard to communal representation on the basis of district population. Preference was to be given to unemployed Assamese youth.[53] On the same principle as is followed in the matter of appointments to Government services, preference being given to unemployed educated youth. The Quit India movement in Assam witnessed the resurgence of a new spirit for a vigorous campaign for prohibition of opium. In an editorial, the *Asamiya* appealed to the people to make the Opium Prohibition Campaign a grand success. 26 February 1941 was declared as 'Opium Prohibition Day'.

Start with a Clean Slate

THE POST-INDEPENDENCE SCENARIO

The Constitution of Independent India included specific provision for prohibition by including it among the Directive Principles of State Policy (Article 47) as follows,

> The State shall regard the raising of the level of nutrition and standard of living of its people and the improvement of public health as among its primary duties and, in particular, the State shall endeavour to bring about prohibition of the consumption except for medicinal purposes, intoxicating drinks and of drugs which are injurious to health.

Development was high on the agenda of the Government, both at the centre and at the states. The post-war reconstruction and development programme had taxed the resources of the governments. Rehabilitation measures were to be implemented in Assam which, however, was plagued by financial crisis. Accordingly, Assam sought increased grants-in-aid under Article 272 of the Constitution.[54] This increased demand was to meet her basic needs and to enable her to continue 'essential development' and welfare schemes. It was sought to place greater emphasis on productive schemes and expenditure on welfare activities were required to be curtailed until the State was in a position to afford them. Measures at rehabilitating the finances of the province were found by compelling the tea industry of Assam to pay their income tax in Assam which could result in a total revenue of around Rs. 2 crore. While the Congress Government in Assam wanted the Centre to furnish her with adequate funds so as to enable her to raise the efficiency of administration and improve the standard of living of the citizens, it faced strong challenge on the ground that the opium prohibition campaign had failed to contain the problem of opium addiction.[55]

During the campaign, drug traffickers had been widely targeted. Available regional data suggests that it had aggravated the situation and smuggling and addiction continued to wrought miseries upon the people, particularly in Dibrugarh and Lakhimpur. The smuggling of opium emerged as a potent threat to salvage the entire scheme of prohibition. The 'division of spheres' launched by the prohibition scheme of 1939 was not conducive to the success of the scheme and with a view to giving a legal status to the non-official organization and to associate it with both the fronts, the Assam Prohibition Act was passed. Under it, some non-officials were given powers of search, seizure and arrest, though its activities were primarily confined to the sphere of propaganda, relief and vigilance. While opium consumption was registering a declining trend, official statistics revealed a concomitant rise in the consumption of *ganja* and liquor throughout the province.[56] Even the *ganja* vendors had failed to account for the rise in the sales of *ganja* in the North Cachar Hills.[57] With a view to gain greater control over the smuggling of opium, the Assam Opium Prohibition Act was passed in 1947, which became effective from 1 April 1948. It was explicitly declared that the aim of the Act was to bring in suitable legislation for reviewing and revitalizing the prohibition scheme.[58] It was specifically aimed at a consumption of opium, except for medicinal purposes (b) smuggling of opium in the province and (c) to give a statutory basis to the non-official organization. This led to the institution of a non-official organization headed by Honorary Prohibition Commissioner.[59]

In September 1948 session of the Assam Legislative Assembly,

Bijay Chandra Bhagabati, moved a special resolution in view of increased smuggling of opium into Assam which was subsequently adopted,

That this assembly is of the opinion that the Government of Assam do move the Government of India to help in making the Opium Prohibition Campaign in Assam a success by making poppy cultivation and traffic in opium illegal and punishable in law all over India, including the states, and to take such effective steps as to stop smuggling of opium into Assam from other provinces and countries.[60]

Elucidating the government policy on opium and liquor, Bhagabati called for the cooperation of the Government of India to ensure success in a 'stupendous task'. The All-India Opium Conference convened in 1949 reiterated its commitment to facilitate and promote greater inter-state cooperation along with the move to evolve uniformity.

Based on the suggestions made at the Conference, a survey of addicts getting opium from illicit sources was undertaken in 1949. This survey was conducted separately by departmental and non-official agencies and was confined to the districts of Kamrup, Darrang, Nowgong, Sibsagar, Lakhimpur, Cachar, Khasi and Jaintia Hills and the Mishimi Hills. The official agency estimated the number of unregistered addicts at 13,919 and with an annual consumption of 94 maunds 18 seers 40 *tolas*.[61] The 'division of spheres' launched by the prohibition scheme of 1939 was not conducive to the success of the scheme and with a view to giving a legal status to the non-official organization and to associate it with both the fronts, the Assam Prohibition Act was passed. Under it, some non-officials were given powers of search; seizure and arrest, through its activities were primarily confined to the sphere of propaganda, relief and vigilance. While opium consumption was registering a declining trend, official statistics revealed a concomitant rise in the consumption of *ganja* and liquor throughout the province.[62] Even the *ganja* vendors had failed to account for the rise in the sales of *ganja* in the North Cachar Hills.[63]

As late as 1958, the matter was put up in the Legislative Assembly of the increased consumption of illegal opium in Dibrugarh and Lakhimpur where it was claimed that the opium business had registered an increase, with the Pathans and Muslim traders involved in smuggling of opium and the Government was accused of patronizing these people. Alleging Government complicity, Gaurishankar Bhattacharya claimed, 'The smugglers have become so powerful that they boast to the extent that they can make or unmake the Government. Even very important State dignitaries pay them respect by visiting them when they go round in their tours. They are ruling supreme in the Dibrugarh subdivision and in the other backward areas of the State.'[64]

Such a claim was by no means a trifling, especially when the Congress Government was being accused of harbouring opium smugglers and criminals and even trying to 'rehabilitate' them by awarding them timber Mahals in the Dibrugarh subdivision.[65] Even the High Court had observed that it would be in the interest of the state to place these people under the Preventive Detention Act. Increase in seizures of opium along with spurt in the number of addict population in Dibrugarh was viewed with great anxiety in the legislature. Gaurishankar Bhattacharya retorted, 'I wonder where is the Government machinery? Where is that enthusiasm which was noticed in 1938-39? Where are those patriotic youngmen-whatever political party they may belong to who fought so stubbornly and valiantly in 1938-39 in the interior parts of Sibsagar and Dibrugarh Subdivisions? Why are they not fighting now?'[66]

The remark is significant yet poignant and intriguing. The general attitude was one of utter regret over the failure of the then government to stem the existing tide of opium smuggling and urged for the resumption of creating awareness and educating the people against addiction.

With the inclusion of Prohibition as one of the Directive Principles of State Policy and the adoption of a socialistic pattern of society as the national objective, the shift towards the financial aspect of the problem assumes significance. Prohibition was viewed as an integral part of the national development plan and for it, the Prohibition Committee of 1955 upheld as that prohibition had to be accorded a high priority. However, the failure of 'Prohibition Movement' in USA in the mid-twentieth century was amply reflected in policy makers avoiding it being enunciated as a

Constitutional obligation. Cultural and social factors differed from province to province and such any move at uniformity was bound to be unacceptable at a time when the country was witnessing the worst phase of divisive tendencies. An Estimates Committee appointed in 1955, to examine the workings of the excise and forest department, recommended that a portion of revenue accruing from the sale of excise opium should be diverted to the treatment centres for opium addicts.[67]

Another significant observation of the Estimates Committee was lack of coordination between the special branch and the general branch of law enforcement created to detect and deal with cases of opium smuggling. The Intelligence Bureau established in 1945 was found inadequate and insufficiently staffed. The Committee recommended that proper wages and improved facilities for the department personnel. It also suggested strengthening of the intelligence branch to deal with rising instances of inter-state opium smuggling.[68]

Conclusion

1939 was a defining moment in the long history of Assam's struggle with opium. It is interesting to note how the maneuvering of the interests of economics and politics consolidated and at the same time undermined the efficacy of the opium eradication scheme. The coalition government was able to build up a consensus on the massive anti-drug campaign, – the rhetoric of reclaiming the *Xonar Axom* (land of golden gardens) which had been defiled by the opium addicts earning it the infamy of a 'black spot'. The rationale of the massive opium eradication programme was the resolve of the government aimed at socio-economic transformation of Assam. It was to build a new provincial identity for the province. Drug suppression was a part of that ambitious programme and certainly not a high priority. Interestingly, the premise of the entire anti-drug campaign was based on self-appraisal rather than the 'poisoning policy' rhetoric that had characterized the early years of the anti-opium movement. Nevertheless, the campaign against opium was a novel initiative which generated much interest in the country.

In 1940, the Central Advisory Board of Public Health convened a meeting in Poona where the representative from Assam was to inform about the effects of the Opium Prohibition Scheme and how it affected the health of addicts in Assam.[69] The 1939 anti-opium campaign was not followed by any further campaign as multi-layered anti-drug campaigns of the type carried out in the China. Post-1947, the issue reverberates less and less in the official debates and discussions. It became more a concern of the excise department and slowly moved away from popular parlance and became part of yet another ambiguity. Ironically, 'opium' was left out of the development agenda of the government. The anti-opium campaign continued till officially Assam was declared 'nil' of opium in 1959.

Notes

1. Ram N. Chopra, 'The Present Position of the Opium Habit in India', *Indian Journal of Medical Research* 16(1928): 389-439. Also refer, Ram N. Chopra and R. Knowles, 'The Action of Opium and Narcotine in Malaria', *Indian Journal of Medical Research*, 5(1930): 13.
2. *Asamiya*, 24 February 1939, DHAS, 9.
3. Ibid.
4. Ibid.
5. Ram N. Chopra and I.C. Chopra, 'Quasi Medical Use of Opium', *Bulletin on Narcotics,* 3(1953): 1-22.
6. John Palmer Gavit (1868-1954) as chief of the Washington Bureau of the Associated Press, had attended the Opium Conferences in Geneva. His book entitled *Opium* is a critical review of the opium conferences in Geneva written in an engaging style, which captures the various perspectives of the problem in an international context.
7. Founded in 1893, it was a prominent liberal newspaper in London. It ceased publication in 1928.
8. Elie Metchnikoff (1845-1916), a Russian scientist, foreign member of the Royal Society of London and Professor at the Pasteur Institute in Paris, was the first to discover phagocytes that could engulf and destroy microorganisms in the body. In 1908, he co-shared the Nobel Prize. However, his best known research work was the 'Immunity in Infectious Diseases' which he conducted during his tenure at the Pasteur Institute at Paris.
9. Elie Metchnikoff, 'Immunity in Infective Diseases', tr. Francis G. Binnie, University Press, 1905.

10. 'For Securing the Effective Control of Opium and Kindred Drugs in Accordance with the Recommendations of the Hague International Opium Convention, 1912', *British Bulletin of the Society for the Suppression of the Opium Trade*, 1925, 23: 2-4, NAI.
11. Richard K. Ries, Shannon C. Miller and David A Fiellin, *Principles of Addiction Medicine*, Philadelphia: Lippincott, Williams and Wilkins, 2009, p. 332.
12. Charles E. Terry and Mildred Pellens, *The Opium Problem*, New York: Committee on Drug Addictions, Bureau of Hygiene, 1928.
13. *Departmental Committee on Morphine and Heroin Addiction,* London: Rolleston Committee, 1926. Available at <http://www.druglibrary.eu/library/reports/rolleston.pdf> (accessed on 12 April 2010).
14. Col. Ram Nath Chopra (1882-1973) is regarded as the Father of Indian Pharmacology. He is respected as a great teacher, keen researcher in Indian indigenous drugs, clinical pharmacologist, and toxicologist and above all a visionary pharmacologist.
15. R.N. Chopra and I.C. Chopra, 'Treatment of Drug Addiction: Experience in India', *Bulletin on Narcotics* 4(1957): 21-33.
16. Ram N. Chopra, 'The Present Position of the Opium Habit in India', *Indian Journal of Medical Research* 16(1928): 389-439.
17. Ram N. Chopra and R. Knowles, 'The Action of Opium and Narcotine in Malaria', *Indian Journal of Medical Research* 18(1930): 5-13.
18. D.N. Campbell, P.J. Olsen and L. Walden, *The Narcotic Farm: The Rise and Fall of America's First Prison for Drug Addicts*, New York: Abrams, 2008. The federal narcotic treatment programme of U.S. launched in and around 1930 has and continued roughly until the 1980s. The farm though designed as rehabilitation centre for internment and treatment, came under heavy criticism for its experiments on the inmates, as part of its drug-testing programme. It had to be shut down.
19. Professor Karl Bonhoeffer, a prominent German psychiatrist in Berlin, advocated the withdrawal of the drug by the 'sudden' method. He was elected chair of the Department of Psychiatry and Neurology at the Charity Hospital, Berlin. Among his studies are his prominent researches on alcoholism, *Die Giesteszustandeder Alkoholddeliranten* which opened up new vistas in the treatment of addiction. Although they were claimed to be successful in Europe and America, it had not been possible to carry it out in India due to lack of infrastructural facilities to deal with post withdrawal complications, if any.
20. Chopra and Chopra, 'Treatment of Drug Addiction', 21-33.
21. Chopra, 'The Present Position of the Opium Habit in India', p. 410.
22. In 1931, Drs R.N. Chopra and J.P. Bose of the School of Tropical Medicine, in Calcutta, had carried out studies on the psychological aspect of opium

addiction on a series of patients in the hospital, which was published in the *Indian Medical Gazette,* 1931. They illustrated a 'predominant psychic element' which could be overcome, 'if the patient is not aware that he is taking opium, the drug can be effectively given for weeks and months for its therapeutic effects and can be stopped at any moment without producing abstinence symptoms.' They concluded that physicians should not hesitate to use opiates in special cases, provided the identity of the drug be concealed from the patient. They also suggested that during the treatment of addicts, opium can be replaced by substances like gentian or *nux vomica* preparations without trouble. Ram N. Chopra and J.P. Bose, 'Psychological Aspects of Opium Addiction', *Indian Medical Gazette*, LXVI(1931): 663.

23. S. Gohain, 'A Brief Report on the Progress of the Scheme for Prohibition of Opium in the Sibsagar and the Dibrugarh Subdivisions, Assam from 15 April to 30 June 1939', File No. A.G.P Excise (1939), ASA, pp. 11-100.
24. The Congress party did not have a clear majority and the Congress High Command was initially skeptical to the idea of coalition ministry. K.L. Barooah, 'Shri Gopinath Bordoloi: A Study', in M.L. Baruah (ed.), *Lokapriya Gopinath Bordoloi*, New Delhi: Gyan Publishing House, 1992, pp. 175-88, 336, 337. The AICC had authorized acceptance of offices in provinces where the Congress party commanded absolute majority in the Legislatures. At a meeting of the Assam Pradesh Congress Committee (APCC) on 14 March 1937, held at Barpeta, G.N. Bordoli, Omeo Kumar Das, Liladhar Barua, Sarbeswar Barchetia, Ghanashyam Das and others, decided in favour of playing the opposition as it did not command absolute majority. This paved the way for the accession to power of the United Muslim party formed with the newly elected Muslim members of the Assembly of the Brahmaputra valley and the Surma valley. Md. Sadullah enjoyed the support of the European bloc. The Ministry was accused of being a congregation of diverse and reactionary elements and of 'setting an example of political muddling of an unhealthy kind.'
25. The report of the 1925 Assam Congress Opium Enquiry Committee had suggested imposing additional taxation on the tea industry to compensate for losses incurred due to the restriction on opium. The tea garden block was apprehensive that prohibition of opium would mean imposing heavy duties on tea. Heramba K. Barpujari, *Political History of Assam*, vol. III, Guwahati: Publication Board Assam, 1999, p. 214.
26. The members of the Congress Coalition Government (19 September 1938-17 November 1939) were, Gopinath Bordoloi (Premier), Akshay Kumar Das, Ramnath Das, Kamini Kumar Sen, Rupnath Brahma, Fakhruddin Ali Ahmed, Mahmud Ali and Ali Hyder Khan, Barpujari, *Political History of Assam*, p. 367. Although the ministry was called the Congress-coalition ministry, it was maintained that 'it was as good as a

sole Congress Government' with unanimity among the partners as regards the objectives and programmes. Some of the measures of this programme were:

(i) progressive eradication of opium, (ii) reduction of land revenue, (iii) restoration of land confiscated by the previous governments for the failure of payment of revenue owing to poverty, (iv) abolition of the Commissioner's establishments, (v) restriction of immigration into Assam and, (vi) Safeguarding the interests of the indigenous population, etc. Refer, Barpujari, *Political History of Assam,* pp. 357-8.

27. Gohain, *A Brief Report on the Progress of Prohibition*, p. 2.
28. The annual consumption of opium in 1938 being about 35 maunds in the Dibrugarh subdivison and about 26 maunds in the Sibsagar subdivision. This far exceeded the standard set by the League of Nations of 30 seers per 10,000 of population for India. This standard had been ratified by the member countries including the Government of India and accepted by the Legislative Assembly of the Provincial Government of Assam.
29. *ALA Proceedings*, *The Assam Gazette*, 16 March 1939, ASA, pp. 348-9.
30. Ibid.
31. As of 1932-3, it was estimated that of the total population of 2,858,651 (1931 census) in the four districts of the Assam valley (Darrang, Nowgong, Sibsagar, Lakhimpur) and the Sadiya Frontier Tract which had been identified as the 'Black Spot, there were a total of 59,674 opium pass holders, the percentage of pass holders to total population being 1 in 48. *Report of the Assam of the Assam Opium Enquiry Committee 1933*, *ACOER*, 1933, ASA.
32. Government notification no. 727-L.S.G. dated 17 February 1941, Report on the Administration of the Excise Department in the province of Assam for the years 1941-2, ASA.
33. *ALA Proccedings*, *The Assam Gazette*, 27 October 1937, ASA, 1120-1.
34. The *Gormur Kani Nibarani Samiti* presided over by *the Sattradhikar* Gormurio Goswami, convened a meeting in the *Sattra* premises following the launch of the Prohibition campaign and called upon the opium addicts to avail of the treatment facilities and 'rid body and mind of the evil.' *Asamiya*, 6 August 1939, DHAS, p. 7.
35. Bilasrai Themani, 'Letter to the Editor', *Asamiya*, 25 February 1939, DHAS, 6.
36. *Asamiya*, 23 September 1939, DHAS, p. 4.
37. Advertisements in the *Asamiya* about the efficacy of an Ayurvedic preparation, prepared at *Gunawan Mahantar Aushadhalay* (the clinic of Gunwan Mahant) at Sibsagar for curing opium addiction. This was being sold for Rs. 5 per 250 gms of medicine. It was claimed that it not only was a cure for opium addiction but also provided instant relief from all

withdrawal symptoms. *Kani Erra Aukhod*, Asamiya, 25 February 1939, DHAS, p. 1.

38. Public Health Reports of the Province of Assam, ASA
39. Withdrawal symptoms included physical and mental discomfort arising from withdrawal from the drug. This included epigastria pain, loss of appetite, insomnia, constipation, nausea, vomiting and cramps, irregular and sinking pulse, headaches and in some cases cardiac collapse. About the second or third day of the withdrawal, the symptoms are at their peak. Ram N. Chopra and Inder C. Chopra, 'Treatment of Drug Addiction. Experience in India', *Bulletin on Narcotics*, 3(1957): 21-33.
40. Dr. Polyvios Modino (1872-1970) was the chief attending surgeon at the European Hospital in Alexandria. He accidentally discovered that injecting fluid from a water blister, such as that raised by a mud plaster, could rid a cocaine addict of his addiction. Dr. Modino's clinical trial of blister fluid on morphine addicts yielded positive results. However, contrary to claims of cure, it appeared to provide only temporary relief. Further, the injection of autogenous serum from a blister on the skin was not considered suitable owing to the risks of septic infections and other complications that had discredited further continuance of the scheme, *ACOER*, 1933.
41. The Lecithin and Glucose method of treatment had been used in China by Ma Wen Chao (1932) and co-workers at the suggestion of Dr. J. Heng Lui, Chairman of the National Opium Suppression Commission in China. They had observed that opium smokers secure comfortable and spontaneous cure by means of a lecithin diet. A daily dose of 60-90 gms., of lecithin from soyabean, administered for around three to six weeks was believed to break the habit. According to Ma, the lecithin treatment afforded a means of suppressing opium habit without the use of military force or elaborate hospital equipment.
42. A Chinese anatomist, Dr Ma Wen Chao and his team at the Peiping Union Medical College in 1931, made a revolutionary discovery for the treatment of opium addicts and other narcotics. The team had concluded that during the withdrawal period, the protein content, especially the 'neuro-protein' was deficient and patients, who were put on a rich protein diet, would facilitate speedy recovery of the patient. In 1932, Ma's experiments on 143 opium smokers where the patients were allowed to smoke opium but they were alongside administered around 20-30 grams of soybean lecithin, three times a day after meals showed that the patients expressed decreased tendency for opium, within 4 to 22 days. National Research Council (US) on Drug Addict. *Report of the Committee on Drug Addiction, 1929-1941*, Washington: National Academies, 1941, pp. 1331-51.
43. 'Instructions Issued by the Civil Surgeon, Lakhimpur to all Medical Officers,' Memo no. 416 P., 12 July 1939, ASA, pp. 316-17.

44. Lt Col. A.M.V. Hesterlow (Director of Public Health, Assam), 'Note on Instructions for the Treatment of Opium Addiction', Memo no. 476 P., August 1939, ASA.
45. *Tinidiniya Asamiya*, 21 April 1939, ASA, p. 3.
46. *ALA Proceedings*, *The Assam Gazette*, 13 May 1939, ASA, 310.
47. *Tinidiniya Asamiya*, 2 December 1939, ASA, p. 4.
48. Ref. figure in Appendix XI
49. Chopra and Chopra, 'Treatment of Drug Addiction', p. 27.
50. Joint sitting of the Assam Legislature presided over by Heramba Prasad Barua, *The Assam Gazette*, 4 August 1939, ASA, pp. 52-60.
51. *ALA Proceedings*, *The Assam Gazette*, 19 March 1940, ASA, pp. 1014-15.
52. Ibid., 15 November 1940, ASA, pp. 1382-3.
53. Under the revised rules, Assamese Hindus were to be classed as distinct from other 'domiciled Hindus'. Also, the members of the Ahom community were to be considered as a separate community and the settlement made on the basis of district population on as shown in the statements appended to appointment and Political Department Circular, dated 7 December 1933. However, under Rule 7, it was laid down that if any of the sitting lessees was given settlement of a shop, he was to share the quota of the community to which he belonged. However, the district officers were informed that these rules were not applicable to the Excluded Areas. 'Letter from the Secretary to the Government to the Commissioner of Excise, Assam', no. 727, LSG, 24 January 1941, ASA.
54. Article 272 of the Constitution provided by legislation, that atleast 75 per cent of Excise duty on tea, petrol and Kerosene should be provided to the states.
55. *ALA Proceedings*, *The Assam Gazette*, 13 March 1950, ASA, p. 311.
56. An enquiry was ordered to be conducted by the Deputy Commissioners of Cachar, Lakhimpur and Naga Hills and the Political officer of the Sadiya Frontier Tract to ascertain the reasons for the rise in the sales of opium consumers are showing any signs of taking *ganja* as a substitute for opium and seek information from the *ganja* vendors as to whether any of their new clients are former opium consumers. The reports failed to conclusively indicate the main reason for a rise in sale of *ganja* consequent to fall in the sale of opium with the Commissioner of Excise claiming on the lack of any conclusive evidence to show that *ganja* and liquor are taking the place of opium to any appreciable extent in the Prohibition areas. Amongst the tea garden coolies there are to be met only a few cases of opium addicts who in place of opium are taking liquor and *ganja* but the number of such cases is by no means large. The rise in the sales of liquor and *ganja* in the shops on the border of the prohibition areas is no sure indication that these intoxicants are taking the place of opium, as their rise is noticeable

almost throughout the province. Various reasons have been attributed to the increase in the sale of *ganja* as the influx of *ganja* consuming foreigners, recruitment of coolies in the Railways Quarries by the Assam Bengal Railway contractors, death and desertion, etc., of the opium consumers. 'Letter from Commissioner of Excise to the Secretary to the Governor of Assam', no. 3514, 11 March 1940. Also refer, 'Letter from Commissioner of Excise, Assam to the Secretary, Government of Assam', 10 May 1940, ASA.

57. Replies received from the *ganja* vendors at Dittokcherra, Langting, Maibong and Haflong at the North Cachar Hills. 'Letter from Ganja Vendors to the Commissioner of Excise, Assam', 22 December 1939, ASA.
58. Political File no. 13, January 1947, ASA.
59. The sphere of his responsibilities was originally limited to fighting against the consumers through propaganda, relief and vigilance. With the enforcement of the Assam Opium Prohibition Act in 1948, the sphere of activities of the non-official section was extended to the field of detection and prevention of smuggling. Although, later these powers were gradually withdrawn and their activities were confined to propaganda, relief and vigilance.
60. *ALA Proceedings*, 25 September 1948, ASA, pp. 1294-5.
61. Comparing the figures as on the date of first introduction of total prohibition as an experiment in 1939 and 1947-8, the number of addicts has been reduced from 30,366 to 15,326 and their ration from 180 to 98 maunds. Based on the average annual reduction for the period between 1938-9 and 1947-8, the total number of addicts and their ration at the end of the year was put at 30,313 and 71 maunds. This includes 2,176 registered addicts with a ration of 7 maunds. *Report on the Excise Administration of the Province of Assam for the Year 1950-51*, ASA.
62. An enquiry was ordered to be conducted by the Deputy Commissioners of Cachar, Lakhimpur and Naga Hills and the Political officer of the Sadiya Frontier Tract to ascertain whether opium consumers were taking *ganja* as a substitute for opium. It was also decided to seek information from the *ganja* vendors as to whether any of their new clients are former opium consumers. The reports failed to conclusively indicate the main reasons for a rise in sale of *ganja* consequent to fall in the sale of opium with the Commissioner of Excise claiming on the lack of any conclusive evidence to show that *ganja* and liquor are taking the place of opium to any appreciable extent in the Prohibition areas. Amongst the tea garden, 'coolies' there were a few instances of opium addicts who had substituted liquor and *ganja* for opium. Various reasons were assumed to have contributed to the increase in the sale of *ganja*. These included the influx of *ganja* consuming foreigners, recruitment of 'coolies' in the railway quarries by the Assam

Bengal Railway contractors, death and desertion, etc., of the opium consumers. 'Letter from Commissioner of Excise to the Secretary to the Governor of Assam', no. 3514, 11 March 1940. Also refer, 'Letter from Commissioner of Excise, Assam to the Secretary, Government of Assam', 10 May 1940, ASA.

63. Replies received from the *ganja* vendors at Dittokcherra, Langting, Maibong and Haflong at the North Cachar Hills. 'Letter from Ganja Vendors to the Commissioner of Excise, Assam', 22 December 1939, ASA.
64. *ALA Proceedings, The Assam Gazette*, 8 April 1958, ASA, pp. 2436-7.
65. Ibid.
66. Ibid, pp. 2440-1.
67. Letter from the Commissioner of Excise to the Secretary to the Government of Assam, no. Ex.174/58/2, 4 September 1958, ASA.
68. The flow of cheap Kachin opium from across the Burma border and the discovery of poppy cultivation in places across Upper Assam had become an additional menace to the campaign for total prohibition of opium. In addition, it was reported that contraband opium was smuggled into Assam from West Bengal, Uttar Pradesh, Bihar, Punjab, Rajasthan, and East Pakistan, Burma and from China. *Report on the Annual Excise Administration of the Province of Assam for the Year 1950-1*, ASA.
69. *ALA Proccedings, The Assam Gazette*, 16 March 1940, ASA, pp. 348-9.

CHAPTER 8

Kaniai Khale Asam Desh: A Reconsideration of the Nationalist Critique of the 'Imperialism of Opium'

Extent of Opiate Consumption

RECONSTRUCTING THE INDEX of 'epidemiologic reality', which could provide a holistic representation of the extent and pattern of opiate consumption in Assam, is complex and intricate. While the official surveys and reports have their limitations, the prevalence of a large number of unregistered consumers who did not wish to reveal their condition is a major deterrent in deciphering the exact nature and prevalence of opium consumption. It is the lack of any independent survey that has made it imperative to draw information from the several government reports; hence, any attempt to corroborate the figures and findings is difficult, if not impossible. Although each type of data has its limitations, it is nevertheless possible to reach certain general conclusions. The reports, both official and the non-official, along with the debates in the floor of the legislature, discussed in a previous chapter, had established that opium addiction was considered a problem of massive dimensions. At the high tide of nationalist agitation, the rhetoric that 'Opium had ruined Assam', moved from the colonial parlance into the realm of the nationalists demand for eradication of the opium evil.

Undoubtedly, Assam had a problem with opium. But there lies a difficulty in an authentic assessment of the proportion of population that was rendered 'useless' due to the opium habit and an evaluation of its affect on the economic productivity of the people, the rural peasantry in particular, if it did at all. To that end, it is necessary to attempt to reconstruct the prevalence and trend of opiate addiction.

Narratives from Prisons

Available literature on the subject of penal policy in colonies illustrates how colonial jails not merely served in 'casting deviance outside spaces of enlightenment'[1] but were also sites of production of knowledge of native 'difference and backwardness'.[2] This is evident from the data collected on the opium eaters incarcerated for various crimes, which served to identify or mark a specific set of populace within the community as 'criminal' due to their association with opium. *The Report on the Jail Administration of Assam*, from the mid-nineteenth century, kept a track of the opium eaters under a separate statement, titled, 'Statement showing the number of opium eaters admitted into the Jails and Subsidiary Jails of Assam'. These statements provide information on the number of convicts who confessed being habituated to the use of opium, quantities that they consumed, treatment that the doctors approved in their case and the effects of stopping the supply of opium. Medical officers did testify to the misery of some newly jailed inmates who had suffered withdrawal symptoms after being deprived of their daily dosage.[3] Most prisoners recovered their health but some who suffered from dysentery or some other diseases were administered opium doses within permissible limits, to prevent collapse or even death. This continued well into the twentieth century when the concept of reform and rehabilitation replaced one of punishment to the opium eaters who were confined in jails – 'correction through segregation'. Officially branded as the 'maintenance programme' for opium consumers in jails, it was, however, characterized by absence of any uniformity in approach. While in some jails, the doctors insisted that no opium was to be provided while in some jails, the doctors advocated 'diminishing doses of opium' to prevent untoward withdrawal symptoms. Based on the statements collected from the jail administration reports for selected years – showing the number of consumers admitted into jail who confessed their use of opium in the jails of Assam for the various years as mentioned in the table in Appendix VII.

While certainly not an index of epidemiologic reality, the above figures are an indicator of the late nineteenth century rhetoric of opium use as deviance and opium users as prone to criminal behaviour. Further, these figures also reveal that an increasing number of opiate users were being incarcerated and subjected to 'experimentation' by varying the treatment procedure from forced abstinence to being allowed opium use in controlled quantities. Opium use was like 'bits of evidence' that could add up to the guilt of the jailed inmates and justify the perpetration of policies aimed at 'disciplining the body', of the opium users to render them into useful and productive subjects. The reports also claimed that majority of the users were the Assamese populace, the 'natives of the Brahmaputra valley'.[4] The percentage of those who confessed using opium and were being treated in jails varied from 10.93 in 1881 to 12.96 in 1882, to around 10 in 1883 with a 8.19 in 1884, 7.22 in 1885, 4.8 in 1893, 4.6 in 1892, 3.9 in 1894, 4.8 in 1895, 4.7 in 1896, 5.1 in 1898, 6.4 in 1899. The success of the 'treatment of opium users in jails' was sought to be publicized in the figures of the amount of daily dose. The doctors claimed that following the phase of incarceration and forced abstinence, even those used to consuming a heavy dose of around 11 to 16 *annas*[5] of opium a day could do with a moderate dose of ½ to 4 *annas* a day.

Extent of Opiate Consumption: Re-examining Official Surveys

Opium 'does not appear responsible for any disease peculiar to itself', declared the 1893 RCO. It contested the claims of the anti-opium campaign led by the missionaries and medical men, for total prohibition of opium. Based on the massive evidence accumulated, the RCO argued against the prohibition of the use of opium citing that its use was part of the cultural and social ethos of India. One should keep in mind that the British, American and Canadian Protestant missionaries were the staunchest of the anti-opium advocates and it was their testimonies that formed the main basis of 'opium as an evil' rhetoric.

Contradicting the claims made by the anti-opium protestors, a lengthy analysis of the evidence from a medical point of view was carried out by William Roberts (1830-99), renowned British doctor and medical researcher. He was the sole medical member of the RCO.[6] The RCO was the first methodical and extensive survey on opiate consumption. It carried details about the number of opiate users and consumption patterns within the limits of the country and area under survey. The districts of Kamrup, Darrang, Nowgaon, Sibsagar and Lakhimpur were found to be worst affected and the habit was mentioned as being widely prevalent among the members belonging to the various castes of Chutiyas, Dom, Ahom, Ganak, Kalita, Keot, Lalung, Mikir, Miri, Salai, Jugi, Koch and Hari.[7]

The percentage of opium eating to total population was estimated around 53.38 in Kamrup, 46.41 in Darrang, 76.37 in Nowgong, 63.79 in Sibsagar and 47.13 in Lakhimpur. Out of a total population of 19,97,478 (figures as per census of 1891), 1,155,520, that is around 57.85 per cent were consuming opium with consumption per head being the highest in Lakhimpur, 4.15 *tolas* followed by Sibsagar, 2.46 *tolas*, Darrang, 2.08 *tolas*, Nowgong, 1.06 *tolas* and Kamrup, 0.76 *tola*.[8] The rising incidence of opium use was linked with an increase in indigenous opium eating Assamese population, which had registered a positive growth in the year 1911 (14.1 per cent increase – up to 2,023,972 in 1911 from 1,773,484 in 1901).

Excise revenue figures from the year 1911 onwards, reveal that increasing sales of *ganja* was occurring while opium sales had reported a dip. Official reports of the District Commissioners claimed that the policy of rationing of opium had resulted in balloon effect – opium users were taking to *ganja*.[9] To allay apprehension, in 1912, a Committee was set up to report on the rising trend of *ganja* use. The Report of the Committee of 1913 appointed to enquire into aspects of Opium and Ganja Consumption (also called the Botham Committee) was another first of its kind, which elucidated a highly overlooked approach to the opium situation in Assam, that of the use of *ganja* which was gaining popularity following the increase in the price of opium. While discussions on this have remained elusive in the course of unearthing the trajectory of opium question in Assam, its significance can hardly be ignored. The Report of the Committee (1913), however, established that moderation was the rule and that excess consumption of opium was found in only 3 to 4 per cent of the population. Official estimates for the first decade of the twentieth century confirmed, 'an 88% increase in the consumption of *ganja* between 1901 and 1911',[10] which far outnumbered the increase in population.[11]

Based on the testimony of witnesses, the Committee observed,

> There is no doubt that the upper class Assamese regards ganja as a less disreputable vice than opium partly on account of its religious associations, partly perhaps and this is the reason he usually gives himself because it stimulates whilst opium tends to indolence. Its cheapness also gives ganja an advantage as compared with opium. In Kamrup, the example of foreigners employed on the construction of railway may have had some effect, as may also the influence of the number of up-country or Bengali sanyasis, who pass through the district on the way to Kamkhya. One of these gentry in particular appears to have established a regular cult of *ganja* smokers in the neighbourhood of Nalbari.[12]

Years later, in 1925, the *Report of the Assam Congress Opium Enquiry Committee* reinforced the image of 'misery, unhappiness, physical and moral degradation which opium habit has caused amongst the Assamese people in general'.[13] The report deplored the official policy of 'maximum revenue and minimum consumption', which had rather resulted in 'maximum revenue and increasing consumption', despite steep rise in per seer of opium issued.[14] The *ACOECR 1925* does not provide any information on the number of users or the percentage of population addicted to the use of opium, yet from the data, it can be safely surmised that in 1921, around 42 per cent of the population (indigenous) was using the drug in one form or another. This appears to be a lower figure than that of the previous years, in 1911, 47 per cent of population; in 1901, 37 per cent of the population (low on account of decrease of population due to diseases); in 1891, 43 per cent of the population and in 1891, around 59 per cent of the population was 'addicted' to opium.

Statistics presented for Assam at the Black Spot Conference[15] provided figures for the total number of registered opium consumers.

In 1927-8, there were 85,976 pass holders (registered consumers); in 1928-9, the number of pass holders was 98,000; in 1930-1, the total number of registered consumers were 83,801; in 1931-2, the number was further down to 74,875. At the end of 1932-3, there were 69,605 registered consumers in Assam.[16] The average dose per pass holder in Assam was 1½ *tolas* a month.

Statistics available from the report on the *Scheme for Prohibition of Opium in the Sibsagar and the Dibrugarh Subdivision, Assam*, is incomplete yet enlightening. The numbers of registered addicts in Dibrugarh were estimated at 6,426 and 3,724 in Sibsagar subdivision.[17] Besides, the registered consumers there were also a very large number of unregistered consumers coming up for treatment. Official estimates confirmed that as of 1929, there was a significant population of unregistered consumers who obtained from illicit sources, estimated between 8,000-9,000 consumers, which are considerable.[18] As per official approximation of 11,000 addicts in the two subdivisions, it was expected that around 1,000 would apply for treatment. The numbers of those who came in for the treatment, however, exceeded the 1,000 approximate figures. The number of addicts treated between 15 April to 30 June 1939, was around 12,850.[19] The figures available for the number of consumers from 1926-7 to 1936-7 are:

TABLE 8.1: NUMBER OF OPIUM CONSUMERS (1926-37)

Year	Total number of opium consumers
1926-7	98,000
1927-8	85,976
1928-9	82,590
1929-30	88,652
1930-1	78,009
1931-2	75,265
1932-3	70,947
1933-4	64,513
1934-5	55,128
1935-6	51,220
1936-7	42,533

Source: Tinidiniya Asamiya, June 1939. DHAS

The data provide inconclusive results on analysis, simply because none of the figures are reliable and they are hard to compare as well. There have been claims that 70 per cent of the total population use opium on a regular basis to almost universal consumption of opium use. Precisely how many, is difficult to gauge. It is a fallacy in the first place to consider that the use of opium was increasing.

The following graphic representation illustrates how the opium consumption per head declined from 1.45 *tolas* in 1873-4 to 1.11 *tolas* in 1880-1. In 1890, it declined further to .77 down to .68 in 1901. From .72 *tolas* in 1912-13, in 1923-4, it was .37 *tolas*.

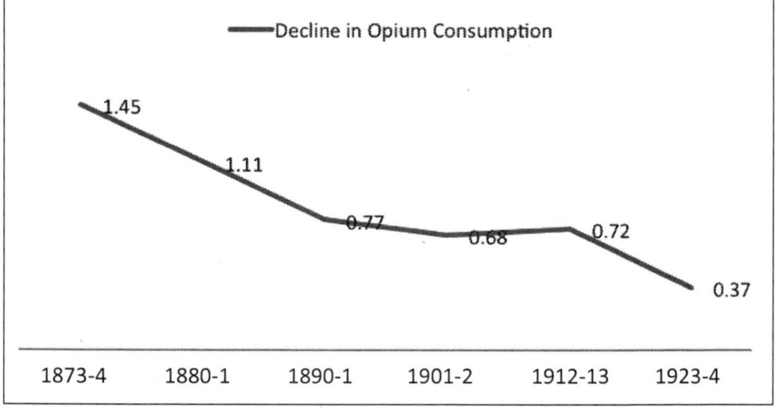

Source: Based on statistics in the Annual Excise Administration Reports

FIG. 8.1: DECLINE IN OPIUM CONSUMPTION

The Myth of the Endemic Opium Affliction

The 'demonization' of opium coincided with a series of enactments all facilitated to benefit the then emerging tea cultivation and to satisfy the imperial taste and culture. Tea symbolized refinement and respectability, opium was its antithesis – it was the symbol of decadence and degradation. Uninhibited poppy cultivation in Assam was moreover held responsible for the stagnant agricultural production.[20] As sensational reports of Assam being contaminated and destroyed by opium made its way to the international arena, the region became a 'black spot on the face of India'.[21] 'Assam is ruined by the opium poison'; 'Opium scourge wracks havoc in Assam'; 'What a ruin has befallen Assam'? – such pathetic and gory imageries of sullen, lazy and incapacitated people reinforced the belief that the opium plague was a scourge of humanity all over and must therefore be eradicated. As a 'narcophobic discourse'[22] established itself within the precincts of international efforts; draconian measures were initiated not only against opium but against 'illicit' drug use all over the world in Europe, Americas and Asia. As the colonial government of India faced increasing international scrutiny, the burgeoning number of opium 'addicts' set in motion political activism and increasing medical intervention to 'reform and cure the addict'. As opposition to opium use in Assam became vocal, anti-opium forces both in Assam and overseas inflated the number of addicts to illustrate more graphically the damage opium was doing to the Assamese people. Late nineteenth century temperance agitations reinforced the image of the Assamese opium eater 'Kaniya' a term still widely used in popular usage in Assam and which is used to describe a lazy person. Interestingly, the image at the core of this belief has rarely been examined at the time either by contemporaries or more recently by historians. Missionaries and later medical men were instrumental in shaping the rhetoric of opium use being detrimental to the health and well-being of an individual; nationalists were eager to find a scapegoat in imperialism by emphasizing the catastrophic effects of opium use.

Oft repeated condemnation of the British indulgence in opium trade have largely been from the viewpoint of analysing the subject as a cause and effect of the imperialist policies. The primary hypothesis that has been proposed by anti-opium proponents is that 'all opium use is harmful and that it leads to addiction and therefore to physical ruin'. The picture drawn by the opponents of opium use is that those who are in the habit of using it are a 'set of degraded, depraved, miserable wretches, enfeebled in mind and body, unfit for the active duties of life'. Any possibility of the existence of a class of moderate and occasional users is completely ruled out. Richard Newman considers it as the greatest fallacy in approach. He argues instead in his excellent article[23] against the oft-repeated assertion of historians of China, who regard it as an innocent victim to the abuse of opium. He attests to the existence of a vast population of low and moderate users of opium in China who led healthy and robust lives, in contrast to the images of the emaciated opium sot.

Opium smokers were not all emaciated and miserable but were often cheerful and healthy; they took up the pipe for various reasons and many of them put it aside without much difficulty. Economic activity may have been no worse, and in some regions could even have been rather better, for the existence of opium. The first International Opium Commission met in an atmosphere of emotion and exaggeration about Chinese opium and became the victim of a myth about the problem it was trying to solve. To the extent that succeeding generations have allowed memories of China influence their attitudes and policies, they too have been victims of that myth.[24]

A major deterrent in establishing the existence of 'moderate users' is that there is a paucity of substantial work on the subject, though 'oppositional histories' combating the 'accommodationist approach' do exist. Analysing a mass of historical evidence in China, Frank Dikotter contends, '[...] very few users were compulsive addicts who had unmanageable lifestyles or suffered from tolerance or escalation of use. There existed a class of intermittent smokers and consumers. Once they reach a point, beyond that most of the users did not increase.'[25]

It is in this context that I have attempted to revisit the 'damage narrative' and analyse the commonly held belief that 'opium had poisoned Assam'. Such 'misinformation' in the colonial period, as Syed Hussein Alatas informs in his excellent treatise[26] reinforced the 'Eurocentric prejudice' against the 'lazy native'.

Opium in Everyday Life of the Assamese

By the mid-nineteenth century, opium as has been elaborated in an earlier chapter had been absorbed as a regular feature of Assamese social life and hospitality. The Assamese used opium in a variety of ways, depending on their means and tastes. The essential product was mixed with taste enhancers as fried betel leaves and tobacco. Every village had its percentage of regular smokers as well as a large number of people who used opium only on special occasions. While cigarettes had replaced opium as the 'drug of choice' of the younger generation of the Assamese towards the early twentieth century, opium was, however, especially attractive to the class of labourers – the cultivator. Although from a clinical point of view, the primary alkaloid of opium-morphine does not act as a stimulant in humans; by removing the dull imitation of routine aches and pains, opium would surely induce a feeling of vigour, alertness and energy.

It's medicinal properties go a long way in explaining the appeal of opium to the peasants. This is especially true in light of the prevailing public health conditions in Assam during the nineteenth century. The dismal public health conditions that prevailed in the province;[27] with outbreaks of kala-azar, cholera, smallpox and malaria resulting in high mortality rates, lack of access to professional medical care and also in part, the 'positive hostility' attached to the use of allopathic medicines, which were considered 'worse than poison', enabled opium to assume the position in popular culture in those times,

> People are for the most part ignorant. They object even to European medicines and European doctors. Even if they do not object, these are not available in every part of the province. There is a great deal of insanitary conditions in the province. A great deal of malaria and scarcity of water. The villages are waterlogged from being in low-lying places and no attempt being made to drain them. Facilities of Communication with Calcutta and other places are not so good.[28]

Under such conditions, opium appeared to be a panacea of sorts. Undoubtedly, it formed part of *Materia Medica* of the Asian and European countries, where it was prescribed for a variety of ailments. In Assam and elsewhere in India, it was used to treat headaches, fevers and chills (including malaria), stomachaches, diarrhoea, dysentery and asthma, tuberculosis (bloody coughing), fatigue and anxiety. Opium was also used for symptoms of venereal diseases and gynecological afflictions, and for pain caused by injuries such as sprains, dislocations and broken bones.[29] Because of its analgesic and other medicinal properties, ingested opium clearly provided relief from the pain associated with these conditions and ameliorated many other symptoms as well. In addition, among a population, in which it was rare for a mature adult to be without aches and pains, of one kind or another, regular opium smoking provided a more general analgesic effect. For many people, opium smoking took the edge off the routine physical discomfort of life.

> [...] when someone smokes a pipe of opium, the morphine swiftly enters the bloodstream through the lungs along with all the other alkaloids. It travels to the brain, where it easily crosses the blood-brain barrier and, by virtue of its bio-chemical similarity to endorphins, attaches to the same receptors in the brain normally reserved exclusively for these euphoric, analgesic neurochemicals. The same effect is achieved each and every time; awareness of pain is first reduced and finally eliminated; tension dissolves from the whole system and the entire body relaxes; blood pressure decreases and respiration slows down and an exquisite euphoria spreads like a gentle breeze throughout the body and mind.[30]

Possibly, this is the explanation for the frequent claim of the opium smokers. Women also ate and smoked opium along with their male counterparts.[31]

Both the European and the Assamese tea planters, who testified before the Royal Commission on Opium, which visited Assam in December 1893, were unanimous of the 'medicinal value of opium',

> It is a known fact that when the daily allowance of opium is stopped, the strongest man will become useless and unfit for hard labour. Most of the opium eaters contract the habit of eating it through sickness, such as bowel complaints, rheumatism, diabetes and malarial fever, which they seem to get rid of by using the drug in one form or other. Among the lower class, opium is a common medicine. To abolish its sale, therefore, will be to take away from them an indigenous medicine.[32]

Such comments should not be ignored out of hand. If we are to understand the true effect of opium on the health of individual consumers and cumulatively on the Assamese society, then we 'must distinguish carefully between those who were addicted; those who were damaged in some way by the addiction and the many light and moderate consumers who were not addicted at all'. Not all were opium addicts. Most of them were opium users, who consumed it as a cure. For many – it was a 'work drug'.

> The people who chiefly use the drug are the people residing in low-lying, marshy and damp places, and those at the foot of the hills where the jungly fever is prevalent, use the drug to ward off disease. People of such places

habituate their children even at very tender ages to use the drug in small quantities. If a census of the opium eaters is taken, I have every reason to believe that two-thirds of the opium eaters will be found among such people. The remaining one-third among the villagers of comparatively healthy localities in the interior because being ignorant of the rudimentary principles of sanitation as well as those of pathology, they know of no other medicine or drug as efficacious as opium as a panacea for all diseases. These people never use it for pleasure sake and hence rarely anyone is found among them to use it immoderately.[33]

This position of the peasantry is strikingly similar to the high incidence of opiate use in 'low-lying marshy Fens' whereas Berridge contends, because of frequent inundations, it was vulnerable to a host of afflictions as cold, coughs, fevers, aches and pains. She observes, – 'high opium consumption may have been to some extent characteristics of agricultural populations in low-lying and marshy areas'.[34] Here, long working hours involved susceptibility to infections with symptoms of high fever, coughs, aches and depression. Interestingly, as Berridge notes, 'opiate use in the Fens was culturally accepted and sanctioned . . . which is striking in such an English setting.' In Assam, where a majority of the population (according to the 1921 census figures), around 89 per cent were involved in agricultural pursuit and three-fourths of them were ordinary cultivators,[35] with women, forming a significant population of the agricultural workforce,[36] the therapeutic use of opium was common, though perhaps the use continued well after the 'strict medical condition' was relieved. It can safely be assumed that prior to prohibition of its 'non-medical uses', opium was used extensively as a legal and social stimulant. It had become deeply ingrained in the culture and social fabric of the people of Assam.

The Assamese peasant did not, however, have a single 'drug of choice'. Ethnographic studies on 'drugs/alcohol and livelihood has opposing views of what brings use'. In a study of poly use in farm settings, the parallel notion that drug use is solely recreational and that it interferes with the work performance has been challenged.[37] Revisiting these concerns, drugs like opium, *ganja*, alcohol and other local practices that support poly-use, serve to offset the physical harshness of the agricultural labour and to mitigate the reduced bodily capacity that originates in physically demanding work. Under such conditions, a few 'puffs also bring with it, a halo of momentary euphoria'. Indeed, opium was probably the world's first authentic anti-depressant.

Unlike other pain-relieving agents, opium does not impair sensory perception, intellect or motor-coordination. Pain ceases to be intrusive and distressing.[38] People working in the fields were relying upon opiates to deal with a whole range of ailments. They were a remedy for fatigue and depression, unavoidable among the life of the peasantry at that time. Research on historic labour systems to explore how alcohol (given limited drug availability) was used to induce recalcitrant men to perform difficult work, to serve as partial/full exchange for labour in lieu of wages and to enhance job performance. The use of opium and liquor as wages and as incentive by the tea garden managers in Assam to retain labour is a reminder of the ambivalent attitude to drug use and users.

Individuals fancied smoking, as it was 'more satisfying and pleasurable'. Smoking, it is believed gives a 'peak effect' immediately while the effect from eating is delayed an hour or two and it is more gradual. Interestingly, opium smoking was a 'wasteful enterprise' as well, since around 80 to 90 per cent of the active compound is lost from fumes going directly into the pipe into the atmosphere and from exhaling of unabsorbed compounds. Unlike smoking, eating also allows virtually all of the active alkaloid compounds in opium, particularly morphine and codeine to be absorbed through the gastrointestinal tract.[39] It is a well-known fact of medical science that opium readily relieves such common conditions as insomnia, hypertension, depression and chronic pain.[40] Despite the fact that opium is generally acknowledged to cause drowsiness and under favourable conditions, sleep, Assamese smokers persistently said that opium gave them energy. Col. Batra IMS, during his tenure as the Civil Surgeon Darrang, opined on the beneficial effects of opium in moderation in dysentery, malaria, neuralgia, and rheumatism, chronic cough, asthma and nervous diseases, which were the bane of those involved in the wet rice paddy cultivation.[41]

William Jankowich and Dan Bradburd's ethnographic study

investigating the relationship between the uses of specific kinds of drug foods and the different tasks of labour,[42] has highlighted a clear relation between the type of activity and stimulant use. They contend that 'the more intensive the subsistence system, the greater the likelihood that a drug food will function as a labour enhancer'. They concluded that those in farming communities were more likely than any other occupation to use some kind of stimulant to allay fatigue and augment labour activity.[43] Among the *Kaibartas* (fishermen) community in Assam, the opium habit was believed to be rampant on account of the nature of their occupation where they were required to be awake all night.[44] A group of opium users aged between 40-80 years who were accustomed to the habit of opium for a very long time belonging to the Koch community were interviewed by the 1913 Botham Committee. They spoke about the factors that brought the onset of drug use. They cited disease followed by work related fatigue as the primary inducers. Most of them consumed between 1½ to 6 *tolas* which they could reduce substantially over the years without any compulsion but voluntarily without any harmful health related problems.[45]

Agricultural statistics for Assam available since 1890 present an interesting analysis of the agrarian productivity and labour activity. With around 82 per cent of the Assamese population[46] who were involved in agricultural pursuits, it will be interesting to understand the extent of the effect of opium consumption on the overall agricultural growth based on certain indicators: (a) Income and Expenditure (b) Rural Indebtedness (c) Areas under different crops and (d) Output of crops.

Though there had been a rapid rise and fall of agricultural prices, the acreage under different crops had shown a steady increase. The average yield of Assam compared favourably with all-India averages. However, considering the excellent climatic conditions, abundant rainfall and fertile soil, the yield per acre is low. The figures for the output of crops are not very reliable. The net sown area more than doubled in the period between 1901 and 1947.[47]

Table 8.3 further illustrates how the yield of some of the principal crops has shown a consistent increase.

TABLE 8.3: ACREAGE UNDER DIFFERENT CROPS (IN THOUSAND ACRES)

Year	Rice	Cereals and Pulses (Inc. Rice)	Rape/ Mustard Seeds	Oilseeds (including Rape and Mustard)	Sugar Cane	Tea	Tobacco	Jute	Cotton
1901–2	1,789	1,869	162	177	30	275	2	5	3
1906–7	2,042	2,154	226	238	33	276	5	45	6
1911–12	2,573	2,682	238	245	30	288	8	58	35
1916–17	2,730	2,867	243	251	30	314	9	80	32
1921–2	2,945	3,118	283	306	37	334	10	76	36
1926–7	3,072	3,252	342	371	36	343	9	167	46
1931–2	3,198	3,400	293	319	28	352	14	95	37
1933–4	3,283	3,526	320	347	32	353	14	144	37
1936–7	3,714	3,949	392	420	38	361	12	146	36
1939–40	3,674	3,922	397	431	36	361	14	286	37
1941–2	3,699	3,668	368	404	42	362	15	277	36
1943–4	4,001	4,268	324	347	47	366	18	201	37
1945–6	4,149	4,403	297	344	54	366	19	159	38
1946–7	3,913	4,167	293	329	54	367	19	184	32
1947–8	4,004	4,259	310	349	60	375	20	210	36
1948–9	4,008	4,220	314	352	61	388	20	225	34
1949–50	4,095	4,351	317	356	59	400	20	231	30
1950–1	4,043	4,244	313	346	58	382	23	249	30
1951–2	4,182	4,355	299	317	59	389	20	311	30
1952–3	4,238	4,459	293	312	68	385	21	313	34
1953–4	4,237	4,454	287	308	64	384	22	284	38
1954–5	4,195	4,431	290	311	60	385	24	282	35
1955–6	4,217	4,457	280	301	63	386	24	333	35
1956–7	4,252	4,507	302	328	64	384	23	298	35

Source: Reproduced from Goswami, *The Economic Development of Assam*, pp. 286–7.

TABLE 8.4: PRODUCTION OF DIFFERENT CROPS (IN THOUSAND TONS)

Year	Rice	Oilseeds (including Rape and Mustard)	Sugar Cane (Gur)	Jute	Cotton
1901-2	574	37	35	3	2
1911-12	825	54	35	36	3
1921-2	945	64	43	48	3
1931-2	1,026	67	32	60	3
1941-2	1,187	84	49	167	3
1946-7	1,255	67	63	117	2
1949-50	1,737	59	70	717	11
1950-1	1,413	55	68	790	12
1951-2	1,510	52	66	840	14
1952-3	1,654	49	76	912	17
1953-4	1,646	49	62	902	19
1954-5	1,692	50	73	750	8
1955-6	1,632	56	66	1212	8

Source: Table of Agricultural Statistics in Goswami, *The Economic Development of Assam*, p. 290.

The problem of inadequate data has been a major constraint at forming proper estimates of agricultural output. Available official estimates reveal significant trends of agricultural productivity in the period under review. It is evident from the statistics compiled in the table that large areas were being brought under cultivation, although it is evident that the agricultural research and institutional support were also highly instrumental in achieving higher production.[48]

While the quantum of agricultural produce is an index of the level of labour and land productivity, the overall economic well-being of the peasant is also reflected in the distribution of agricultural indebtedness (as in Table 8.5)

Social ceremonies like marriage, *shradha* (funeral ceremonies) account for one-tenth to one-fifth of the total loans and productive purposes like purchase of cattle, seeds, implements, etc., and improvement of land, only for 15-30 per cent. The proportion of loans for education of children and medical expenses are quite insignificant.

The Provincial Banking Enquiry Committee, 1929-30 estimated

TABLE 8.5: EXTENT OF INDEBTEDNESS IN RURAL AREAS IN ASSAM

Districts of Regions	% of Indebtedness to total families in the Sample	Average debt per family (in Rs.)	Average debt per indebted family (in Rs.)
A. Provincial Banking Enquiry, 1929-30			
Darrang	81.5	188	229.0
Nowgong	78.0	183	235.0
Jorhat Subdivision	83.5	120	145.0
Goalpara	62.0	111	180.0
Cachar	90.0	179	200.0
B. Rural Economic Surveys, 1948-9			
Darrang District	42.2	96.0	227.0
Sibsagar	39.1	66.1	173.2
Lakhimpur	31.0	57.7	186.5
Nowgong	39.2	74.4	189.7

Sources: (i) Provincial Banking Enquiry Committee Report, 1929-30 (ii) Rural Economic Surveys, 1948-9 in Goswami, *Economic Development of Assam*, p. 57.

in that the average debt per family in Assam was Rs. 205 and per indebted family Rs. 242; the figure of indebtness in 1929-30 was over 22 crores. Two-fifths of the total number of rural families were under debt even in 1948-9 though the burden was much relieved. The annual gross value of the principal crops, rice, jute and mustard was calculated approximately at 34 crores, i.e. around 54 per cent more than the estimated debt of 22 crores.[49] While the excise reports frequently mentioned about the increase in purchasing power capacity with a direct impact on the increased sale of opium, the increase in the population as well as the increase in the treasury price of opium per seer did certainly account for a great measure in the increase in revenue, though the observations of the 1948-9 Rural Economic Surveys as regards rural expenditure is worth a mention here,

Food and clothing account for about 75 per cent of the total expenditure of a rural family- food alone taking around 65 per cent. Much of the expenditure on food is on rice alone, leaving very little for vegetables, fish, meat and milk. Fuel and lighting take about 2 to 3 per cent and the miscellaneous expenses the rest (from 9 to 17 per cent). With its meagre income, the family finds little scope for expenditure on education, medical services, repairs of homestead, etc. In the drudgery of life, the little amount a peasant spends on tea, tobacco and drugs cannot be considered as extravagant. Contrary to common belief that the Indian peasant spends too much on ceremonies and litigations, in Assam, the expenses under such headings account for only 5 to 7 per cent of the total annual family expenditure. In absolute terms, the amounts are insignificant. [50]

The surveys did not regard the use of stimulants – 'tea, tobacco and other drugs' as extravagant. The intake of opium as a stimulant should not be overlooked and ignored. In Assam, it was consumed as a stimulant. Contemporary observers believed that opium was a necessity. All consumers of opium, moreover, did not turn into 'enfeebled and useless workers'. The opium used was in its crude form. Further, by using crude products, the addicts absorbed comparatively smaller quantities of the active principles which were responsible for producing the euphoric, narcotic and toxic effects. The heaviest dose was half a *tola* a day. [51]

If we are to understand the true effect of opium on the health of individual consumers and cumulatively on the Assamese society, then we must distinguish carefully 'between those who were addicted; those who were damaged in some way by the addiction and the many millions of light and moderate consumers who were not addicted at all'. This is evident from the statements of the Assamese opium lessees before the Assam Opium Enquiry Committee Report 1933 as – 'All are not consumers, some take as consumer, some take for other purposes.'[52] The existence of a class of casual consumers, who consumed opium only on celebrations as during *Bihu* and *Hatidhara*[53] is attested to by the *mahaldars* (opium lessees). They constituted a part of unregistered consumers, approximately numbering around 25 per cent of the total population of opium consumers, which included also the 'so called gentlemen and ladies' who 'do not like to take opium pass out of shame and they have to purchase surplus opium from the *mahaldar* at high rates'.[54] The statement of Gopinath Bordoloi, then advocate, on the various categories of opium eaters to the 1933 Opium Enquiry Committee is illuminating, 'The first are those who are seriously thinking that opium is a great evil and that they would do well to give it up. Others there are who admit that it is a bad habit but do not seriously think of giving it up. And there is a third class who are fortunately few in number who wish to go on with it. With them, the habit becomes inexorable and they cannot give it up.'[55]

There were opium eaters like Bhagothi aged 70 years and Kakhom aged 80 years and many more like them who were accustomed to taking 2 to 4 *tolas* of opium and completely gave up the habit without any harmful effects and by free will.

An essential step in 'demythologising' the Assam opium problem is to understand the scientific evidence about the drug's impact, or lack of it, upon the health of the individual consumer. Were all users/consumers of opium 'addicts?' Dikkoter's remark offers a perspective, 'the element of opium myth is the refusal to accept that most opium use in Europe, the Middle East and Asia was light and moderate'.[56]

A series of scientific studies on opium poppy and the analysis of the etiology and demographics of drug addiction in India were carried out by Col. Chopra and his team at the School of Tropical Medicine, Calcutta. The scientific investigations and its conclusions were illuminating. As per the investigations into causation of the opium habit the report identified fatigue and stress as reasons for opium use in the country particularly by individuals over 40 years of age,

> [...] Small doses of opium or alcohol, or a few whiffs of 'ganja' smoke remove the feeling of hunger and fatigue for a while, and give a feeling of self-satisfaction and forgetfulness to a person, who generally takes them towards the evening, after a day's hard work. He becomes content, and relaxes into an easy mood. As the effects of a single dose last only for a few hours, a desire to repeat it at frequent intervals becomes irresistible and the next dose is only foregone if its acquisition is beyond his means. Opium is believed to stimulate physical energy. The living and working conditions of laborers' in tea gardens, rice and wheat fields are often hard, and opium is sometimes used to mitigate the exhaustion due to the work and the heat....[57]

Around 33.33 per cent of those used to taking drugs usually use it to thwart fatigue and stress. The reports found the addicts in 'normal health' who could be 'easily persuaded to give up the habit', since their average dose was low. It was observed that most of the consumers in India started taking it in the later years of their life, that is after the age of 40 years, sustaining on a dose of around half a grain in the management of joint pains, bowel ailments and respiratory infections. This corroborated the evidence in Assam of the causative factors of using opium.

> [...] they suffered from diseases as dysentery and malaria, bowel complaints, rheumatism and pain in the chest etc. the habit is generally acquired about the age of 40 years though there are some cases where it has been acquired earlier. I do not think that the use of opium is resorted to as luxury but as a remedy against disease. The moderate use of opium does not tend to make the consumer weak and indolent on the contrary; it gives them vitality and sustaining power for hard work.[58]

Further, the findings of the report are illuminating and reveal the properties of opium poppy, which render it a beneficial stimulant.

> Poppy seeds are demulcent and nutritive also mild astringent. Poppy capsules are astringent, somniferous, soporific, sedative and narcotic, they promote talkativeness. Externally, they are used as anodyne and emollient. Opium is first stimulant, then narcotic, anodyne and antispasmodic, also aphrodisiac, astringent and myotic. In overdoses, it is a powerful narcotic poison. *Hakims* have described opium as an anesthetic and pain reliever. Locally, opium relieves pain and allays spasms. As astringent, it checks hemorrhages, lessens bodily secretions and restrains tissue changes. Large doses such as 1 or 2 gm can be given to a man without producing marked toxic effects.[59]

There, remains, however, the impact of opium consumption on the economy of individual families. The fluctuating incomes of the Assamese peasants were very much a deterrent and played a major role in influencing the quantity of opium consumed. Smokers who were not addicted could limit their consumption to what they could afford while some of those who were addicted were wealthy enough to pay for their habit. Interestingly, in China in the late 1930s, when China was also witnessing a phase of inflationary price-rise, most users had halved their consumption of opium. The following table offers an interesting insight into the sources of average annual Income and annual expenditure of a rural family in Assam, based on the Rural Economy Surveys (1948-9),

TABLE 8.6: SOURCES OF AVERAGE ANNUAL INCOME PER FAMILY, 1948-9.

(*in Rs.*)

Sources	Darrang	Sibsagar	Lakhimpur	Nowgaon
A. Sources of Gross Income				
1. Agricultural Produce	794.2	800.8	733.9	1,048.8
2. Milk and Milk Produce	19.5	41.9	17.9	24.5
3. Cottage Industries	9.0	21.8	16.0	7.8
4. Trade, Services and Profession	119.1	133.7	114.6	94.9
5. Wages	35.1	81.2	84.8	93.1
6. Miscellaneous	46.8	58.0	43.9	74.9
Total Gross Income	1,074.0	1,137.0	1,011.0	1,344.0
B. Net Income	1,054	906	906	1,168
C. Number of Persons per family	6.2	6.5	6.8	6.8
D. Per Capita Net Income	170.0	147.7	133.2	171.8

Source: Reproduced from P.C. Goswami, *Economic Development of Assam,* p. 276.

TABLE 8.7: AVERAGE ANNUAL EXPENDITURE PER FAMILY, 1948-9.

Items of Expenditure	Darrang	Sibsagar	Lakhimpur	Nowgong
1. Food				
Rice	562.7	599.9	560.6	600.2
Pulse	36.2	19.3	21.3	28.5
Potatoes and Vegetables	35.4	21.5	24.9	24.4
Fish and Meat	26.5	15.1	24.9	25.9
Salt and Spices	23.0	20.7	20.6	25.0
Mustard Oil	42.1	27.7	30.0	43.9
Sugar and Gur	39.2	28.5	20.0	23.3
Milk and Milk Products	35.9	26.7	19.7	18.5
Total on Food	801.0	759.3	721.9	789.7
2. Clothing	92.1	78.8	88.2	116.2
3. Fuel and Lighting	21.3	15.7	30.9	28.3

4. Tea, Tobacco and Drugs				
Tea	21.7	16.7	19.1	40.5
Betel Nuts	31.6	37.1	19.3	38.1
Tobacco	36.6	32.7	24.8	21.7
Liquor	35.1	19.6	14.2	13.9
Total	125.0	106.2	77.4	114.5
5. Miscellaneous				
Medicine	12.8	11.6	9.0	12.0
Interest	11.8	5.1	5.3	11.2
Repairs of Homestead	19.7	25.8	17.9	11.4
Education	5.0	13.4	15.9	11.6
Marriage and Ceremonies	44.6	57.1	32.9	33.5
Travelling	6.9	12.8	9.9	6.5
Litigation	5.3	2.2	3.8	4.4
Ornaments	11.0	8.8	9.5	8.5
Wages	...	7.3	11.8	31.8
Others	11.6	13.9	34.1	87.0
Total	128.7	158.0	150.1	28.1
Grand Total	1,160.0	1,118.0	1,068.0	1,267.0

Source: Reproduced from Goswami, *Economic Development of Assam,* p. 277.

Conclusion

Historiography of Assam has demonized opium use – in a striking similarity to what happened with opium in China in the eighteenth and the nineteenth centuries. However, it is fallacious to assume that opium was a 'forbidden fruit' all along. Much before aspirin was made available as a painkiller by Bayer around 1899, opium was the 'universal analgesic'. Opium's impact on health has been exaggerated to do away with the practice of self-medication first and second to facilitate the rise of modern medicine. Following the advancements in medical science, indigenous medical knowledge and usage was suppressed.

The popular culture in the Assamese society centering on opium use was the natural outcome of it being raised in almost every Assamese *bari*. Its use continued and extended well after the strict medical condition was relieved. There were, as available data and literature suggests – 'opium addicts' of modest means who ruined their families or fell into crime in order to satisfy their craving. Opium smokers undoubtedly produced some addicts and some of these were reduced to pitiable conditions. It is this fluidity that is used to explain the 'existence of addiction'. But though its use in Assamese society was universal, addiction was not. There were users smoking and drinking opium 'peaceably'. It was their favourite indulgence, pastime activity, stimulant and medicine. Indeed, before the onset of the 'politics' of prohibition, the production and consumption of opium were for most people, 'normal' rather than 'deviant' activities. As Richard Miller suggests, 'drug use is a voluntary decision. It is no more an epidemic than is choosing a bunch of unhealthy fast food.'[60]

Notes

1. Anoma Pieris, *Hidden Hands and Divided Landscapes: A Penal History of Singapore's Plural Society*, Honolulu: University of Hawaii Press, 2009.
2. Michel Foucault, *Discipline and Punish*, London: Allen Lane, 1977. Foucault talks about the punishment as a 'complex social function' rather, a 'political tactic', – a way of enacting power.
3. Severe symptoms lasting a few days to as much as weeks included 'looseness of the bowels, dejection and misery, restlessness and loss of sleep, failure of appetite, aching of the bones, lassitude and misery'. *Report on the Jail Administration of the Province of Assam for the Year 1885*, ASA, p. 54.
4. *Report of the Jail Administration of the Province of Assam for the Year 1885*, ASA.
5. An *anna* is 1/16th of a rupee.
6. His Memorandum on the *General Features and the Medical Aspects of the Opium Habit in India*, forms an important basis of the Commission's pronouncement of the 'relative harmlessness of opium' on the Indian populace.
7. Refer Table in Appendix I.
8. Although Goalpara district was considered the first district in Assam where poppy was sown by the *burkandez* – the mercenary soldiers accompanying the Mughal force who introduced poppy cultivation in Assam, opium use was reduced to minimal by the end of the nineteenth century. The Assam Congress Opium Enquiry Committee dealt with the 'Problem of Goalpara' in a separate Appendix, which offers interesting insight into the case of Goalpara. Its affinity to the Bengali population as it was situated close to the Bengal border, also it was the only district in Assam which was under Permanent Settlement. It was inhabited largely by the Kacharis who were

by temperament inclined to consumption of *laopani* (rice beer) and alcohol and not opium. Another plausible explanation was the presence of emigrants from East Bengal who were 'free from the opium habit and their presence and strong competition with the Assamese agriculturists undoubtedly effected a great change in the opium habits of the Assamese indigenous race itself.' For Details, refer, Appendix XV, *ACOECR*, 1925, ASA, pp. 134-6.

9. 'Letter from J.T. Rankin, Secretary to the Board of Revenue, Eastern Bengal and Assam to P.G. Melitus, Secretary to the Government of Eastern Bengal and Assam.' Municipal Department, no. 244, Shillong, 27 May 1910, ASA.
10. James H. Mills, *Cannabis Britannica: Empire, Trade and Prohibition, 1800-1928*, Oxford: Oxford University Press, 2003.
11. The consumption of *ganja* in Kamrup district increased from 68 maunds in 1904-5 to 125 maunds in 1909-10. *Report of the Administration of Excise in the Province of Assam for the Year 1911-12*, ASA.
12. Ibid., p. 9.
13. *ACOECR*, 1925, p. 9.
14. Table showing the figures for consumption and revenue for selected years from 1875-1921.

Year	Price per seer (in Rs.)	Opium Consumption (in maunds)	Opium Revenue (in Rs.)
1875-6	22	1874	12,25,141
1885-6	32	1446	16,75,363
1895-6	37	1377	16,75,363
1905-6	37	1415	19,55,706
1915-16	45	1560	30,53,933
1919-20	65	1748	38,37,125
1920-1	65	1614	44,12,308

Source: Assam Congress Opium Enquiry Committee Report, 1925, ASA, pp. 23-4.

15. Separate local committees had been appointed after the Geneva Convention of 1924-5 to investigate the areas where consumption of opium exceeded 30 seers per 10,000 inhabitants. After the committees submitted their reports, a Conference was convened at Simla in 1930. A 'Black Spot' was defined as an area where the consumption exceeded 30 seers per annum per 10,000 of the population. The standard of consumption set by the League of Nations was set at 6 seers per 10,000 of the population (600 mg per head per annum). This standard was fixed for the needs of countries where the use of opium was confined to medical or scientific purposes. It was not to apply to India where opium had been used in traditional

societies as an indulgence and stimulant and the standard for India was fixed at 30 seers per 10,000 of population. *Opium 'Black Spots' Conference*, 1930. Central Board of Revenue. R.Dis. no. 491, E.O. 26, NAI.

16. *Report on the Administration of the Excise Department in the Province of Assam for the Year 1930-31*, ASA.
17. Ibid. The area of the Dibrugarh subdivision under Prohibition was 2,040 sq. miles with a total population of 5,30,178. The area of the Sibsagar subdivision under prohibition is 1,012 sq. miles with a total population of 3,31,052. Thus, the total area put under prohibition was 3,052 sq. miles with a population of 8,61,230.
18. Ibid, p. 2.
19. Table showing the number of addicts treated and the distribution in centres and subdivisions:

Centres	Dibrugarh Subdivision		Sibsagar Subdivision	
	Total	Per cent	Total	Per cent
Ordinary centres	7,060	59.94	4,290	33.38
Tea estates	900	7.00	600	4.67
Total in Subdivisions	7,960	61.94	4,890	38.05
Total in Area	12,850			

From this table, it is seen that in the Dibrugarh subdivision, the number of addicts treated in the ordinary centres as well as in the tea gardens was half as much as again in the number treated in Sibsagar. The excess over the estimated 11,000 was about one-sixth. Refer, 'Correspondence from Lt. Col. A.M.V. Hesterlow to the Secretary to the Government of Assam in the Education and the Local Self-Government Departments', SRB, no. 11,823, 19 August 1939, ASA.

20. Private cultivation of poppy was prohibited from 1 May 1860. The sale of *abkaree* (excise opium sold from government treasuries) opium almost doubled between 1851-2 and 1858-9 which was allowed to continue on revenue grounds even hereafter. Guha, *Medieval and Early Colonial Assam*, p. 170.
21. 'Opium Black Spots Conference, 1930', Central Board of Revenue, R.Dis. no. 491, E.O. 26, NAI.
22. Frank Dikotter, Lars Lamaan, and Xun Zhou, *Narcotic Culture: A History of Drugs in China*, Hong Kong: Hong Kong University Press, 2004, p. 93.
23. Richard K. Newman, 'Opium Smoking in Late Imperial China: A Reconsideration', *Modern Asian Studies* 4(1995): 765-94.
24. Newman, 'Opium Smoking in Late Imperial China', p. 769.
25. Frank Dikotter, '"Patient Zero": China and the Myth of the "Opium

Plague,"' Inaugural Lecture delivered at the School of Oriental and African Studies, University of London, 24 October 2003.

26. Alatas H. Syed, *The Myth of the Lazy Native: A Study of the Image of the Malays, Filipinos and Javanese from the 16th to the 20th Century and Its Function in the Ideology of Colonial Capitalism*, Routledge: New York and London, 1977.
27. The census returns of the years 1881-1901 depict a 5.4 per cent of decrease in the population (indigenous inhabitants of Assam proper, comprising the districts of Lakhimpur, Sibsagar, Darrang, Nowgong, Kamrup and Goalpara, Balipara Frontier Tract and Sadiya Frontier Tract which formed part of Darrang and Lakhimpur districts also contained small number of Assamese populace), *ACOECR*, 1925, p. 14.
28. Testimony of Madhav Chandra Bordoloi, RCO, 1893, ASA.
29. 'Analysis and Report on Original Documentary Evidence Concerning the Use of Opium in India, Part IV', *British Medical Journal*, 1721(1893): 1399-1400.
30. Peter Lee, *Opium Culture: The Art and Ritual of the Chinese Tradition*, Rochester, Vermont: Park Street Press, 2006, p. 46.
31. An official survey estimated around 30 per cent of the female population working at some occupation other than a homemaker. It was asserted that more than 15 per cent render help in the family land with a small number also working as 'farm servants' and 'farm labourers' in tea gardens, etc. *Report of the Assam Provincial Banking Enquiry Committee 1929-30*, Shillong: Government Press, 1930, ASA, p. 30.
32. Testimony of Munshi Rehmat Ali, Tea Planter, Puranigudam, Nagaon to RCO, 1893, ASA.
33. Testimony of J.J.S. Driberg, Commissioner of Excise Assam before the RCO, 1893, vol. VI, ASA, p. 80.
34. Fenland covered part of rural England in the nineteenth century. This covered parts of Lincolnshire, Cambridgeshire, Huttingdownshire and Norfolk in rural England. Malaria was rampant in the Fenland and opium was used to control the symptoms. Virginia Berridge and Griffith Edwards, *Opium and the People: Opiate Use in Nineteenth Century England*, London: A. Lane, 1981.
35. As per the Report of 1921 Census, occupations per mile was as follows, Ordinary Cultivators, 761, Tea, 115, Fishing, 8, Trade, Industry and Transport, 68, Professions and Arts, 17, Others, 31. *Report of the Assam Provincial Banking Enquiry Committee 1929-30*, p. 7.
36. The women in the districts of Lakhimpur, Sibsagar, Darrang and Nowgong work in the fields, transplanting and reaping. *Report of the Assam Provincial Banking Enquiry Committee 1929-30*, p. 12.

37. Keith V. Bletzer, 'Modulation of Drug Use in Southern Farming Communities. Social Origins of Poly Use', *Human Organization*, 3(2009): 340-9.
38. William Osler, 'Natures Own Medicine', < www.asis.com/re/CoverStory.pdf> (accessed on 07.04.2013).
39. Joseph Westermeyer, *Poppies, Pipes, and People: Opium and its Use in Laos*, California: University of California Press, 1983.
40. Lee, *Opium Culture,* p. 3.
41. 'Testimony of Lieutenant Colonel, H.L. Batra IMS, to the 1933 Assam Opium Enquiry Committee', p. 177.
42. William Jankowiah and Dan Bradburd, 'Using Drug Foods to Capture and Enhance Labour Performance: A Cross-Cultural Perspective', *Current Anthropology,* 4(1996), pp. 717-20.

Occupation	Yes	No	Total
Fishing	1	11	12
Hunter-Gatherer	3	8	11
Pastoralist	2	6	8
Simple Horticulturist	16	3	19
Advanced Horticulturist	8	4	12
Industrial Labour	10	0	10
Agriculturist	27	0	27

43. Reproduced from Jankowiah and Dan, 'Using Drug Foods to Capture and Enhance Labour Performance', p. 719.
44. 'Testimony of Rohini Kumar Choudhary to the Assam Opium Enquiry Committee 1933', p. 152.
45. Statements of opium eaters before the Assam Opium Enquiry Committee Report, 1933.
    Bhagothi – age 70 years – I used to take 2-3 *tolas*. I gave up this habit in Magh last year. I gave up because of economic depression.
    Kakhom – age 80 years – I gave up the habit of opium eating a year ago. I do not know whether it is good or bad but I will not take it up again. I was taking 4 *tolas* but the last amount I have been taking before giving up was 1 or 2 *tolas*.
    Andhar – age 60 years. Formerly my ration was 3 *tolas* but now I take only 1½ *tolas*. I don't feel any difficult after reducing my intake.
    Maghur – age 50 years. I started it when I got a pain in my stomach. I gave it up voluntarily without any outside persuasion.
    Sumbora Kachari – age 40 years. I took it originally because I was suffering from some disorder of the bowels.
46. The Rural Economic Surveys 1948-51 put the percentage of rural population in Assam dependant on agriculture between 75 and 85 per cent.

The figure is as mentioned in the Report on Intensive Surveys of Agricultural Labour: Employment, Wages and Levels of Living, vol. II, 1955, cited in P.C. Goswami, *The Economic Development of Assam*, pp. 46-50.

47. The net sown area increased from 2.40 million acres in 1901-2 to 4.73 million in 1946-7. Rice, the principal crop was under irrigation by private canals, tanks and wells in the districts of Darrang and Kamrup. Ibid., pp. 174-7.
48. Arupjyoti Saikia, Kawal Deep Kour and Gopal Sharma, 'Estimate on Crop Production in Assam: 1881-1950', Proceedings of North East India History Association, Nagaon (2009): 409-20.
49. The official figures for the years ending 1922-3 for the agricultural produce was approximate 128 crores, which was pegged at 42 per cent more than the total debt. *Report of the Assam Provincial Banking Enquiry Committee, 1929-30*, p. 15.
50. Goswami, *Economic Development of Assam*, p. 55.
51. Chopra and Chopra, 'Treatment of Drug Addiction', pp. 21-33.
52. Testimony of Maulvi Muhammad Rafique, who also identified a large percentage of people taking much less opium than they do previously used to (down from 25 seers to only 3 seers) which he attributed to economic hardships. *ACOECR*, 1925, pp. 25, 36.
53. Testimony of Girish Chandra Barua, opium lessee, *Hatidhara* refers to elephant catching. Whenever an elephant was caught some opium must be smoked in its honour by the *kanikhowa*.
54. *AOECR*, 1933, p. 143.
55. Ibid., p. 187.
56. Frank Dikotter, 'Patient Zero: China and the Myth of the Opium Plague'. www.frankdikotter.com/publications/the_myth_of_opium.pdf> (accessed on 19 July 2012).
57. Chopra and Chopra, 'Treatment of Drug Addiction', pp. 21-33.
58. Evidence of C.J.F. More, Extra Assistant Commissioner, Jorhat, *RCO*, 1893, ASA.
59. G.S. Chopra and P.S. Chopra, 'Studies on 300 Indian Drug Addicts with Special Reference to Psycho-social Aspects, Etiology and Treatment', *Bulletin on Narcotics* 1(1965): 1-9.
60. Richard L. Miller, *Drug Warriors and their Prey: From Police Power to Police State*, Westport, Connecticut: Praeger, 1996.

CHAPTER 9

Conclusion

THE HISTORY OF modern Assam is shockingly silent about the narrative of opium being a part of the revolutionary transformation in Assamese politics of the period under review. In doing so, it has preferred to obliterate the significance of opium in the nationalist discourse. If, 'to forget history is treachery', it would indeed not be going too far to acknowledge that after the language question, the opium issue was equally potent and which reverberated in the struggle for identity and sovereignty. The vitriolic protests of nationalists like Nilmoni Phukan and Bijoy Chandra Bhagawati, in the mid-twentieth century, against Assam's identification and portrayal as a 'black spot on the face of India' is reminiscent in many ways of the 'racialized construction' of the people in the mid-nineteenth century when notions of racial degeneration and racial tendencies were central to the colonial ideology of governance. They challenged the Government of India to understand that Assam would not accept such double-dealing. To deal with the crisis, they argued that a concerted effort at the national level was a prerequisite.

The campaign against opium was, by the time of independence, a century and more old. Opium revitalized the national freedom movement in Assam. Opium had brought Assam within the ambit of the national freedom struggle and it became M.K. Gandhi's main plank in ensuring Assam integration in nationalist politics. Intriguing then, that the stories of freedom movement do reverberate but opium's role in nurturing the rancour against imperialist tendencies is understudied. The trajectory of opium use, regulation and control is a narrative of the imperial exploitation of the Assamese peasantry, the disorganization of the Assamese social life and the persistant attempts of the Assamese intelligentsia of the times to highlight the trepidations of opium at the highest levels of narcotics control and surveillance.

Within an imperialism centered paradigm, this volume has been an attempt to unearth a critical relationship between a crucial lever of colonialism in Asia and a frontier province laced with tea gardens and on a route laden with opium poppy. Tea and opium were the two most valuable commodities of trade in the nineteenth century. The trajectory of the opium question has facilitated a perspective into delineating a province in the heydays of Western imperialism and colonialism and its abyss in the post-independence period. Opium's introduction and naturalization is part of the inherent dynamics of the trajectory of acceptance, assimilation and abhorrence, which is unique to all mind-altering substances. Ever since it was absorbed as a part of the Assamese socio-cultural life in around the eighteenth century, opium has had a firm hold on the Assamese society for two centuries and more.

It is this facet of understanding a story of opium and modern Assam that has been explored in-depth in Chapter 1. While most of the work on Assam has focussed on tea, opium has endowed a fresh pair of lens with which to view Assamese society, culture and politics of the period under review. Exploring this vital dimension of the impact of addictive commodities in shaping patterns of dominance, the economics of opium and the politics of the empire effected a metamorphosis of the frontier landscapes and the way of life of the people. Imperial expansion was intertwined with the dynamics of trade and networks of production, consumption and exchange of psychoactive substances. It was through the networks of distribution that the stories of sugar, tea and opium were set to intersect and entwine to the British colonial Empire in Asia. The agrarian landscape of medieval and pre-colonial Assam had to now yield way to the plantation culture of tea and many other commercially viable crops. The romance of the enervating tea was soon contrasted with the opium-induced indolence and this reverberated in the colonial opium policies.

If we are to believe Bernard Cohn that the British Empire building in South Asia was a cultural project; knowledge was an important component of the structure of colonialism. Chapter 2 is a dive into the development of the knowledge of the 'opium disease' within the precincts of colonial ideology of governance. Science and medicine served as catalysts towards facilitating the undertaking and 'conquest' of the geography of disease. The medical profession's hostility to its use and its subsequent 'demonization' in the nineteenth century was in essence a moral and a political attempt at perpetration of the myth of the colonial subjects as prone to infectious diseases and which was the marker of difference between the 'savage' and the 'civilized'; the 'primitive' and the 'modern'. As hybrid theories of addiction spawned up images of the opium user as diseased and the deviant, prevention and protection mechanisms ranged from medical intervention to punitive. This was ideally, what opium symbolized.

How opium became the 'opiate of the people' in Assam is difficult to ascertain as the patterns emerge haphazardly. The Arabs brought it to India and it came to Assam via war and conquest. The Mughals mercenary soldiers, the *burkandez*, brought it to Assam or was opium's introduction in Assam a rejoinder of its 'genealogical intimacy with South and South-East Asia'. Imperial concerns were quick to identify a culture of consumption with commercial significance in a colonial frontier. Chapter 3 weaves together the intricate networks of commerce and consumption patterns, which witnessed the entrenchment of colonial interests in Assam and its integration within the configurations of opium imperialism of the East India Company. Exploratory surveys proved Assam was invaluable – opium was all over the frontier with direct access to Yunnan (China). From the early years of the twentieth century, British opium trade with China was clearly on the decline. With direct routes to China under threat, the search for alternative passages was intensified. The imperial eye struck gold with the discovery of tea in a frontier province – Assam. Though certainly not central to the local economy, opium undeniably weaved the politics and commerce of the north-east frontier of British India into a story of surveillance and control. The variant patterns of usage enabled in exploring the 'indigenous usage of psychoactive' alongside mirroring the society's level of political complexity. Colonial investigative modalities defended British colonial interests and opium was inextricably linked to the process of empire building in India.

It certainly was a favourite indulgence, which was cherished by the users as is evidenced by the distinctive mode of preparation, which imparted to it a distinctive characteristic. It provides an interesting perspective to the place of opium in colonial Assam economy, its culture and society. It would not be incorrect to say that people within the scope and area of this study has been extensive users of 'mild narcotic' throughout their recorded history. *Pan-tamul* (areca nut and betel leaves) have been used as stimulant while the hookah was an important part of the social life of the Assamese much before the Assamisization of opium. The prevalence of a tradition of experimentation with various stimulants – from rice beer to tobacco and betel nut chewing which certainly facilitated opium's easy infiltration into the social and cultural life of the Assamese. The shift from *paan-tamul* and hookah to *afing* was reminiscent of significant economic and social changes. Towards the end of the eighteenth century, i.e. sometime around 1770, extensive cultivation of poppy was reported. Interestingly, it was not merchandise until colonial intervention identified the potential of opium poppy farms in Assam on similar lines, as in Bengal and Bihar. The discovery of tea turned the tables against poppy. A harmless social stimulant was now derided. Users of opium became *kania* – the lazy one. Such identification spawned up the propaganda of the 'civilizing mission' ushering in a new era of material exploitation and political domination.

The 'Imperialism of Opium' commenced with the inclusion of opium within the *abkaree* (excise). The inclusion of opium within the excise is important to understand because it illustrates a dynamic of British colonial rule in India. Chapter 4, explains the shifts in colonial opium policies as with the establishment of opium as an excise good/*abkaree*, the auctioning of privileges to get commercial benefits began at a rapid pace. As official and non-official surveys confirmed a qualitative as well as quantitative shift in the extent and pattern of use, it coincided with attempts at greater regulation and control. This is identifiable with the administrative origins of colonial prohibition. This can, however, be construed as a component of the increasing international surveillance and the global identification and acceptance of opium as 'scourge of humanity'. As with so many other problems that faced Assam in the twentieth century, Assam being labelled a 'black spot' stirred a wave of nationalist protest against what was termed as the 'poisoning policy' of the colonial government. In chapter 5, opium took centre-stage in the surcharged political atmosphere. Opium was regarded as the very symbol of slavery and subjection to a foreign yoke. Led by the middle class Assamese intelligentsia, the battle against opium was now attempted to be won with stringent laws. Despite an array of prohibitive measures as prohibition on opium smoking, rationing of opium and registering of opium users, opium eating and smoking was allowed to be used in some contexts. Its use for medical purposes and by men/women over fifty years of age was still allowed. These ideas continued to co-exist with the more modern views of opium and drugs as harmful and destructive of the health and prosperity of a nation.

In 1939, as a final assault, the Congress-coalition Government in Assam decided to launch a *Total Prohibition of Opium* campaign. Chapter 6 discusses the emerging politico-medical discourse during the mid-twentieth century, which placed priority on the importance of state participation with medical collaboration to deal effectively with a menace to public health. Scientific investigations and studies had confirmed that opium addiction could be effectively treated with the help of medical involvement. This was emblematic of the shifts in the treatment of alcoholism and narcotic addiction developing during mid-twentieth century. The government appeared unlikely to have missed this opportunity of rebuilding Assam and restoring provincial pride. The classification of the Assamese people as physical and mental degenerates, had struck at the core of Assamese identity. This battle against opium was an important landmark in the history of the emergence of Assamese nationalism, which received stimulus with the up-and-coming Assamese intelligentsia in the latter half of the nineteenth century.

Literary outpourings of eminent Assamese litterateurs, such as Hemchandra Barua and Laksminath Bezbaruah, against a malady that threatened to sap the vitality of the Assamese peoples, reached their culmination with the *Nikaniakaran Parva* (Festival of Temperance) during the 1939 medico-legal orientation of the anti-opium campaign. The propaganda against opium was, in a sense, an act of purification and defence and, simultaneously, an assertion of Assamese pride and identity and the rebuilding of a *Sonar Asom* (Golden Land of Assam).

While Assam clamoured for integrated efforts at all India level to curb the menace of smuggling at the All India Opium Conference in 1949, failure to evolve consensus sabotaged any such concerted and joint effort at an all-India level. Post-independence, attempts at enforcing total prohibition were enmeshed with contemporary political and economic realities. Following the inclusion of prohibition as one of the Directive Principles of State Policy, the prohibition of intoxicating liquors and narcotic drugs was viewed as an integral part of the national development plan. Despite fervent pleas by representatives from Assam to prohibit the cultivation of opium in other provinces to prevent its smuggling into Assam, no constitutional obligation was resolved for uniformity in the implementation of the Prohibition in India. Finance seems to have been a decisive factor in policies on prohibition and continues to be so until this day. The phasing out of opium because of the massive campaigns for opium eradication and opium prohibition left tobacco without any major competitors. Cigarette smoking was promoted and encouraged as part of the 'modernity' which was eulogized as a direct product of colonial rule.

Chapter 7, echoes in many respects the contemporary concerns and issues which reverberates in the challenges that are now posed to the 'narcophobic discourse' and in the tacit acceptance of the failed 'War on Drugs'. It is difficult to make a comparison between Assam and China because statistics are inadequate and partly also because cultural contexts of the use vary. We need to remind ourselves that a substantial proportion of these people, who used opium, led normal lives. How was the expansion of opium smoking symptomatic of the weakening of social controls during this period is a question with wide ramifications, which cannot be answered except to observe that for many millions of moderate smokers the controls appear to have been effective still. Wilder accounts of rampant Assamese opium consumption cannot be correct. The stereotypical addict of the missionary literature was only one small part of a varied cast of opium users. Most opium smoking was in Assam a mild and recreational social indulgence. Punitive prohibitive regimes have only accentuated the knotty issues of drug use and their regulation. Opium did not die natural death with the *Opium Eradication Campaign* of 1939 or the Opium Prohibition Act of 1947. In its state of invented hibernation, it was changing contours and meanings – heroin and amphetamines as synthetic and lab-based substitutes of plant based opium. Recent Narcotics Control Bureau reports point to organized criminal gangs operating in Assam, with quantities of pod being smuggled through the porous Indo-Myanmar border further on to Myanmar, Thailand and Laos, for the manufacture of heroin. Smugglers have been routing the contraband from Myanmar into Manipur and thence into Guwahati.

As Berridge and Edwards, rightly contend in *Opium and the People*,

> The market stalls or the chandler may no longer be selling opium, but tranquilizers are multinational business.... All the reasons which formerly made opium so popular for symptomatic medication are still society's common pain and tribulations, but with a variety of drugs now taking a role in different areas-analgesics in particular in place of opium for pain relief or ill-defined malaise, varieties of cough medicine where opium was previously the sovereign remedy, and tranqulizers and anti-depressants as present day substitutes on a huge scale for opium's role as a psychoactive drug for the relief of nervous tribulations and the stress of life.

With around 2.4 million people afflicted with cancer in India and requiring opioids (opium-based preparations) for pain relief the clamour for a relaxation of the stringent narcotic policy from one of prohibition oriented to public health oriented continues to mount. Despite potential risk environment, the increasing demand for medical and scientific purposes in the international market is a quest for reviewing the draconian measures and punitive prohibition regimes and the need of developing consensus for a humane and health based drug policy.

The empirical basis for the analysis of archival sources have facilitated a theoretical understanding of the 'multivalent role' of opium in nineteenth and twentieth century colonial Assam. Involvement with opium was crucial to the sustenance of the Asian enterprise and it is interesting to note the intersection of competing interests with concerns of safeguarding strategic economic interests and discourse on surveillance and control. Opium, or for that matter any psychoactive, provides a rich analytical category with which to view culture, politics and the level of societal complexity. Pharmacological definitions have invariably influenced and shaped our attitudes towards acceptance or rejection of certain drugs as 'licit' and 'ilicit'. It is in these shifting attitudes and meanings that lay the most vexing observation: the acceptability and assimilation of one while the denial and rejection of the other with the use and the user both shunned and stigmatized. Equally significant is their impact on scholarship, which has evaded engaging with the crucial issues such that 'historical and cultural record is often distorted and understood poorly'. My visits to the fringe villages of Mamoroni and Kengya (in Tinsukia district of upper Assam) have reaffirmed the latter observation. It was hardly surprising that some members of the Moran community were sceptical of the terminology 'opium addicts'. A *Kania* was a user of opium, not addicted to opium – 'We are not addicts. We have been traditionally using opium for centuries. We are not ready to speak to any person who is not clear of this misconception. We are opium users, not addicts.'

It has sufficiently highlighted the need to revisit some important issues relating to the use of intoxicants including opium use in our society.

Scholarship needs to let go its 'drugphobia' to evaluate in a correct perspective the role of psychoactives within a socio-cultural milieu and its myriad effects. Historical studies borrowing from anthropology can help uncover and place use of drugs in a society in their proper perspective. There is, for example, an extensive literature on opium but relatively less on betel, tobacco and cannabis. Interestingly, in India, there is a dearth of historical works on the subject. Unearthing the trajectory of cannabis use and its subsequent influence on opium use and policy is an important area of future research. We have scant idea of the role of rice beer (*laopani*) and betel leaf and areca-nut (*paan-tamul*) and the social contexts of their production, consumption and distribution. Historical perspectives of tobacco production, consumption and circulation remains a remote subject of discussion in academic circuits until this date. Virtually nothing is known about the history of use of liquor and wine in Assam. Perhaps the most vexing issue relates to the fluid frontiers between legal and illegal substances and an explanation of the shifts in the attitude that affect political and cultural decisions. A fresh perspective of their role in influencing 'social relations, on economic systems of exchange and on political power and privileges' is required.

This is especially important considering that the story of poppy and colonialism in British India which has been explored so far both in historical writings and fictional works as in Amitav Ghosh's *Sea of Poppies* has been located in the midst of peasant production of opium, the story of indentured labour and the anti-opium ranting. Locating the history of opium use in Assam against this backdrop is like locating a missing piece of a jigsaw; moving beyond production and trade; of profits and power into understanding how opium use easily found its way into the socio-cultural and religious life of a people.

The language of opium intoxication enabled a common meeting ground for both the nationalists and the colonialists. Both argued that they wanted the opium habit driven out of the country as it was physically and morally decapacitating. Both faltered through. Even M.K. Gandhi could not deny its inherent therapeutic properties, although he maintained his prohibition stance, 'I must admit that its [opium] place in the *materia medica* is incontestable. It is impossible to do without this drug as a medical agent.'[1]

The very fact that India still today is the only exporter of crude raw opium in the world testifies and attests the statement made around 120 years ago by the Royal Commission on Opium on the medicinal value of opium; that cannot be countenanced without an authentic assessment of the 'all opium use is evil' argument. Unveiling the local histories of opium consumption in British India is thus imperative as it would open up new vistas of understanding and exploring the multi-stranded issue of opium production, circulation, consumption and regulation. The present work has attempted to add one such perspective to the opium story in India.

Note

1. Mohandas Karamchand Gandhi, *Key to Health,* tr. Sushila Nayyar, Ahmadabad: Navjivan Publishing House, 1948, p. 38.

APPENDICES

APPENDIX I

Consumption of Opium in Assam by Persons of Different Tribes Castes and Tribes

Districts	Population	Consumption	Chutiya	Dom	Ahom	Ganak	Kalita	Keot	Lalung	Mikir	Miri	Salai	Jugi	Hari	Proportion of opium eating to total population
Kamrup	6,34,249	150	1036	14,826	475	5,967	129,939	34,239	2,375	13, 595	218	7,832	17,406	3,725	53.38%
Durrung	3,07,761	200	3546	7,988	3135	8,121	19,468	14,239	22	2,362	2,749	1,065	18,795	1,846	46.41%
Nowgong	3,44,141	211	10,468	26,223	5,265	248	24,034	20,553	46,658	47,881	243	207	21,792	2,997	76.37%
Sibsagar	4,57,274	357	54,487	23,564	97,465	2,081	34,470	20,615	5	1,144	15,579	6	6,221	2,595	63.79%
Lakshmipur	2,54,053	329	17,206	12,185	46,869	170	4,694	2,457	569	21	18,940	5	948	879	47.13%
Total	19,97,478	1,247	86,743	84,786	1,53,209	16,587	212,605	90,103	49,629	65,003	37,429	9,115	65,162	2,042	57.85%

Source: Reproduced from Royal Commission on Opium, 1893, vol. II.

APPENDIX II

Statement Showing the Number of Shops for the Vend of Opium and the Consumption in Assam, Since the Formation of the Province

Year	Maximum Number of Shops Licensed for the Vend of Opium	Consumption of Opium			Duty on Opium per seer (in Rs.)
		(mds.	srs.	ch.)	
1874-5	3,997	1837	11	0	23
1875-6	3,151	1874	38	0	23
1876-7	2,833	1793	38	0	24
1877-8	1,271	1034	16	0	24
1878-9	1,342	1655	19	0	24
1879-80	1,367	1618	32	0	26
1880-1	1,397	1685	33	7	26
1881-2	1,404	1582	37	6	26
1882-3	1,373	1738	10	13	32
1883-4	1,318	1404	9	7	32
1884-5	1,283	1482	10	0	32
1885-6	1,250	1446	16	5	32
1886-7	1,175	1446	36	1	32
1887-8	1,067	1416	32	3	32
1888-9	989	1411	17	15	32
1889-90	990	1494	24	15	32
1890-1	934	–	–	–	37

Source: Adapted from the Papers relating to the Consumption of Opium in India. Finance and Commerce Department, no. 99, 8 January 1892.

APPENDIX III

Increasing Revenue and Diminishing Consumption. Statistics for the Period 1873-4 to 1894-5

Year	Population of the Province	Number of shops	Treasury price of opium (per seer)(Rs.)	Total consump. (Mds s c)	Total Revenue Collections (Rs.)	Consumption per head of population (in *tola*)	Revenue per head of population	Revenue per *tola* of consumption
1873-4	4,094,972 (1872)	5,137	22 and 23	1856 32 0	11,71,815	1.15	17	32
1881-2	4,881,426 (1881)	1,404	26	1582 37 6	15,53,600	1.03	51	111
1891-2	5,433,199 (1891)	977	37	1369 25 4	19,16,369	.80	57	611
1894-5	5,433,199 (1891)	845	37	1376 28 11	19,36,037	.81	58	79

Source: Report on the Excise Administration of the Province of Assam 1895. ASA.

APPENDIX IV

Population, Consumption and Revenue at Each Census

Year	Assamese Speaking Population	Percenatge of Growth or Decrease	Assam Valley Population	Total for Assam	Total Consmption for Assam (mds)	Total Revenue
1881	1,920,726	–	2,353,495	5,129,391	1582	15,53,600
1891	1,826,849	-5.4	2,587,228	5,447,880	1308	18,11,610
1901	1,773,484	-2.9	2,742,162	6,126,945	1291	18,04,382
1911	2,023,972	+14.1	3,248,319	7,060,521	1511	24,90,828
1921	2,113,569	+4.4	3,991,682	7,990,246	1614	44,12,308

Source: Reproduced from Assam Congress Opium Enquiry Committee Report, 1925.

APPENDIX V

Table Showing the 'Black Spots' of Assam-consumption in the Four Upper Assam Districts (League of Nations Standard = 6 Seers per 10,000 of Population)

District	Consumption (in seers) 1926-7	Consumption (in seers) 1932-3
Sadiya Frontier Tract	175	94
Lakhimpur	153	62
Sibsagar	91	45
Darrang	72	22
Nowgong	119	27

Source: Reproduced from the Assam Opium Enquiry Committee Report, 1933, ASA.

APPENDIX VI

Consumption of Opium in British India, 1924-5

Provinces	Consumption of Opium (in seers) per 10,000 population
Burma	25.6
Assam	49
Balasore district of Bihar and Orissa	56
Godavari district of Madras	59
Ferozepur district of Punjab	61
Calcutta (including all the suburbs and towns including Howrah and Bareilly	88

Source: Hansard Archive, 8 February, 1926.

APPENDIX VII

Selected Year Wise Statistics of the Jailed Inmates Who Confessed Habitual Use of Opium

Location	Year																			
	1881		1882		1884		1885		1893		1894		1895		1896		1898		1899	
	t	u	t	u	t	u	t	u	t	u	t	u	t	u	t	u	t	u	t	u
Guwahati	100	30	379	48	134	25	187	28	197	24	181	21	120	22	128	23	158	6	135	36
Barpeta	39	2	117	7	87	1	95	2	53	1	100	(-)	115	7	54	(-)	401	1	36	(-)
Tezpur	181	21	379	25	209	51	142	24	158	12	114	8	145	10	159	18	170	4	165	4
Mangaldai	96	32	245	31	186	56	136	28	153	12	117	11	105	14	109	8	80	6	89	15
Nowgong	196	42	468	34	195	37	152	24	187	23	158	20	238	22	211	43	170	48	151	26
Sibsagar	138	12	369	26	196	23	156	23	275	32	267	25	331	20	254	26	207	35	195	48
Jorhat	110	21	346	28	116	16	268	13	178	17	204	14	173	18	189	9	196	14	178	16
Golaghat	100	16	184	12	74	10	95	12	198	11	154	15	72	10	163	18	190	13	135	36
Dibrugarh	266	32	630	30	290	25	236	23	314	28	468	21	440	42	476	27	391	37	365	43
Lakhimpur	59	64	67	6	32	6	42	23	79	15	69	12	83	7	102	7	58	7	87	13

Notes: *t: total number of those admitted into prisons

*u: total number of those who confessed the use of opium

*implies record not available for the jails during the year

Source: Table constructed from data/statistics available in the Annual Jail Administration Reports, ASA.

APPENDIX VIII

‘Assamese in the Clutches of Opium.’ ‘What a Ruin has Befallen! Opium has Destroyed Assam’ (Translation Mine)

Courtesy: Tinidiniya Asamiya, 1939, DHAS.

APPENDIX IX

'Opium has Brought the Society on the Brink of Degradation' (Translation Mine)

Courtesy: Asamiya, 1942, DHAS.

APPENDIX X

Newspaper Article on the Announcement of Opium Eradication Campaign by Congress Coalition Ministry in 1939

আগৰ কথা

কানিৰ গ্ৰাসত অসমীয়া

Courtesy: Tinidinya Asamiya, 1939, DHAS.

APPENDIX XI

'The Vision of Opium Eradication Campaign in Assam' (Translation Mine)

অসমত কানি-বৰ্জ্জন আন্দোলনৰ পৰিকল্পনা

Courtesy: Tinidiniya Asamiya, 1939, DHAS

APPENDIX XII

'Medicine for Giving up Opium Use' (Translation Mine)

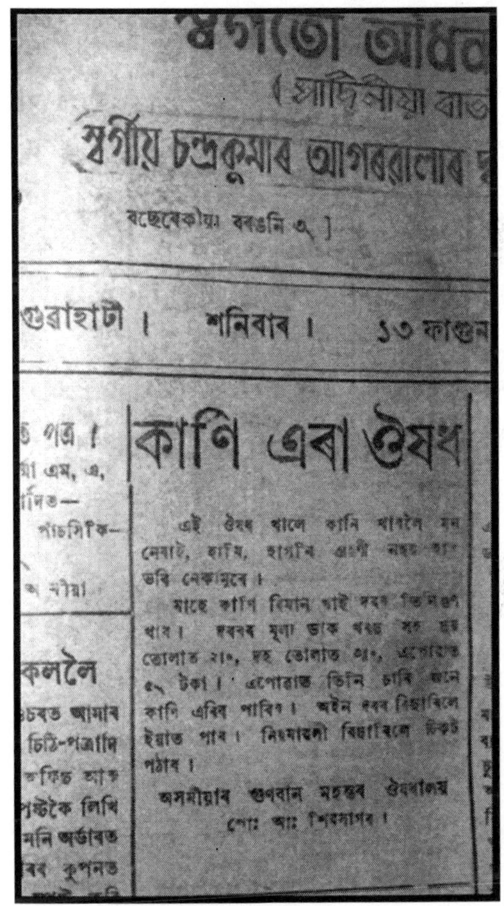

স্বৰ্গীয় চন্দ্ৰকুমাৰ আগৰৱালাৰ

গুৱাহাটী । শনিবাৰ । ১৩ ফাগুন

কাণি এৰা ঔষধ

অসমীয়াৰ গুণবান মহন্তৰ ঔষধালয়
পোঃ আঃ শিৱসাগৰ ।

Courtesy: Asamiya, 1939, DHAS.

Bibliography

Primary Sources

Assam State Archives

Annual Assam Administration Reports, 1874-1947.
Annual Excise Administration Reports, 1874-1947.
Annual Excise Revenue Reports, 1874-1947.
Annual Jail Administration Reports, 1874-1947.
Annual Public Health Reports of Assam, 1880-1947.
Annual Reports on the River-Borne Trade of Assam, 1900-1912.
Annual Reports on the Trade between Assam and the Adjoining Foreign Countries, 1881-1902.
Assam Legislative Assembly Proceedings, 1937-1955.
Files on the Political History of Assam (PHA), 1826-1947.
Finance and Commerce Department Proccedings, 1905-1937.
Finance Department (Revenue) Proceedings, 1905-1937.
Home Department Proceedings, 1937-1947.
Home Department, Police Branch Proceedings (SB), 1935-1947.
Local Self-Government Department Proceedings, 1905-1912.
Memorandums on Excise Administration in India, 1874-1947.
Revenue and Agriculture Department Proceedings, 1921-1937

National Archives of India, New Delhi

Central Board of Revenue (Excise and Opium Branch) Proceedings, 1934-1946
Central Board of Revenue, 1924-1946.
Commerce and Industry Department Proceedings, 1905-1947.
Criminal Intelligence Gazette, Assam Excise Supplement Notes, 1946
External Affairs Department Correspondence Notes, 1947-1955.
Finance and Commerce Department (Separate Revenue Branch) Proceedings, 1879-1905.
Finance Department, Central Revenues, 1905-1947.
Foreign and Political Department Notes, 1914-1937.

Government of Bengal, Revenue Department 'OPIUM' (1891-1912).
Home Department Proceedings, 1800-1932.
Local Self-Government Department, Separate Revenue Branch, 1881-1946.
Opium Proceedings, 1790-1793 (August 1790-December-1791 and January 1792-April 1793).

National Medical Library, New Delhi

British Medical Journal, 1840-1975.
Bulletin of the Indian Institute of the History of Medicine, 1974-1985.
Bulletin on Narcotics, UNODC, 1952-1975.
Indian Medical Gazette, 1937-1955.

Documents and Memoirs

Aitchson, C.U. (ed.), *A Collection of Treaties Engagements and Sanads etc.*, vol. II: *Relating to Burma, Nepal, Eastern Bengal and Assam, Bhutan, Sikkim, Tibet, Siam and the Eastern Archipelago*, Calcutta, Superintendent Government Printing, India, 1909.

Allen, B.C., *Assam District Gazeteers*, Shillong, Baptist Mission Press, 1905-7.

Allen, B.C. et al., *Imperial Gazeteer of India Series,* Calcutta, Superintendent Government Printing, India, 1909.

———, *Assam: Sketch of its History, Soil and Productions, with the Discovery of the Tea Plant and of the Countries Adjoining Assam*, London, Smith, Elder and Co., 1839.

Butler, J., *Travels and Adventures in the Province of Assam*, London, Smith, Eldern and Co., 1855.

———, *Consumption of Opium in India: A Critique of the memorandum Presented by Sir William Roberts-1895, as Medical Member of the Royal Commission on Opium, 1893-1894*, Indian Medical Record, 1895.

Cooper, T.T.A., *Pioneer of Commerce in Pigtail and Petticoats or an Overland Journey from China Towards India,* London: John Murray, 1871.

Dey, Kanny Lall, *The Indigenous Drugs of India; or Short Descriptive Notices of the Medicines, Both Vegetable and Mineral, in Common Use Among the Natives of India,* Calcutta: Thacker, Spink & Co., 1867.

Leslie, J., *A Sketch of the Medical Topography of Gowhattee, with an Account of the Prevailing Diseases*, Calcutta: G.H. Huttmann, 1834.

———, 'Liquor Shops and the Outstill System in Assam', Memo by J. Buckingham, Chairman of the Assam Branch Indian Tea Association.

M'Cosh, J., *Topography of Assam*, Calcutta: Bengal Military Orphan Press, 1837.

Mackenzie, Alexandar., *The North-East Frontier of India*, 1st pub. 1884 entitled *History of the Relations of Government with the Hill Tribes of the North East Frontier of Bengal*, New Delhi: Mittal Publications, 2008 (rpt.).

Martin, M., *The History, Antiquities, Topography and Statistics of the Eastern India*, vol. III, London: W.H. Allen and Co., 1838 (1st pub.).

Mills, A. J. Moffat, *Report on the Province of Assam*, 1854, republished by Publication Board Assam, Guwahati, 1984.

———, *Physical and Political Geography of the Province of Assam*, Shillong: Assam Secretariat Press, 1896.

Pemberton, R.B., *Report Upon the Countries on the Eastern Frontier of the British Territories*, 1835, New Delhi: Mittal Publications, 1979 (rpt.).

Raynal, A., *A Philosophical and Political History of the Settlements and Trade of the Europeans in the East and West Indies*, translated from French by J. Justamond. vol. II, Book V., London: A Stratahan, 1776.

Royle, F. J., *Essay on the Productive Resources of India*, London: W.H. Allen & Co., 1840.

Robinson, W., *A Descriptive Account of Assam*, 1841, Calcutta: Sanskaran Prakashak, 1975 (rpt.).

Samuel, Morewood, *A Philosophical and Statistical History of the Maritimes and Customs of Ancient and Modern Nations in the Manufacture and Use of Inebriating Liquors*, Edinburgh: Fraser and Company, 1838.

Scott, Anna Kay, *Korno Siga, the Mountain Chief; or Life in Assam*, Philadephia: The American Sunday-School Union, 1889.

Tavernier, B.J., *Travels in India*, translated from the original French Edition Le Voyageur Tavernier of 1676 with a Biographical Sketch of the Author with notes, Appendices, etc. by V. Ball, vols. I & II, London: Macmillan & Co., 1889.

Ward, K.F., *The Land of the Blue Poppy: Travels of a Naturalist in Eastern Tibet*. Cambridge: Cambridge University Press, 1913.

Welsh, T., *Report on Assam*, 1794, with Additional Observation by David Scott, 1826, reproduced with A. Mackenzie, *History of the Relations of the Government with the Hill Tribes of North-East Frontier of Bengal*, Calcutta, 1884 (1st pub.), New York: Cambridge University Press, 2012 (rpt).

Official Reports and Contemporary Accounts

PUBLISHED

Allen, B.C., *Report on the Trade between Assam and Adjoining Foreign Countries for the Three Years Ending 1902*, Shillong: Assam Secretariat Printing Office, 1903.

Brent, H.C.E. Carter and J. Albert, *Report of the Committee Appointed by the*

Philippine Commission to Investigate the Use of Upium, Jose Albert: U.S. Bureau of Insular Affair, 1905.

Excise (Opium) Administration, Government of India, *Opium in India*, Calcutta: Government Printing Office, 1892.

Government of Assam, *The Assam Opium Enquiry Committee, Evidence*, vol. III: *Sylhet, Silchar and Haflong,* Shillong: Assam Secretariat Press, 1933.

Government of India, *Collection of Papers Relating to the Excise Administration of India*, Bombay: Government Gazzette, 1890.

———, *Collection of Papers, Relating to the Report of the Royal Commission on Opium, 1894,* Calcutta: Superintendent of Government Printing, 1896.

———, *Royal Commission on Opium,* 1893, Appendix XXXXV (accessed from Secretariat Library), London: His Majesty's Stationery Office 1895.

———, *Royal Commission on Opium, January 3-January 27, 1894,* vol. III (accessed from Assam State Archives).

———, *Royal Commission on Opium, January 29-February 22, 1894*, vol. IV (accessed from Assam State Archives), Shillong: Assam Secretariat Library.

———, *Indian Hemp Drugs Commission Report*, Simla: Government Central Printing Office, 1894.

———, Finance Department (Central Revenues), *Report on the Traffic in Opium and other Dangerous Drugs, 1934,* Simla: Finance Department of India, 1934.

———, *Memorandum on CISE (Opium) Administration in India for 1934-35,* Excise (Opium) Administration, India, 1930.

———, *Report by the Representative of India to the Opium Advisory Committee, 1938*, Government of India (Finance Department, 1938).

———, *Report on Chronic Cannabis Intoxication*, Bulletin on Narcotics, 1940.

———, *Report of Taxation Enquiry on Assam, 1953*, Shillong: Assam Secretariat Press, 1953.

———, *Opium Revenue, 1924-25* (accessed from Assam Secretariat Library), Simla: Finance Department, Government of India, 1926.

———, *Report of the Committee Appointed to Enquire into the Quinine Supply and Cinchona Cultivation in Assam*, Shillong: Assam Secretariat Printing Office, 1925.

———, *Report of the Statutory Commission on the Powers of the Government of India and the Provincial Governments with Regard to Introduction of Prohibition*, New Delhi: Logos Press, 1988 (rpt.).

———, *Report by the Government of India for the Calendar Year 1934 on the Traffic in Opium and other Dangerous Drugs,* Shillong: Assam Secretariat Press, 1934.

———, *Memorandum on Excise (Opium) Administration in India, Finance Deptt. (Central Revenue), 1932-3,* India Finance Department, 1933.

———, *Report of the Committee Appointed to Report on Questions Relating to the Consumption of Opium and Ganja in Assam,* Shillong: Government Press, 1913.

———, *Assam Congress Opium Enquiry Committee Report*, Shillong: Government Press, 1925.

———, *Report of the Select Committee Appointed to Enquire into the Progress and Prospect and the Best Means to be Adopted for the Promotion of European Colonisation and Settlement in India, especially in the Hill Districts and Healthier Climate in the Country as well as for the Extension of our Commerce with Central Asia, ordered by the House of Commons*, Great Britain: Parliament, House of Commons, 1860.

———, *The Assam Provincial Banking Enquiry Committee*, 1929-30, Shillong: Assam Secretariat Press, 1930.

———, *Report of the Opium 'Black Sopts' Conference*, 1930.

———, *Report of the Drugs Enquiry Committee*, 1930-1.

———, *Report of the Convention for Limiting the Manufacture and Regulating the Distribution of Narcotic Drugs*, 1931.

Hunter, W.W., *A Statistical Account of Assam*, vols. I & II (1st pub. in 1879), New Delhi: Spectrum, 1990 (rpt.).

League of Nations, *Interim Report of the Indian Delegation to the Eight (Ordinary) Session of the Assembly of the League of Nations*. Geneva, 1927.

———, *Opium Advisory Committee: Annual Report on Opium and other Dangerous Drugs for 1933*, London: His Majesty's Stationery Office, 1933.

———, *Report of the Geneva Opium Convention*, Geneva, League of Nations Secretariat, 1925.

Mackenzie, Alexandar, *The North-East Frontier of India* (1st pub. in 1884), Delhi: Mittal Publications, 1979.

Mills, A.J.M., *Reports on the Province of Assam*, Calcutta: Government of Bengal, 1854.

Pemberton, B.R., *Report on the Eastern Frontier of British India*, Guwahati: Department of Historical and Antiquarian Studies, 1966, 1st pub. 1835.

Planning Commission, Government of India, *Prohibition Enquiry Committee*, 1954, Planning Commission, Government of India, 1954.

Reply to Major the Hon. E. Baring's Budget Speech in the Legislative Council of his Excellency the Governor-General of India on 8 March 1822 published for the Society by Dyer Brothers, Amen Corner, Peternoster Row, 1822.

Report of the Assam Opium Enquiry Committee, Shillong: Assam Secretariat Press, 1933.

———, *The Assam Opium Enquiry Committee, Evidence*, vol. I, *Jorhat and Dibrugarh*, Shillong: Assam Secretariat Press, 1933.

———, *The Assam Opium Enquiry Committee, Evidence*, vol. II, *Nowgong, Tezpur and Gauhati*, Shillong: Assam Secretariat Press, 1933.

Report of the Committee Appointed by the Phillipine Commission to Investigate the Use of Opium and the Traffic Therein, 1905.

Rules, Ordinances and Laws Towards Regulating Intoxication

Government of Assam, *Assam Temperance Act*, Shillong: Assam Secretariat Press, 1926.

———, *Assam Opium Smoking Act*, Shillong: Assam Secretariat Press, 1927.

———, *Assam Opium (Amendment) Act*, Shillong: Assam Secretariat Press, 1933.

———, *The Assam Dangerous Drugs Rules*, 1937, Shillong: Assam Secretariat Press, Shillong, 1937.

———, *The Assam Opium Prohibition Act, 1947*, Shillong: Assam Secretariat Press, 1940.

———, *The Assam Drugs Control Act, 1950*, Shillong: Assam Secretariat Press, 1950.

———, *The Assam Opium Amendment (Autonomous Districts) Act, 1954*, Assam Secretariat Press, 1954.

———, *The Assam Ganja and Bhang Prohibition Act, 1958*, Assam State Prohibition Council, 1958.

———, *The Assam Ganja and Bhang Prohibition Rules, 1960,* Assam State Prohibition Council, 1960.

Government of India, *The Drugs Act 1940*, Government of India, 1940.

———, *Opium Act 1878*, Government of India (Superintendent of Calcutta, 1878).

———, *Eastern Bengal and Assam Act I of 1910* (Regulations Department, Government of East Bengal and Assam, 1910).

Digitized Version of Contemporary Periodical and other Journals (accessed from Gale Digital Library)

British Medical Journal, United Kingdom.

Church Missionary Gleaner, Gale University Library.

Friend of India and Statesman, Statesman and Friend of India Office, Calcutta.

Gleanings in Science, Asiatic Society of Bengal.

Indian Quarterly Register, The Annual Register Office, Calcutta.

The Eclectic Review, United Kingdom.

The Calcutta Review, now published by Calcutta University Press.

The Economist Historical Archive, 1840-2000 (accessed from Gale Digital Archives)

The Times Digital Archive (accessed from Gale Digital Archives).

19th Century U.K. Periodicals (accessed from Gale Digital Archives).

Assamese Works

UNPUBLISHED

Hazarika, Dutiram, *Rasik Puran*, Guwahati: Department of Historical and Antiquarian Studies, 1877.

PUBLISHED

Adhikari, Gajendra, *Asamar Itihaas*, Mirza: Brahmaputra Books, 2005.

Barbarua, Hiteswar, *Ahomar Din*, Guwahati: Asama Prakashan Parishada, 1981.

Barmudoi, Purabi, *Rupowali Noir Sunowali Ghaat*, Dibrugarh: Banalata Prakashan, 2011 (rpt.).

Barua, B.K., *Asamar Loka Sanskriti*, Guwahati: Lawyer's Book Stall, 1961.

Barua, Hemchandra, *Kaniar Kirtan: A Play in Assamese on the Evils of Opium-Eating*, Guwahati: Hem Chandra Prakashan, 2003 (rpt.).

Barthakur, Padmanath, *Swadhinata Ranar Sangsparat*, Dibrugarh: Kaustubh Prakashan, 2006 (rpt.).

Baruah, H. (ed.), *Bharatar Mukti Yugat Asam*, Guwahati: Publication Board Assam, 1902.

Baruah, Usharani, *Hemchandra Barua Aru Gunabhiram Barua Kritti Aru Krittitva*, Dhemaji: Kiran Prakashan, 2006.

Bezbarua Granthavali, vol. I., Guwahati: Sahitya Prakash, 1968.

Bezbaroa, Lakhsminath, *Mur Jiwanar Suwaran*, Banalata: Dibrugarh, 2008 (rpt.).

Bhattacharyya, Basanta K., *Arunodoi Yugor Sahitya*, Guwahti: Chandra Prakash, 2006 (rpt.).

Bhuyan, Suryya K., *Kamrupar Buranji*, Guwahati: Department of Historical and Antiquarian Studies, Assam, 1987 (rpt.).

———, *Kavita Sangrah*, Guwahati: Department of Historical and Antiquarian Studies, 1993.

———, *Asamar Padya Buranji*, Guwahti: Department of Historical and Antiquarian Studies, 2008 (rpt.).

———, *Mirjumlar Asam Akraman*, Guwahati: Bani Mandir, 2009 (rpt.).

———, *Padshah Buranji*, Guwahati: Bani Mandir, 2009 (rpt.).

Bora, Mahendra and J. Goswami, *Ananda Chandra Agarwalla Granthavali*, Jorhat: Assam Sahitya Sabha, 1974.

Chaudhari, Pratap C., *Asama Buranjisaar*, Guwahati: Department of Historical and Antiquarian Studies, 1991 (rpt.).

Das, D., *Asamar Swasthya Parampara*, pts. I-II, Guwahati: Dhrupad Publishers, 1996.

Das, O. and L. Barua, *Asamat Mahatma*, Guwahati: Assam Prakashan Parishad, 1969.

Deka, K. (ed.), *Atul Chandra Barua Rachnavali*, Guwahati: Baruah Prakashan, 1996.

Dutta, Nanu, *Swadhinat Andolonot Axom*, Guwahati: Lawyers Book Stall, 1998.

Gohain, Hiren, *Bharatar Swadhinata Sangramat Biplabvadi Sakalar Avadaan*, New Delhi: National Book Trust, 1998.

Gohain Barua, Padmanath, *Asamar Buranji*, Guwahati: Publication Board Assam, 2004 (rpt.).

Goswami, H., *Kamaratna Tantra*, Shillong: Assam Government Press, 1928.

Goswami, Apurba B., *Namboror Pora Myanmaroloi (From Nambor to Myanamar)*, Golaghat: Jagaran Printers, 2007.

Hazarika, Anee, *Asamar Itihasat Shri Shri Anirudhdeva Aru Mayamara Vaisnav Sampraday*, Guwahati: Lawyers Book Stall, 2000.

Goswami, Jatindranath (ed.), *Nakul Chandra Bhuyan Rachana Samagra*, Guwahati: Lawyers Book Stall, 1995.

Goswami, P., *Karmavir Nabin Chandra Bordoloi Grantha*, Guwahati: Assam Prakashan Parishad, 1975.

Lekharu, Upendra C., *Katha Gurucharit*, Guwahati: Dutta Baruah Publishing Co., 2006 (rpt.).

Phukan, Lakhinath, *Matmahar Pora Rupkonwaroloi*, Guwahati: Lawyer's Book Stall, 1962.

Saikia, N. and J. Goswami (eds.), *Chandradhar Barua Granthavali*, vols. I-II, Jorhat: Assam Sahitya Sabha, 1975.

Sarma, B., *Kamngrecar Kanchiali Rodat*, Guwahati: Assam Publication Board, 1969.

Sarma, Krishnanath, *Krishna Sharmar Diary*, Guwahati: Assam Publication Board, 1972.

Sarma, S., *Ambikagiri Raychaudhari Rachanavali*, Guwahati: Assam Publication Board, 1985.

Sarma, Shashi, *Katha-Gurucharit (Ati Samiksha)*, Guwahati: New Book Stall, 2001 (rpt.).

Sharma, Benudhar, *Majirpara Meijalai: An Autobiography of Part 1*, Guwahati: Assam Jyoti, 1985.

Talukdar, Nanda, *Lambodar Bara Rasanavali*, Guwahati: Lawyers Book Stall, 1983.

Tayyebulla, Mohammad, *Karagarar Ciithi*, Guwahti: Assam Publication Board, 1962.

Tyagvir Hem Baruah Smriti Grantha, Tezpur: Unknown, 1971.

Journals and Newspapers (in Assamese, accessed from Department of Historical and Antiquarian Studies, Guwahati)

Avahan, 1933-58.

Asamiya, 1925-55.

Tinidiniya Asamiya, 1938-42.

Newspaper accessed from The District Library, Guwahati

The Assam Tribune, 1949-60.

Books on Assam and North-East India

Antrobus, H.A., *A History of the Assam Company, 1839-1853*, Edinburgh: T.A. Constable, 1957.

Barooah, Nirode K., *David Scott in North-East India, 1802-1831: A Study in British Paternalism*, New Delhi: Munshiram Manoharlal, 1970.

———, *Indian Constitution and Centre-Assam Relations*, Guwahati: Publication Board, 1980.

Barpujari, Heramaba K., *Political History of Assam*, Guwahati: Assam Publication Board, 1977.

———, *Assam in the Days of the Company 1826-58*, New Delhi: Spectrum Publications, 1980.

———, *An Account of Assam and her Administration, 1603-1822*, New Delhi: Spectrum Publications, 1988.

Barpujari, Heramba K. (ed.), *The Comprehensive History of Assam*, vol. I, Guwahati: Publication Board Assam, 1990.

———, *Political History of Assam*, Guwahati: Publication Board Assam, 1999.

Barua, Hem, *The Red River and the Blue Hills*, Guwahati: Lawyers Book Stall, 1960.

Barua, Prafulla C., *Fundamentals of Assamese Culture*, Guwahati: Lakhimi Printing Press, 1965.

Barua, Golap C. (ed. and tr.), *Ahom Buranji: From the Earliest Times to the End of the Ahom Rule,* Guwahati: Spectrum Publications, 1985.

Baruah, Manjeet, *Frontier Cultures: A Social History of Assamese Literature*, London and New York: Routledge, 2012.

Baruah, Sanjib, *India Against Itself: Assam and the Politics of Nationality*, New Delhi: Oxford University Press, 1999.

Baruah, Swarnalata, *A Comprehensive History of Assam*, New Delhi: Munshiram Manoharlal, 1995.

Bhattacharjee, Arun, *Assam in Indian Independence*, New Delhi: Mittal Publications, 1993.

Bhattacharjee, Jayanta B. (ed.), *Studies in the Economic History of North-East India*. New Delhi: Har Anand, 1994.

Bhattacharjee, Jayanta B., *Trade and Colony: The British Colonisation of North East India*, Shillong: North East History Association, 2000.

Bhattacharyya, Birendrakumar, *Humor and Satire in Assamese Literature*, New Delhi: Sterling Publications, 1962.

Bhuyan, Arun (ed.), *Nationalist Upsurge in Assam*, Guwahati: Jisnu Barua, 2000.

Bhuyan, Suryya K., *Early British Relations with Assam*, Guwahati: Assam Government Press, 1949.

———, *Atan Buragohain and His Times*, Guwahati: Lawyers Book Stall, 1957.

———, *Studies in the History of Assam*, Jorhat: Lakheswari Bhuyan, 1964.

———, *Anglo-Assamese Relation's 1771-1826*, Guwahati: Lawyers Book Stall, 1974.

———, *Tungkhungia Buranji, 1681-1826*, Guwahati: Department of Historical and Antiquarian Studies, 1990 (rpt.).

Borua, Prafulla C., *A Short History of Assamese Newspapers*, Guwahati: Sahitya Ratna Prakashan, 1997.

Bose, Mani L., *Social History of Assam*, New Delhi: Concept Publishing, 2003 (rpt.).

Chakravarty, Birendra C., *British Relations with the Hill Tribes of Assam Since 1858*, Calcutta: Firma K.L. Mukhopadhyay, 1964.

Chaube, Shibani K., *Hill Politics in Northeast India*, Delhi: Orient Longman, 1999 (rpt.).

Chatterjee, Suniti K., *The Place of Assam in the History and Civilisation of India.* Guwahati: Banikanta Kakati Lectures, 1956.

Chevalier, Jean B., *Historical Memoirs and Journal of Travels in Assam, Bengal and Tibet (1752-1765)*, tr. Caroline Dutta-Baruah and J. Deloche, Guwahati: LBS, 2008.

Chutia, D., *Benudhar Sarma Commemoration Volume*, Guwahati: Kamrup Anusandhan Samiti, 1987.

Das, Jogesh, *Folklore of Assam*, New Delhi: National Book Trust, 2005 (rpt.).

De, Ranjit K., *The Barak Valley: A Survey of Documents on the Economic History, 1832-1947*, New Delhi: Mittal Publications, 2006.

Dev, Bimal J. and Dilip Lahiri, *Assam Muslims: Politics and Cohesion*, New Delhi: Mittal Publications, 1985.

Dutt, Keshab N., *Landmarks of the Freedom Struggle in Assam*, Guwahati: Lawyers Book Stall, 1958.

Gait, Edward A., *A History of Assam*, London: Thacker, Spink and Co., 1906.

Ganguly, Jalad B., *An Economic History of North East India, 1826-1947*, New Delhi: Akansha Publishing House, 2006.

Gogoi, Padmeswar, *Tai-Ahom Religion and Customs*, Guwahati: Publication Board Assam, 1976.

Goswami, Shrutidev, *Aspects of Revenue Administration in Assam*, New Delhi: Mittal Publications, 1987.

Goswami, Praphulladatta, *Ballads and Tales of Assam: A Study of the Folklore of Assam*, Guwahati: Gauhati University Department of Publication, 1970.

Goswami, Mamoni R., *The Moth-eaten Howdah of the Tusker*, New Delhi: Rupa, 2006.

Goswami, Prafulla C., *The Economic Development of Assam*, New Delhi: Kalyani Publishers, 1994.

Goswami, Priyam, *Assam in the Nineteenth Century: Industrialization and Colonial Penetration,* New Delhi: Spectrum Publications, 1999.

Gohian, Hiren, *The Magic Plant*, Guwahati: Lawyers Book Stall, 1992.

Guha, Amalendu, *Medieval and Early Colonial Assam: Society, Polity Economy*, Calcutta: K.P. Bagchi, 1991.

———, *Planter-Raj to Swaraj: Freedom Struggle and Electoral Politics in Assam, 1826-1947,* New Delhi: Indian Council of Historical Research, 1998.

Hamilton-Buchanan, Francis, *An Account of Assam*, tr. Surya Kumar Bhuyan, Guwahati: Department of Historical and Antiquarian Studies, 1987.

Jenkins, Francis, *Report of the Northeast Frontier of India,* ed. Heramba K.Barpujari, New Delhi: Spectrum, 1995.

Kakati, Banikanta, *Assamese: Its Formation and Development*, Guwahati: Lawyers Book Stall, 1987 (rpt.).

Lahiri, Rebati M., *The Annexation of Assam: 1824-1854*, Calcutta: General Printers and Publishers, 1954.

Misra, Tillottama, *Literature and Society in Assam: A Study of the Assamese Renaissance*, Guwahati: Bhabani Print and Publications, 2011 (rpt.).

Nathan, Mirza, *Baharistan-i-Ghaybi*, tr. Moidul Islam Borah, Guwahti: Department of Historical and Antiquarian Studies, 1992.

Neog, Maheswar, *Lakshminath Bezbaroa: The Sahityarathi of Assam*, Guwahati: Gauhati University Publication Department, 1972.

Saikia, Arupjyoti (ed.), *Orunodoi: Collected Essays between the Period 1855-1868*. Nagaon: Krantikaal Prakashan, 2002.

Saikia, Rajen, *Social and Economic History of Assam, 1853-1921,* New Delhi: Manohar, 2001.

Sarma, Anjali, *Among the Luminaries in Assam*, New Delhi: Mittal Publications, 1990.

Sarma, Satyendranath, *Neo-Vaishnavite Movement and the Satra Institution of Assam*, Guwahati: Lawyers Book Stall, 1999 (rpt.).

Sen-Deka, Nilamoni, *Mitha Xenir Titta Kotha*, Nalbari: Journal Emporium, 2010.

Sharma, Anil K., *Quit India Movement in Assam*, New Delhi: Mittal Publications, 2007.

Sharma, Jayeeta, *Empire's Garden: Assam and the Making of India*, Duke: Duke University Press, 2011.

Talesh, Shihabuddin, *Tarikh-e-Aasham (1662-1663*), tr. Mazhar Asif, Department of Historical and Antiquarian Studies, Assam, 2009.

Sharma, S.K. and U. Sharma, *Documents on North-East India*, vol. 3, New Delhi: Mittal Publications, 2006.

Books on Regional and Global Studies

Adamson, Walter L., *Hegemony and Revolution: A Study of Antonio Gramsci's Political and Cultural Theory*, Princeton: Princeton University Press, 1980.

Ahmad, Diana L., *The Opium Debate and the Chinese Exclusion Laws in the Nineteenth Century American West*, Nevada: University of Nevada Press, 2007.

Allen, Nathan, *An Essay on the Opium Trade*, Boston: John P. Jewett & Co., 1853.

Alexandar, R., *The Rise and Progress of British Opium Smuggling*, London: Judd and Glass, 1856.

Andrew, Charles F., *The Opium Evil in India: Britain's Responsibility*, London: Student Christian Movement, 1926.

Arnold, David, *Colonizing the Body: State, Medicine and Epidemic Disease in Nineteenth-Century India,* California: University of California Press, 1993.

———, *Warm Climates and Western Medicine: The Emergence of Tropical Medicine, 1500-1900,* Amsterdam-Atlanta: Rodopi B.V.,1996.

———, *Science, Technology and Medicine in Colonial India*, Cambridge: Cambridge University Press, 2000.

———, *The Cambridge History of India*, vol. III, Cambridge: Cambridge University Press, 2004.

Aquilar, Filomeno V., *Clash of Spirits: The History of Power and Sugar Planter Hegemony on Visayan Island*, Honolulu: University of Hawaii Press, 1998.

Baber, Zaheer, *The Science of Empire: The Scientific Knowledge, Civilization and Colonial Rule in India*, Albany: State University of New York Press,1996.

Bandopadhyay, Shekhar, *From Plassey to Partition: A History of Modern India*, New Delhi: Orient Longman, 2004.

Baumler, Alan, *Modern China and Opium: A Reader*, USA: University of Michigan Press, 2001

———, *The Chinese and the Opium Under the Republic: Worse than Floods and Wild Beasts*, Albany: State University of New York Press, 2007.

Bavry, Stimmel, *Evaluation of Drug Treatment Programs*, New York: Haworth Press, 1983.

Bello, David A., *Opium and the Limits of Empire: Drug Prohibition in the Chinese Interior*, Harvard: Harvard University Asia Centre, 2005.

Bichel, William K. and Dhume J.R. Grandpe, *Drug Policy and Human Nature: Psychological Perspectives on the Prevention and Management*, Germany: Springer, 1996.

Bernard, Semmel, *Rise of Free Trade Imperialism*, Cambridge: Cambridge University Press, 1970.

Bernstein, J.W., *A Splendid Exchange: How Trade Shaped the World*, New York: Atlantic Monthly Press, 2008.

Berridge, Virginia, *Opium and the People: Opiate Use and Drug Control Policy in Nineteenth and Early Twentieth Century*, London: Free Association Books, 1999 (2nd edn.).

Bergsma, Harold, *The Opium Eaters*, Bloomington, Indiana: Author House, 2009.

Boon, Marcus, *The Road of Excess: A History of Writers on Drugs*, Cambridge: Harvard University Press, 2005.

Brewer, Tony, *Marxist Theories of Imperialism: A Critical Survey*, New York: Routledge, 1990.

Brodie, Janet F. and Marc Redfield, *High Anxieties: Cultural Studies in Addiction*, California: University of California Press, 2002.

Brook, Timothy and Tadashi B. Wakabayashi, *Opium Regimes: China, Britain and Japan 1839-1952*, California: University of California Press, 2000.

Bull, Melissa, *Governing the Heroin Trade: From Treaties to Treatment*, Fornham: Ashgate Publishing, 2008.

Burns, Cecil D., *International Politics*, London: Methuen & Co., 1920.

Burton, Antoinette M., *Politics and Empire in Victorian Britain: A Reader*, New York and Basingstoke: Palgrave, 2001.

Buxton, Julia, *The Political Economy of Narcotics: Production, Consumption and Global Markets*, Nova Scotia: Fernwood Publishing, 2006.

Cain, P.J. and Mark Harrison, *Imperialism: Critical Concepts in Historical Studies*, London: Routledge, 2001.

Calkins, Alonzo, *Opium and the Opium Appetite: With Notices of Alcoholic Beverages, Cannabis Indica, Tobacco and Coca and Tea and Coffee in their Hygienic Aspects*, Philadelphia: J.B. Lippincott & Co., 1871.

Campbell, Nancy D., *Discovering Addiction: The Science and Politics of Substance Abuse Research*, Michigan: University of Michigan Press, 2007.

Carmath, Tom and Ian Smith, *Heroin Century*, London: Routledge, 2000.

Cox, Howard, *The Global Cigarette: Origins and Evolution of British American Tobacco, 1880-1945*, Oxford: Oxford University Press, 2000.

Curtin, D. Philip, *Cross-Cultural Trade in World History*, Cambridge: Cambridge University Press, 1984.

Chandra, Bipan, *Essays on Colonialism*, New Delhi: Orient Longman, 1999.

Chatterjee, Piya, *A Time for Tea: Women, Labour and Post-Colonial Politics of an Indian Plantation*, Duke: Duke University Press, 2001.

Chatterjee, S.K., *Legal Aspects of International Drug Control*, Hague: Martinus Nijhoff Publishers, 1981.

Chaudhari, Kirti N., *The Economic Development of India Under the East India Company 1814-58: A Selection of Contemporary Writings*, Cambridge: Cambridge University Press, 1971.

———, *The Trading World of Asia and the English East India Company 1660-1760*, Cambridge: Cambridge University Press, 1978.

Chouvy, Pierre A., *Opium: Uncovering the Politics of the Poppy*, London: I.B. Tauris and Co., 2009.

Chung, Tan, *China and the Brave New World*, Durham, NC: Carolina Academic Press, 1978.

Cohn, Bernard, *Colonialism and its Forms of Knowledge: The British in India*, Princeton: Princeton University Press, 1996.

Collingham, Elizabeth M., *Imperial Bodies: The Physical Experience of the Raj, c. 1800-1947*, Cambridge: Polity Press, 2001.

Conrad, Peter and Joseph Schneider, *Deviance and Medicalization: From Badness to Sickness*, Philadelphia: Temple University Press, 1992.

Constantine, Stephen, *The Making of British Colonial Development Policy, 1914-1940*, London: Frank Cass and Company, 2005.

Courtwright, David T., *Dark Paradise: A History of Opiate Addiction in America*, Cambridge: Harvard University Press, 2001.

———, *Forces of Habit: Drugs and the Making of the Modern World.*, Cambridge: Harvard University Press, 2001.

Cowan, Brian, *The Social Life of Coffee: The Emergence of the British Coffeehouse*, Yale: Yale University Press, 2003.

Darwin, John, *The Empire Project: The Rise and Fall of the British World System*, Cambridge: Cambridge University Press, 2009.

Dikotter, Frank, *Exotic Commodities: Modern Objects and Everday Life in China*, New York: Columbia University Press, 2006.

Dikotter, Frank, Peter Lars Laamann and Zhou Xun, *Narcotic Culture: A History of Drugs in China*, London: C. Hurst & Co., 2004.

Dunn, Frederick S., *The Practice and Procedure of International Conferences*, Baltimore: John Hopkins Press, 1929.

Escohotado, Antonio, *The General History of Drugs*, Chile: Graffiti Militante Press, 2010.

Edney, Matthew H., *Mapping an Empire: The Geographical Construction of British India, 1765-1843*, Chicago: University of Chicago Press, 1997.

Edkins, Joseph, *Opium: Historical Note*, American Presbyterian Mission Press, 1898.

Elwin, Verrier, *India's North-East Frontier in the Nineteenth Century*, Madras: Oxford University Press, 1959.

Fairbank, King J. and Denis C. Twichett, *The Cambridge History of China*. Cambridge: Cambridge University Press, 2008.

Farooqui, Amar, *Smuggling as Subversion: Colonialism, Indian Merchants and the Politics of Opium 1790-1843*, Lanham: Lexington Books, 2005.

———, *Opium City: The Making of Early Victorian Bombay*, New Delhi: Three Essays Collective, 2006.

Feldman, Herman, *Prohibition: It's Economic and Industrial Aspects*, New York: D. Appleton & Co., 1927.

Feuer, Lewis S., *Imperialism and the Anti-Imperialist Mind*, New Jersey: Transaction Publishers, 1989.

Foxcroft, Louise, *The Making of Addiction: The 'Use' and 'Abuse' of Opium in Nineteenth-Century Britain*, Farnham: Ashgate Publishing, 2007.

French, Roger K. and Andrew Wear, *British Medicine in an Age of Reform*, Abingdon: Routledge, 1991.

Frenk, Hanan and D. Reuven, *A Critique of Narcotine Addiction*, South Holland: Kluwer Academic Publishers, 2000.

Friedman, Jonathan, *System, Structure and Contradiction: The Evolution of Asiatic Social Formations*, London: Sage, 1998.

Furnivall, John S., *Colonial Policy and Practice*, Cambridge: Cambridge University Press, 1948.

Grob, Gerald N., *Narcotic Addiction and American Foreign Policy: Seven Studies, 1924-1938*, New York: Arno Press, 1981 (rpt.).

Gaber, Rudolph J., *Legalizing Marijuana: Drug Policy Reform and Prohibition Politics*, London: Greenwood Publishing Group, 2004.

Gandhi, M.K. and Bharata Kumarappa (eds.), *Drink, Drugs and Gambling*, Ahmadabad: Navjivan Publishing House, 1952.

Gerristen, Jan W., *The Control of Fuddle and Flash: A Sociological History of the Regulation of Alcohol and Opiates*, Leiden: Brill, 2000.

Giles, Herbert, *Some Truths about Opium*, Cambridge: W. Heffer & Sons, 1923.

Goldberg, Ted, *Demystifying Drugs*, Basingstoke, Hampshire: Palgrave MacMillan, 1999.

Goodman, Jordan, *Tobacco in History: The Cultures of Dependance*, New York: Routledge, 1993.

———, *Consuming Habits: Drugs in History and Anthropology (Consumption and Culture in 17th and 18th Centuries)*, London: Routledge, 1995.

Goodman, Jordan and Paul E. Lovejoy, *Consuming Habits: Global and Historical Perspectives on How Cultures Define Drugs*, New York: Routledge, 2003.

Gootenberg, Paul, *Cocaine: Global Histories*, New York: Routledge, 1999.

Green, Ewen, *Ideals of Empire: Political and Economic Thought, 1903-1919*, London: Routledge/Thoemmes Press, 1998.

Gupta, D.B. Jyoti (ed.), *History of Science: Philosophy and Culture in Indian Civilization*, vol. XV, pt. I: *Science, Technology, Imperialism and War*, New Delhi: Pearson Longman, 2007.

Hanes, Travis and Frank Sanello, *The Opium Wars: The Addiction of One Empire and the Corruption of Another*, Illinois: Sourcebooks Inc., 2002.

Haq, Emdad ul, *Drugs in South Asia: From the Opium Trade to the Present Day*, Basingstoke, Hampshire: Palgrave Macmillan, 2000.

Harcourt, Freda, *Flagships of Imperialism: The P&O Company and the Politics of Empire From it's Origins to 1867*, Manchester: Manchester University Press, 2006.

Hawkins, John A., *Opium Addicts and Addiction*, New York: Arno Press, 1981 (rpt. edn.).

Headrick, R. Daniel, *Tentacles of Progress: Technology Transfer in the Age of Imperialism, 1850-1940*, Oxford: Oxford University Press, 1988.

Hines-Davenport, Richard, *The Pursuit of Oblivion: A Global History of Narcotics*, New York: W.W Norton & Co., 2004.

Hubert, Jean F. and Donald Wigal, *A Mystique of Opium*, Sirrocco: Park Stone International, 2004.

Hubbard, H. Frederick, *The Opium Habit and Alcoholism*, New York: Arno Press, 1981 (rpt. edn.).

Inglis, Brian, *The Forbidden Game: A Social History of Drugs*, New York: Charles Scribner's Sons, 1975.

Irving, Sarah, *Natural Science and the Origins of the British Empire*, London: Pickering and Chato, 2008.

Janin, Hunt, *The India-China Opium Trade in the Nineteenth Century*, North Carolina: McFarland & Company Inc., 1999.

Jasanoff, Sheila, *States of Knowledge: The Co-production of Science and Social Order*, New York: Routledge, 2004.

Jay, Mike, *The Emperor of Dreams: Drugs in the Nineteenth Century*, Sawtry: Daedalus, 2002.

Jennings, John M., *The Opium Empire: Japanese Imperialism and Drug Trafficking in Asia, 1895-1945*, London: Greenwood Publishing Group, 1999.

Jehangir, Rustom P., *A Short History of the Lives of the Bombay Opium Smokers*, Bombay: B. Marzban & Co.'s Steam Printing Works, 1893.

Johnson, Robert, *British Imperialism*, New York: Palgrave MacMillan, 2003.

Jordan, David C., *Drug Politics: Dirty Money and Democracies*, Oklahama: University of Oklahama Press, 1999.

Kane, Hubble, *Drugs that Enslave*, New York: Ayer Publishing, 1981.

Kapoor, L.D., *Opium, Poppy: Botany, Chemistry and Pharmacology*, London: Routledge, 1995.

Keinholz, Mary, *Opium Traders and their World: A Revisionist Expose off the World's Greatest Opium Traders*, Bloomington: Iuniverse.com, 2008.

Kiple, K.F. and K.C. Ornelas (eds.), *The Cambridge World History of Food*, Cambridge: Cambridge University Press, 2000.

Knipe, Ed (ed.), *Culture, Society and Drugs: The Social Science Approach to Drug Use*, Long Grove: Waveland Press Inc., 1995.

Kumar, Dharma (ed.), *The Cambridge Economic History of India*, vol. 2: *c.1757-1970,* Cambridge: Cambridge University Press, 1983.

Laffey, John F., *Imperialism and Ideology: A Historical Perspective*, Quebec: Black Rose Books, 2000.

Lebesco, Kathleen and Peter Nacarto, *Edible Ideologies: Representing Food and Meaning*, New York: State University of New York Press, 2000.

Lee, Peter, *Opium Culture: The Art and Ritual of the Chinese Tradition*, Rochester, Vermont: Park Street Press, 2006.

Lenson, David, *On Drugs*, Minnesota: University of Minnesota Press, 1995.

Levine, Philippa, *Prostitution, Race and Politics: Policing Venereal Diseases in the British Empire*, New York: Routledge, 2003.

Light, Arthur B., *Opium Addiction: Philadelphia Committeee for the Clinical Study of Opium Addiction*, New York: Arno Press, 1981.

Lodwick, Kathleen L., *Crusaders Against Opium: Protestant Missionaries in China, 1874-1917*, Kentucky: The University Press of Kentucky, 1996.

Loue, Sana, *Diversity Issues in Substance Abuse Treatment and Research*, New York: Kluwer Academic/Plenum Publishers, 2003.

Lowes, Peter D., *The Genesis of International Narcotics Control*, New York: Arno Press, 1981.

Lu, Hong and Bin Liang, *China's Drug Practices and Policies: Regulating Controlled Substances in a Global Context*, Abingdon: Ashgate Publishing, 2009.

Mackenzie, John, *Imperialism and the Natural World: Studies in Imperialism*, Manchester: Manchester University Press, 1990.

Madancy, Joyce A., *The Troublesome Legacy of Commissioner Lin: The Opium Trade and Opium Suppression in the Fujian Province, 1820's to 1920's*, Cambridge: Harvard University Asia Center, 2003.

Mannheim, Karl, *Ideology and Utopia*, New York and London: Routledge, 1936.

Marez, Curtis, *Drug Wars: The Political Economy of Narcotics*, Minnesota: University of Minnesota Press, 2004.

Markovits, Claude, *The Global World of Indian Merchants, 1750-1947: Traders of Sind from Bukhara to Panama*, Cambridge: Cambridge University Press, 2000.

Mathee, Rudi P., *The Pursuit of Pleasure: Drugs and Stimulants in Iranian History, 1500-1900,* Princeton: Princeton University Press, 2005.

McAllister, William B., *Drug Diplomacy in the Twentieth Century: An International History*, London: Routledge, 2000.

McKenna, Terence, *Food of the Gods: A Radical History of Plants, Drugs and Human Evolution*, New York: Bantam New Age Books, 1993.

McMohan, Keith, *The Fall of God of Money: Opium Smoking in Nineteenth Century China*, Lanham, Maryland: Rowmann and Littlefield, 2002.

Meier, Kenneth J., *The Politics of Sin: Drugs, Alcohol and Public Policy*, New York and London: M.E. Sharpe, 1994.

Melancon, Glenn, *Britain's China Policy and the Opium Crisis*, Fornham: Ashgate Publishing, 2003.

Meyer, Kathryn and Terry Parssinen, *Webs of Smoke: Smugglers, Warlords and the History of the International Drug Trade*, Lanham: Rowmann and Littlefield Publishers Inc., 2002.

Miligan, Barry, *Pleasures and Pains: Opium and Orient in Nineteenth Century British Culture*, Charlottesville: University Press of Virgina, 1995.

Mills, James H. and Patricia Barton, *Drugs and Empires: Essays in Modern Imperialism and Intoxicants c. 1500-1930*, Basingstoke: Palgrave Macmillan, 2007.

Mintz, Sidney W., *Sweetness and Power: The Place of Sugar in Modern History*, City of Westminster: Penguin Books.

Mitchell, Tim, *Intoxicated Identities: Alcohol's Power in Mexican History and Culture*, New York and London: Routledge, 2004.

Moraes, Francis and Debra Moraes, *Opium*, Berkeley: Ronin Publishing, 2005.

Musto, David F., *The American Disease*, New Haven: Yale University Press, 1973.

Ng, Rick, *Drugs: From Discovery to Approval*, New Jersey: John Wiley and Sons, 2004.

Owen, David E., *The British Opium Policy in China and India*, New Haven: Yale University Press, 1934.

Padwa, Howard, *Social Poison: The Culture and Politics of Opiate Control in Britain and France, 1821-1926*, Baltimore: John Hopkins University Press, 2012.

Parker, N. James and Philips M. Parker, *Opium*, Nevada: ICON Group International, 2004.

Paul, Winther C., *Anglo-European Science and the Rhetoric of Empire: Malaria, Opium and the British Rule in India, 1756-1856*, Oxford: Lexington Books, 2003.

Peiris, Anoma, *Hidden Lands and Divided Landscapes: A Penal History of Singapore's Plural Society*, Hawaii: University of Hawaii Press, 2009.

Peter, Fay W., *Opium War, 1840-1842: Barbarians in the Celestial Empire in the Early Part of the Nineteenth Century and the War by which they Forced her Gates*, Carolina: The University of North Carolina Press, 1998.

Polacheck, James M., *The Inner Opium War*, Harvard: Harvard University Press, 1992.

Pomeranz, Kenneth and Steven Topik, *The World that Trade Created: Society, Culture and the World Economy, 1400-Present*, New York: M.E. Sharpe, 1999.

Porter, Roy, *The Cambridge History of Science*, vol. 4, Cambridge: Cambridge University Press, 2008.

Purpura, Philip P., *Criminal Justice: An Introduction*, Boston: Butterworth-Heinemann, 1997.

Quincey, Thomas D., *Confessions of an English Opium-Eater*, New York: Cosimo Inc. 2010 (originally pub. in 1821).

Miller, Richard L., *Drug Warriors and their Prey: From Police Power to Police State*, Santa Barbara: Praeger, 1996.

Renard, Ronald D., *The Burmese Connection: Illegal Drugs and the Making of Golden Triangle: On the Impact of the Illegal Drug Trade*, vol. 6, London: Lynn Rienner Publishers, 1996.

Robbins, Nick, *The Corporation that Changed the World: How the East India Company Shaped the Modern Multinational*, London: Pluto Press, 2006.

Rock, Paul E., *Drugs and Politics*, New Jersey: Transaction Publishers, 2006.

Schaler, Jeffrey A., *Addiction is a Choice*, Chicago: Open Court Publishing, 2004.

Schur, Edwin E., *Narcotic Addiction in Britain and America: The Impact of Public Policy*, London: Tavistock Publications, 1963.

Seaman, Lewis B.C., *Victorian England: Aspects of English and Imperial History, 1837-1901*, London: Routledge, 1995.

Semmell, Bernard, *The Rise of Free Trade Imperialism: Classical Political Economy of the Empire*, Cambridge: Cambridge University Press, 2004.

Soluri, John, *Banana Cultures: Agriculture, Consumption and Enviornmental Change in Honduras and the United States*, USA: University of Texas Press, 2005.

Sharma, Jayeeta, *Empire's Garden: Assam and the Making of India*, Duke: Duke University Press, 2011.

Singh, Narayan P., *The East India Company's Monopoly Industries in Bihar with Particular Reference to Opium and Saltpeter, 1773-1833*, Muzaffarpur: Sarvodaya Vangmaya, 1980.

Slack, Edward R., *Opium, State and Society: China is Narco-Economy and the Guomindang, 1924-1937*, Hawaii: University of Hawaii Press, 2001.

Smith, Wesley, *The Hippocratic Tradition*, Philadelphia: Cornell University Press, 2002.

Smith, R. Woodruff, *Consumption and the Making of Respectability 1600-1800*, New York: Routledge, 2002.

Spink, Wesley W., *Infectious Diseases, Prevention and Treatment in the Nineteenth and Twentieth Century*, Minnesota: University of Minnesota Press, 1978.

Stares, Paul B., *Global Habit: The Drug Problem in a Borderless World*, Washington DC: Brookings Institutions, 1996.

Steinberg, K. Michael, J. Joseph Hobbes and Kent Mathewson, *Dangerous Harvests: Drugs, Plants and the Transformation of Indigenous Landscapes*, New York: Oxford University Press, 2004.

Sunderland, Jalez T., *India in Bondage*, New York: Lewis Copeland and Company, 1929.

Syed, Altatas H., *The Myth of the Lazy Native: A Study of the Image of the Malays, Filipinos and Javanese from the 16th to the 20th Century and its Function in the Ideology of Colonial Capitalism*, London: Routledge, 1977.

Szasz, Thomas, *Ceremonial Chemistry: The Ritual Persecution of Drugs, Addicts and Pushers*, Syracuse: Syracuse University Press Edition, 2003.

Tagliacozzo, Eric, *Secret Trades, Porous Borders: Smuggling and States Along a Southeast Asian Frontier, 1865-1915*, Yale: Yale University Press, 2005.

Terry, Charles and Mildred Pellens (ed.), *The Opium Problem*, Chicago: The American Medical Association, 1928.

Timothy, Hickman A., *The Secret Leprosy of Modern Days: Narcotic Addiction and Cultural Crisis in United States, 1870-1920*, USA: University of Massachussets Press, 2007.

Trocki, Carl, *Opium, Empire and the Global Political Economy: A Study of the Asian Opium Trade 1750-1950*, New York: Routledge, 1999.

Varma, Ram D., *The Art and Science of Healing Since Antiquity*, Bloomington: Xlibris Corporation, 2011.

Waley, Arthur, *The Opium War through Chinese Eyes*, California: Stanford University Press, 1958.

Walker, William O. (ed.), *Drug Control Policy: Essays in Historical and Comparative Perspective*, Pennsylvania: Pennsylvania State University, 1992.

Wayne, Morgan H., *Drugs in America: A Social History, 1800-1980*, New York: Syracuse University Press, 1981.

Wesley, Spink W., *Infectious Diseases: Prevention and Treatment in the Nineteenth and Twentieth Centuries*, Minnesota: University of Minnesota Press, 1978.

Westermeyer, Joseph, *Poppies, Pipes, and People: Opium and its Use in Laos*, Oakland, California: University of California Press, 1982.

Wilner, Daniel M. and Gene Kassebaum (eds.), *Narcotics*, New York: McGraw-Hill, 1965.

Winther, C. Paul, *Anglo-European Science and the Rhetoric of Empire: Malaria, Opium, and British Rule in India, 1756-1895*, Lanham: Lexington Books, 2003.

Willoughby, Woodbury W., *Opium as an International Problem: The Geneva Conferences*, New York: Arno Press Inc., 1976.

Wong, Y.J., *Deadly Dreams: Opium and the Arrow War*, Cambridge: Cambridge University Press, 1998.

Yangwen, Zheng, *The Social Life of Opium in China,* Cambridge: Cambridge University Press, 2005.

Zhou, Yonming, *Anti-Drug Crusades in the 20th Century China: Nationalism, History and State Building*, Lanham: Rowmann and Littlefield, 1999.

Articles

Ahmed, Nisar, 'Assam-Bengal Trade in the Medieval Period: A Numismatic Perspective', *Journal of the Economic and Social History of the Orient*, 33(1990): 169-98.

Bailey, W. and L. Truong, 'Opium and Empire: Some Evidence from Colonial-Era Asian Stock and Commodity', *Journal of Southeast Asian Studies*, 32(2001): 173-93.

Banerjee, Arun, 'British Rule and the Indian Economy: Agenda for Fresh Searches', *Economic Political Weekly*, 19(1984): 1273-84.

Bard, Solomon, 'On Opium and Tea' (paper presented at the International Conference on Lin Zexu, Opium War and Hong Kong, Hong Kong, December 1998).

Beer, George L., 'British Colonial Policy, 1754-1765', *Political Science Quarterly*, 1(1907): 1-48.

Berridge, Virginia, 'The Origins of the English Drug "Scene" 1890-1930', *Medical History*, 32(1988): 51-64.

Bletzer, Keith V., 'Modulation of Drug Use in Southern Farming Communities: Social Origins of Poly-Use', *Human Organization,* 68(2009): 340-49.

Caroll, Lewis, 'The Temperance Movement in India: Politics and Social Reform', *Modern Asian Studies*, 3(1976): 417-47.

Colton, Arthur, 'On Communication between India and China by the Line of the Burhampooter and the Yang-Tse', *Proceedings of the Royal Geographical Society of London*, 11(1866-7): 255-9.

Crawford, John, 'On the History and Migration of Cultivated Plants Producing Coffee, Tea, and Cocoa, etc.', *Transactions of the Ethnological Society of London*, 7(1869): 197-206.

Dixon, W.E., 'A Clinical Address on Drug Addiction, given at the Annual Meeting of the British Medical Association', *British Medical Journal*, 2(193): 19-24.

Farooqui, Amar, 'Colonialism and Competing Addictions: Morphine Content as Historical Factor', *Social Scientist*, 32(2004): 21-31.

Fielder, Charles H., 'On the Rise, Progress and Future Prospects of Tea Cultivation in British India', *Journal of Statistical Society of London*, 1(1869): 29-37.

Flynn, Dennis O. and Arturo Giraldez, 'Cycles of Silver: Global Economic History through the Mid-Eighteenth Century', *Journal of World History*, 13(2002): 391-427.

Fry, Edward, 'China, England and Opium', *Contemporary Review,* 27(1876): 447-59.

Gray, Errol, 'Journey from Assam to the Sources of the Irrawadi', *Geographical Journal*, 3(1894): 221-8.

Grinëv, A.V., 'The Distribution of Alcohol Among the Natives of Russian America', *Arctic Anthropology* 47(2010): 69-79.

Ghosh, Suniti K., 'Indian Bourgeoisie and Imperialism', *Economic Political Weekly*, 23(1998): 2445-58.

Harley, Vaughan, 'Sugar as a Food', *British Medical Journal*, 2(1895): 1282-9.

Higman, Barry W., 'The Sugar Revolution', *Economic History Review*, 53(2000): 213-36.

Jankowiah, William and Dan Bradburd, 'Using Drug Food to Capture an Enhance Labour Performance: A Cross-Cultural Perspective', *Current Anthropology*, 4(1996): 717-20.

Logan, John F., 'The Age of Intoxication', *Yale French Studies*, 50(1979): 81-94.

Madancy, Joyce, 'Unearthing Popular Attitudes Toward the Opium Trade and

Opium Suppression in Late Qing and Early Republican Fujian', *Modern China*, 5(2001): 436-83.

Markham, C.R., 'Travels in Great Tibet and Trade between Tibet and Bengal', *Proceedings of the Royal Geographical Society of London*, 5(1874-5): 327-47.

Mathee, Rudi, 'Coffee in Safavid Iran: Commerce and Consumption', *Journal of the Economic and Social History of the Orient*, 1(1994): 1-32.

Meredith, David, 'The British Government and Colonial Economic Policy, 1919-1939', *The Economic History Review*, 3(1975): 484-94.

Misra, Tillotama, 'Social Criticism in Nineteenth Century Assamese Writing: The Orunodoi', *Economic Political Weekly*, 20(1985): 1558-66.

Motte, Ellen, 'The Opium Problem', *The American Journal of Nursing*, 7(1929): 791-4.

Palsetia, Jesse S., 'Parsis of India and the Opium Trade in Chin', *Contemporary Drug Problems*, 4(2008): 647-78.

Richards, John F., 'The Indian Empire and Peasant Production of Opium in the Nineteenth Century', *Modern Asian Studies*, 1(1981): 59-82.

———, 'Opium and the British Indian Empire: The Royal Commission of 1895', *Modern Asian Studies*, 2(2002): 375-420.

Reid, Anthony, 'From Betel-chewing to Tobacco Smoking in Indonesia', *Journal of Asian Studies*, 3(1985): 529-47.

Reins, Thomas D., 'Reforms, Nationalism and Internationalism: The Opium Suppression Movement in China and the Anglo-American Influence, 1900-1908', *Modern Asian Studies*, 1(1991): 101-42.

Saldanha, Indira M., 'On Drinking and Drunkenness of Liquor in Colonial India', *Economic and Political Weekly*, 37(1973): 2323-31.

Smith, Henry M., 'British India', *Journal of Comparative Legislation and International Law*, 3(1929): 159-67.

Smith, Woodruff R., 'Complications of the Common-place: Tea, Sugar and Imperialism', *Journal of Interdisciplinary History*, 2(1992): 259-78.

Stanley, Brian, 'Commerce and Christianity: Providence Theory, the Missionary Movement and the Trade, 1842-1860', *The Historical Journal*, 1(1983): 71-94.

Wright, Hamilton, 'International Opium Conference', *American Journal of International Law*, 4(1912): 865-89.

Sharma, Jayeeta, 'British Science, Chinese Skill and Assam Tea: Making Empire's Garden', *Indian Economic and Social History Review*, 4(2006): 429-55.

Articles Retrieved in Electronic Format

Contractor, Farok J., 'How a Soothing Drink Changed Fortunes and Incited Protests: Tea's History Reveals Globalisation Best and Worst Sides: Trade, Prosperity, Migration and War', in *Yale Global*, 2011.

———, 'The Story of Globalisation: From the Neolithic Era to the Tea-Opium Countertrade of the 19th Century', in *Insights*, 20 March 2012 <http://www.rutgersinasia.com/beijing/sites/default/files/HowOldisInternational BusinessArticleforAIBInsightsMarch20,2012.pdf rutgers inasia> (19 May 2012).

Publications

RESEARCH PAPER (IN EDITED VOLUME)

Kour, Kawal D., 'The Opium Question in Colonial Assam', in Harald Fischer-Tine and Jana Tschurenev (eds.), *A History of Alcohol and Drugs in Modern South Asia: Intoxicating Affairs*, Abingdon: Routledge, 2014.

RESEARCH PAPERS (IN JOURNAL)

Kour, Kawal D., 'Imperial Tastes and Imperial Rule in India', *Palgrave Encyclopedia of Imperialism and Anti-Imperialism*, Palgrave Macmillan (2016): 353-8.

———, 'Taste Making and Trend Setting: The Practice of Opium Consumption and Experience in India (1757-1895)', in Neil Price, ed., *Imperial Additions: Cultural Archaeologies of Opium in the Indian Ocean World*, Ohio: Ohio University Press, 2019.

———, 'On the Evils of Opium Eating: Reflections on Nineteenth Century Assamese Literary Reformist Discourse', *European Academic Research,* 2(2013): 138-56.

———, 'A Virtuos Gratification, A Baneful Luxury: Contesting Notions Over Popular Use of Opium in Colonial Assam', *Indian Streams Research Journal*, 3(2013): 58-61.

———, 'From Modinos Cure to Lecithin Treatment: Detoxification and Withdrawal Management in the State Sponsored Mass Treatment Scheme for Opium Addicts in Assam, 1938-39', *National Medical Journal of India* 25(2012): 296-300.

———, 'Opium, Empire and Assam – A History', *The Newsletter* (IIAS, Leiden) 60(2012): 11.

RESEARCH PAPERS (IN CONFERENCE PROCEEDINGS)

Kour, Kawal D., 'Imperial Interest and the Lure of the Opium Trade in Colonial Assam', *Proceedings of the National Seminar on Indian Business through Ages Organized by the Faculty of Mangement Studies,* 12-13 December 2011, Delhi.

———, 'Addictive Consumables and Networks of Commerce-Opium in Assam', *Proceedings of the 8th International Conference of Young Scientists in Humanities and Social Sciences*, 24-6 November 2011, Lviv, Ukraine.

———, 'Internationalization of the "Narcotic Threat": An Analysis of its Repercussions on the Opium Question in Colonial Assam', *Proceedings of the 30th Session of the North East India History Association*, 2010.

Saikia, Arupjyoti, Kawal D. Kour and Gopal Sharma, 'Crop Production in Assam, 1890-1947: A Preliminary Estimate', *Proceedings of the 29th Session of the North East India History Association*, 2009.

PUBLICATION IN ONLINE FORMAT

Kour, Kawal D., 'What is Opium: Exploring the Meanings of Opium from "Exotic Plant" to a "Forbidden Fruit"', 2011 <http://www.narcoinsa.com/pdf/exploring-the-meanings-of opium-kawaldeep.pdf.>

Index